MW01132404

THE WAY
OF THE
ESSENES

THE WAY
OF THE
ESSENES
CHRIST'S
HIDDEN LIFE
REMEMBERED

ANNE AND DANIEL
MEUROIS-GIVAUDAN

Destiny Books
Rochester, Vermont

Destiny Books
One Park Street
Rochester, Vermont 05767
www.InnerTraditions.com

Destiny Books is a division of Inner Traditions International

First published in French under the title *De Mémoire d'Essénien, l'autre visage de Jésus* by Arista Editions, Plazac, 1989

First U.S. edition 1993

Library of Congress Cataloging-in-Publication Data

Meurois-Givaudan, Anne.
    [De mémoire d'essénien, English]
    The way of the Essenes : Christ's hidden life remembered /
Anne and Daniel Meurois-Givaudan.—1st U.S. ed.
      p.   cm.
    Translation of: De mémoire d'essénien.
    ISBN 978-0-89281-322-3
    1. Essenes—Miscellanea. 2. Jesus Christ—Miscellanea.
I. Meurois-Givaudan, Daniel. II. Title.
BF 1999.M495 1992
133.9'3—dc20
                                        92–6240
                                            CIP

Printed and bound in the United States

20   19   18   17   16   15

CONTENTS

INTRODUCTION

The Essenes! Many a time those on the path of self-questioning have come across this still mysterious name. Ever since the discovery of the Dead Sea Scrolls, it has been mentioned the world over, raising many questions left unanswered.

Who were the Essenes? In spite of the most recent work carried out by archaeologists and other scholars, official history so far has told us precious little.

There is talk of a religious sect, with which the name of Jesus is often associated. But just what is the truth about all that? This book is an attempt to answer these questions—rather to begin to answer them—for the field is vast.

The following does not represent the work of a historian, but is an eye-witness account, the testimony of events truly experienced. As a matter of fact, no documents of any sort have gone into its composition.

The rational mind, of course, denies that the past can be investigated outside the traditional methods of historical inquiry. And yet, is it rational to impose limits on the new horizons which nowadays challenge mankind as a whole? Aren't the frontiers of the "impossible" endlessly receding?

We do not pretend to any revolutionary discovery in our approach to writing about the past. This account was based on a technique handed down by the ancient Egyptians and the Himalayan mystics. It is the fruit of a patient reading of the Akashic Records.

And what are the Akashic Records? They might be said to represent the memory of the universe, but that would still be rather vague. The word *akasha* is a Sanskrit term referring to one of the constituents of the natural world, the other ones being the earth, water, fire, and air. According to ancient tradition, it is an infinitely subtle substance, a form of energy in which the universe bathes, and which is capable of storing the visual and auditive memory of all life. *Akasha* is something like the photographic plate of the universe, or to use a more modern metaphor, a natural video tape, which may in certain circumstances reveal the memory of the past.

The consultation of these records took place beyond the confines of our physical world, through a series of astral or out-of-body journeys.

This kind of reading has nothing to do with a spontaneous visual phenomenon, but involves a long and demanding preparation, an individual process of a spiritual nature. No technique by itself would be sufficient. It is but the finishing touch to a long preparation, a cleansing of the various bodies that no set of instructions can accomplish, for it is founded on love.

The consultation of the Akashic Records depends furthermore on the permission granted by the spiritual entities who guard them and who must be assured of the purity of the travelers' intentions, as well as of their capacity for absorption of new ideas. Finally, such research should never be intended to achieve any personal, selfish goal.

The following account takes the readers back some two thousand years to ancient Palestine, into the heart of the Essene community. It is not an easy task to relive one's own past and in this case, one's previous life; nor has it always been pleasant to talk about ourselves.

Through the description of our existence within the Essene

Brotherhood, the readers are offered a firsthand vision of the personality and the teachings of Jesus, of his life and the lives of his disciples.

We are aware that some of the following revelations may surprise or even shock, and we are conscious of the responsiblity implied by their publication. Nevertheless, the time has come to unveil certain truths.

We do not claim that everything we present here is new; we are but adding one more stone to the edifice that is being erected. Nor have we attempted to relate the totality of facts in this domain that have been hidden until now, as the moment for revealing them has not yet come.

We must insist on one point: nothing in our account has been arranged or altered for literary or other purposes. The readers will no doubt be surprised by the quantity of details involved in the descriptions of landscapes, portraits, and conversations. Astral memory is characteristically photographic, and it may be that the eyes of the soul are sharper than those of the flesh.

Nothing that we have written is approximate. We have taken great care to relate what we have seen and heard; and as for conversations, we have taken them word for word.

We would also like to give further details about the reading of the Akashic Records. The scenes were relived with astonishing accuracy, the words perceived in the language of the time and understood as if we had a complete mastery of this language. As far as we are concerned, the sensation of a lived reality was such that we encountered emotions and perceptions that are foreign to our present-day personalities.

Some will take our account for a novel, and others may pass it off as mystical delirium. This matters little. We have written it with our hearts, exactly as we lived it, from day to day for the better part of two years. And we pass it on to your hearts.

Some of you know this already, and time will tell . . . if time there is!

Although Books One and Three were more specifically written by Simon/Daniel and Book Two by Myriam/Anne, most of the scenes described were relived together.

· BOOK ONE ·

BOOK ONE

CHAPTER 1

ZERAH

I had just turned four. My parents and I lived in a small village in Galilee, a two-day walk from Joppa. Joppa was the big city, full of adventure. One of the things I liked to do best was to stand on the little stone wall that encircled our small dwelling and watch the long lines of camels as they listlessly made their way toward Joppa. I would imagine the merchants lifting down the mysterious huge baskets that were strapped to the camels' backs as they set up their stands at the marketplace. I had witnessed this spectacle only once in my life, but it had remained deeply engraved in my childhood thoughts and imagination.

The strange bustle of the stifling alleyways—full of craftsmen's stalls, merchants' shops smelling of spices, and cattle bellowing along—was in striking contrast to the calm and perfectly ordered way of life in our village. My father was a potter and went but rarely into Joppa; even then, he had to be begged to do so. He preferred the throbbing rhythm of his wheel to the exhortations of the merchants. I inwardly held this against him. Wasn't there any other reason for going to Joppa than to buy grain, once a year? It was my mother who tried to talk some sense into me at these times. She, too, was used to the hard and simple life of the country. After all, she had grown up here, like everybody else in the village, the village of the Brothers, as it was called by the people of Joppa.

Whose brothers, I had no idea. But my father and the people who lived in the neighboring houses often said that we were all brothers. I was supposed to have great respect for this name. I didn't really question this; in spite of the occasional moments of uneasy curiosity characteristic of the awakening mind of a child, I felt a warm sense of security in the midst of our little community. Exactly how many of us there were in the sprawl of daub and stone dwellings perched on the hillside, I cannot say: a hundred and fifty, or two hundred, at the very most.

Our village was encircled by what seemed to me at the time to be a real fortification, but was in fact no more than a little gray stone wall, at most a meter high in some places. My father used to tell me again and again—as if to assure himself that his words would be forever etched in my mind—that this was the sacred wall, and all that lived and grew within its shadow was protected and blessed.

Each of the dwellings in the village was surrounded by a plot of land large enough to provide for the daily needs of the household. Farther down the hill, on either side of the road to Joppa, we all worked much bigger fields. As I remember, we worked them together, in common. It never occurred to anyone to say, "This is my land, and that is yours." Instead we said, "This is our land."

Disputes were rare, as each harvest was shared fairly and immediately. As a result, we lived in peace; and thus it was that in the first few years of my life, I came to love my village and its Brothers. It seemed to me that we lived according to a law that others—the people of the city and the merchants who came and went—did not obey. It was a vague feeling that I was never able to put into words.

I used to go with my mother to fill the water jugs, several hundred meters down a narrow path that twisted its way among low brushwood and led us out of the village. From down there our home, as well as all the others, was lost to sight. Only a few yellow-gray cubical forms could be glimpsed through the holm oaks and the pomegranate trees.

Long before, there had been a spring gushing up right in the center of the village; but Nature had changed her mind, and several times a day we had to go outside our sacred wall. Going with my mother to get water was like a game. I would stroll through the vineyards or among the fig trees, according to the seasons. Farther down, near the road, there was a crisscross of broad alternating blue and gold ribbons of land. These were the fields of flax and wheat. I used to throw pebbles toward them to try my arm and test my strength, as if to point the way I intended to go, later on, to sow and harvest.

Every day I made a game out of going to fetch water. It never entered my mind then that my mother's water jug would pass to my own shoulders in some years' time. For his work, my father was always in need of water, and there were only one or two donkeys in the village. Watching him form shapes from nothing but a little clay and much skill was a game too, one that intrigued me. I could feel a sort of magic in the repetitive movements of his hands and feet. Judging from his smile and the keen twinkle in his eyes I knew he took pride in making even the smallest of the pieces that took form in his hands. The things he created were noble, however plain and commonplace. They were the bowls out of which we ate, the jars in which the grape juice from our vineyard fermented, and all kinds of other objects.

His work was sufficient to supply our small community, and now and then a merchant would stop by our house to buy a few bowls and some jugs. If one of the Brothers in the village happened to be in need of some cookware my father would offer it to him, and in exchange, the Brother would care for our vines or do some bit of stone- or woodwork for us. There was a continual exchange of services and everyone profited by it. My parents taught me that this was the rule, a rule that made up part of our strength. This helped to awaken in me the vague but powerful feeling that we were somehow "different." As I walked on the dusty paths that served as streets in our village along with the other children of my age, I often noticed groups of serious-looking men and women with strangely deep and thoughtful eyes. Many of the faces were unfamiliar, and I soon came to understand that our community must have been some sort of stopping place where Brothers from far away were welcome after their long journeys.

Their arrival in our small community always amused and intrigued me. It was like a ritual—something I was used to and never wanted to miss. No sooner had one of these wayfarers crossed the threshold of the village, his forehead burnt by the sun and his back bent by leagues of stony paths, than a whole gang of us children would be upon him. We would always be scattered by one or two of the women of the village who would bring the stranger into a little courtyard shaded by a daub wall or some hanging vine. There, they would remove his sandals, wash his feet with a clean linen, and offer him a piece of fruit to eat; all this without a word. This was not a task assigned to the women only; often I saw men doing the same. Among our people, in fact, no sort of work was considered to be base nor was one sort of work set aside for women rather than men. This, I was quick to learn.

Once refreshed, the guest would lie down, face to the earth, with his arms outstretched in the shape of a cross. He would kiss the ground several times then get up, and over the crown of his head would be draped an ample white linen. Then he would be escorted into the home of his host. Children were rarely allowed to attend the interview that followed the arrival of a stranger in the village. While this was not strictly forbidden, it was an unspoken rule for which there were reasons, and it was not to be questioned.

Forbidden fruit, however, is the most tempting, and I remember having once managed to slip into the shadows of the doorway behind one such eternal traveler who had come to be a guest in our home. I saw my father go down on one knee before him, crossing his right arm over his left upon his chest. He lowered his head, and the stranger laid one hand on his crown.

I was so surprised by this that I jumped up and ran out of the house, my awkwardness attracting the attention of the two men. That evening my father came looking for me where I sat on the little stone wall, which I used as a retreat for my chilhood dreams. A cool wind was blowing through the fig trees and the flames of the few oil lamps scattered around the village were flickering beneath its breath. As we made our way home I dragged my feet a bit, for I was reluctant to speak with my father, whom I had confusedly thought to have caught in a position of inferiority. When we got home, he sat me up on a great wooden trunk and looked me in the eyes.

"Simon," he began, "I have a question to ask you: Which of the two, the master or the servant, is the most important?"

I could not grasp what he was trying to tell me.

"Both of them," he answered slowly, insisting on each syllable. "Both, for they are like the two hands of a single body, the two eyes of one face. They are the wind and the sail, the sword and the shield. One is only the half of itself if the other does not exist."

I still couldn't quite understand, and he must have felt this, as he hugged me close against him. As he went on, his voice was warmer.

"Simon," he said, "it is now time you learned about our way of life. Tomorrow I will take you to see Zerah, the man with the long beard, who lives by the old well. He will tell you many things that will surprise you."

Over my father's shoulder I could see my mother looking at me. She was squatting on a little mat in the half-light, absentmindedly preparing the next day's meal, wheat cakes and olives.

Something was about to happen. My quiet little life that had seemed to flow on in its uneventful way, spiced only by the desire to sow flax or to run along after the camel trains on the road to Joppa, would be unsettled. I had a fleeting sensation that I had never really understood what was happening around me, or that my parents had been keeping everything hidden from me and taking me for a child when I had the right to know what was going on.

The next morning, the warm sluggish buzzing of the first bees drew me from my sleep. My mother had already been down to fill the water jugs and was washing herself in the courtyard. The creaking of his wheel bore witness to the labors of my father.

I was so impatient that in just a few moments I was scrambling down the path beside my father, winding through the bushes and olive trees, on the way to the house by the old well.

Zerah was an old man with a long gray beard that the sun and the years had turned to a rusty color in places. I had often seen him as I played about the village and I knew that many people accorded him respect and a certain admiration. He had one of those ancient, parchmentlike faces, furrowed with many deep wrinkles, with eyes which were at once soft and piercing. When he spoke, his words were at times enigmatic and at other times very simple and clear. He was one of those venerable wise men who peopled the stories of the wandering merchants.

"Peace be with you, Joshua," he said to my father, who prodded me forward. "I knew it wouldn't be long before you brought this boy to me."

Zerah stood in his doorway, dressed in a long, faded white robe, and he stretched out his arms to me. He took one of my hands in his, and I was so surprised by the grip of his large calloused hand that I didn't notice that my father was no longer following us into the cool darkness of the house.

The dwelling of the old man seemed to me to be even poorer than our own, which itself contained nothing more than the barest essentials. By the warm and dusty sunlight that filtered through a tiny window in the single room, I could make out only two or three mats and a few things lying on the hard dirt floor.

Zerah calmly motioned to me to sit down and then sat facing me, his legs folded beneath him. On the wall behind him my glance had just time to rest on a sort of star with eight branches. I was hardly surprised by it; we had one just like it at home.

"Simon," he said, "you are now old enough to know what you are here for, and who we are. Listen to me closely: Have you ever paid attention to the way we are dressed?"

"Yes," I replied, "our clothes are white. They're not like those worn by the people of the city, and they scratch, but my father says that's all right; he says I'll get used to it."

With a slight smile the old man went on: "The thing isn't that they scratch, Simon, it's that they are different from other people's. The clothes worn by the soldiers and the men and women who live by the law of the city are blue and yellow and red and many other colors. It's good that you have noticed the difference. But do you know why this is? It's because the people of Joppa do not speak the same language as we do, they do not speak the gentle tongue."

"But I can understand them!" I burst out.

"You can understand their words, yes," he replied, "but soon you will find that you cannot hear their hearts and that if you want to get close to them, you have to work very hard. And this is difficult, for even if you want to hear the beating of their hearts, they don't often want to hear yours. But now, Simon, you haven't come here to listen to bitter words, you have come to learn to observe and think.

"For some time now you have understood that we do not live like the people in the cities, or like the merchants with their camels; now it is time you understood why. Imagine a great field of flax that is shared by all the members of a big family, who as time goes by, get married and have many children. There are Saul's children, and Jacob's children, and many, many more. There are so many children after a while that they don't even know each other anymore, and they fight. Some of them lose their little plot of land and in order to survive they must seek shelter with the others, who can hardly tolerate their presence.

"The whole earth, you see, is like this flax field, and we here in this village, and in several others, are like survivors from an ancient war in which we lost the worldly goods handed down to us by our fathers. We are in exile, living with kinfolk who have forgotten our common beginnings. We are the survivors of a time when the face of the sun shone less than it does today, though its rays warmed the hearts of men far more. We are also a thorn in the heel of a giant. But do not look at me with such eyes; you will realize this for yourself only too soon."

Zerah paused for a moment, seeing my perplexity, then laid his big hands heavily on my shoulders and went on.

"You must know, Simon, that we are not among the sons of Abraham and Jacob. Our fathers fought each other many moons ago, many more than you can imagine. Look closely at the star on the wall behind me. It is one of the symbols of our people. You will find it wherever you meet people who place their hands over their hearts when they speak. It is a sign, and you must recognize it. There are many others that you will learn later.

"Many peoples live in this land. I do not say that we are the best among them, but our spiritual Father has given us a word, and we have kept the word, neither adding nor taking away an iota. It is for His glory and for the glory of all your human brothers that you must be able to hear the word, and to repeat it. Then, like all the rest of us here in this village, you will earn the right to wear the long white robe, and you will speak the gentle tongue, and with it you will heal."

"I will heal?"

"Yes, you will heal, as do many of us who have sworn to do so. But you will heal not only the bodies that suffer, you will apply yourself to the healing of the souls."

"The souls?" I asked, "What's a soul?"

"The soul, Simon, is . . . it's the great force that is alive in you and that enables you every morning to say something like, 'I am I, and my name is Simon.' It is the flame that goes out from you every night and travels through a land from which it brings back dreams—and many other things. This is a land without borders, where . . ."

"The flame? I've never seen that flame!"

"You will learn to see it, and believe me, you'll even be able to touch it."

It wasn't easy to understand what Zerah was saying in his warm velvet words, but I had a confused feeling that he was opening doors before me, doors that opened on to other doors that opened on to still other doors. It was as if he were stirring some ashes, to revive the forgotten little flame whose name he had just mentioned.

"But how can a flame be ill, Zerah?" I asked, wide-eyed.

"It can become ill when it strays too far from the fire that gave it birth. Remember this well, Simon. When this happens, it burns whatever it touches, instead of warming it. It's all really very simple, but we make it all seem so complicated."

The old man then took my left wrist, and with infinite care he tied a thin black string around it, a symbol for the sacred trust he had just passed on to me and for the edifice whose first stone had thus been laid.

CHAPTER 11

PURIM

The months flowed by, punctuated by my frequent visits to Zerah. The old man who lived in the house by the old well seemed to have taken me under his wing and no longer spoke to me as an instructor, but more as a grandfather speaks to his grandson. More than a habit, seeing him became a necessity, and his humble dwelling was like a second home for me.

My parents looked on from afar but never said a word to me about my visits to the old man. Nonetheless, I could sense that they were far from displeased.

My father spoke less to me of the work in the fields, insisting rather that I often come to watch him knead and shape the clay to which he gave life. As for my mother, she decided that I was no longer to enter the house without first washing my hands and feet in the water from a jug kept in the courtyard for this purpose.

I didn't object at all to this—I was even flattered. My father, his friends, every traveler coming from afar, old Zerah and all those who wore the long white robe, had always done this. As I was now required to do the same, I felt I had been accepted among the adults and that I shared in some real secret. I said nothing of this to the other children with whom I played.

For three years I spent my time listening to Zerah's teachings, watching my father at work and . . . admiring the almond trees as they grew and blossomed from season to season. I rarely found time to play with the other children my age. Only Myriam, the weaver's daughter, came often to share my dreams where I used to sit in the shade of a lemon tree I had chosen as a companion, because it afforded an excellent view of the road to Joppa. She had long, curly red hair and a sort of wild air about her, and she always wore a faded ochre dress that looked too big for her. I thought of her as a "little girl" though I was hardly any older than she was. My attitude changed the day I noticed that she, too, purified her hands and feet before entering one of the houses in the village.

So she knew the secret too! I wondered if she was seeing Zerah as well and couldn't help asking her.

"No, Simon," she answered, "my father told me to do that. He says that our houses and even our bodies are like temples in which there's a little flame burning, and that's why we must keep them clean and what he says is true. I saw the little flame once. It shines like the sun." I looked deep into her gray eyes, and saw a half-mocking, half-serious look, but I didn't dare ask her another question.

So this "little girl" had already seen what Zerah was spending morning after morning describing to me. I had been dreamily listening to the old man as if he were telling fables or stories from ancient times. I thought I knew so much, and in fact, I didn't know anything. I hadn't even seen the flame, while Myriam . . . .

Before I could open my mouth to speak, she took me by the hand and led me though the dusty village to her parents' shaky dwelling, which was the color of earth and which leaned unsteadily against a big, lichen-covered rock.

"Look," she whispered into my ear, as she pointed toward one of the daub walls. I stepped closer and discovered, slightly hidden behind a bush, a little place that had been hollowed out in the form of a sun in one side of the house. A star was engraved in it like the one on the wall at Zerah's.

"That's your flame?" I muttered, somewhat disappointed.

"Hush!" she breathed, "look closer."

Out of the hollow she drew a tiny metal cup, blackened with age, from which timidly rose a wisp of pale white smoke. Without a word she lifted a flat stone out of the back of the cavity, revealing another vessel containing a coarsely ground powder and some dried leaves. Carefully, she took a pinch of this powder and put it in the bottom of the first cup. A thick, bluish white smoke crackled up, filling the air we breathed with a rich and heavy scent.

It was a scent I knew; it often floated on the air among the streets of the community. Although invisible, it was like a living presence—one of the beings peopling our universe and mingling with the fragrance of the acacia flowers and the baskets of coriander carried by the merchants' donkeys.

"Is that your flame?" I asked again. "It's just incense. Zerah buys it from the camel drivers who come from the land of the Red Earth* far over the mountains, where there's a big river. So that's all your flame is!"

"It helps you to see the flame," Myriam replied. "My father told me that I should burn the incense every day and sit quietly for a while with my eyes closed and breathe as if I were drinking up all the scents in the world. So I did, and one day I saw the little flame. It was blue, very blue, right before my eyes, and it shone brighter and brighter until it got so bright I had to stop looking at it."

She stopped, and we stayed there for a long while, watching the thin ribbons of smoke spiral up over our heads. Only then did I realize that Zerah's words were not just fables; the little girl who sat with me under the lemon tree had come with her hand over her heart to tell me this.

From that day on, this moment was engraved upon my memory as being the time of my birth, the coming into the world of the little spark that was to change my whole life.

It was on the eve of Purim,† and I remember watching the

---

*Egypt.

†Feast of the fourteenth of Adar, the twelfth month of the Jewish year, which celebrates the deliverance of the Jews by Esther.

Brothers of our village busily climbing up the narrow path with bales of flax on their shoulders, chanting a strange melody in a language I didn't understand.

This was the same day that a new family came to settle among us. The only child, a boy, looked a bit younger than I. The man was much older than his wife, and his features revealed both great authority and the habit of working hard beneath the hot sun of Galilee. My parents told me he was a woodworker, and was often called over the hills from one place to another, to help other Brothers build their homes or hospices where sick people could be cared for.

Myriam and I noticed right away that he was accorded great veneration. We had even seen old Zerah down on one knee before him, his arms folded over his chest. It was Zerah, in fact, who had first hurried to greet them as they entered within the sacred wall. He had given them the triple embrace of welcome in front of the whole village. This was felt to be an important sign, considering that Zerah was beginning to falter under the burden of his years and could hardly even walk anymore.

The wife of our new Brother had a narrow face with fine features. She was still very young but was treated with equal respect. As soon as she entered the village, my mother and several of her friends rushed to spread before her a long white sheet of linen for her to walk on. She seemed embarrassed by so much attention and stammered a few words of excuse.

I had caught up with Zerah, who told me she had been a "dove"* in a very important temple. There, she had led a very pure life, keeping the secret and the rites of one of our people's ancient traditions.

Myriam and I were filled with wonder by all this. Gripped with the curiosity that comes naturally to children, we decided that the best way to find out more was to question the young boy. This would have to wait, however, for Joseph, as he was called, was the center of the Brothers' attention and they pressed around him. Myriam couldn't contain a startled exclamation when she saw one of them kiss the ground before him. This gesture seemed to dis-

---

*A vestal.

please—or at least to startle—Joseph; he took a few steps backward and stared deeply into the eyes of the one who had so honored him.

"Ehli um," he said, almost in a whisper, "El com." And he burrowed his head into his father's cloak, his eyes on the dust on which he had walked.

The following day promised to be a happy one, and though we did not celebrate Purim, I had told myself that I would go down as far as the road to admire the long procession of worshipers as they made their way to the little neighboring village.

The first glimmer of dawn saw me up from my mat. I crawled out of the heavy cloak I rolled up in every evening, knotted the belt of my robe, and went sliding down the steep rocky path in my bare feet.

Up and down the road there were already small groups of people hurrying on their way to the temple. They jogged along behind the mules and the donkeys, blowing trumpets: a motley crowd full of joy at the prospect of making a sacrifice at the temple.

A young man in a striped robe called out to me, smiling, "Hey, little one, aren't you coming?"

Another intervened saying, "Leave him alone, can't you see he's a Nazarite?" He pulled along his companion who was now looking at me with a scornful little smile.

A Nazarite? I wasn't a Nazarite! Why were they looking at me like that? I stood there, by the edge of the road to Joppa, as if frozen, struck dumb, incapable of showing the least joy before the growing column of merry people.

After a moment I turned back to the steep rise that led to the village. Through the fig and olive trees, I could only catch a glimpse of a few terraces. On the path, old Zerah's words were echoing in my ears: "You must know, Simon, that we are not among the sons of Abraham and Jacob." Looking up, I saw Zerah, high up on the hill, sitting upon the stone wall where the path entered the village. He was watching me as I stumbled, gasping, up the hill.

"Zerah," I burst out, as I reached him, "is it true that I'm a Nazarite?"

"Who told you that, Simon?" he asked. "Those people down there? No, you're not a Nazarite, but there would be no shame in being one." He paused. "You see, often, the people of the city and of the countryside around it don't understand those who don't think as they do, those who don't call the Father by the same name.

"Come here and sit down. I want you to listen to me and to remember what I say."

Reassured by the words of my old friend, I hopped up onto the wall. The stones were already warm in the morning sunlight.

"They call anybody a Nazarite who doesn't claim to be descended from Abraham and Moses, Simon. It is as if they were calling them 'heretics' or saying they were 'impure'. But it doesn't matter. Later on, they'll call you all sorts of names. You'll often be called Nazarene, and that will be untrue, too. Your real name, the only name you or any of us here are entitled to, is Essania,* which means—in the ancient language of our race—'Son of the Sun.' You won't hear this name often, though, as few people know of it. The people of Jerusalem call us Nazarenes, because for them this name sums up a lot of things, such as not cutting your hair, or wearing the rosary made of one hundred and eight grains around your neck, or . . ."

"But why is our hair so long, Zerah?" I asked.

"That is in memory of the time when the sons of the Father, the people of the stars, came to show us the path. . . . But I cannot tell you any more for the time being."

Below in the valley a single, low, drawn-out cry was being repeated over and over. It was the shepherd Brother calling to his flock that it was time to move out. It reminded me, too, that time was passing and that I had to help Zerah back to his home.

When we reached the old well I saw that Myriam was already there, sitting on the ground. She was talking with Joseph, our new companion of the day before. I left Zerah's side in an instant, and his laugh let me know I was forgiven. I hurried to join them.

"My mother is my mother," Joseph was saying slowly, enigmatically, weighing his words. "One day, my father told me that she had been a 'dove' in a great temple kept by our people. Her father was the high priest there. It was in Jerusalem, I think, the temple of light of the Brothers.† Nobody could touch her, and she was forbidden to set foot on the ground.

*Today, Essene.
†The Temple of Helios.

Joseph's voice, though it was particularly soft, filled the little square where we were sitting and his light blue eyes, as luminous as two pearls set into the dark complexion of his face, were laughing. He, too, had long hair like the Nazarites or the Nazarenes, slightly auburn and very thick. It fell in fine curls on his shoulders, which seemed surprisingly well developed for a child of his age.

He was wearing a blue robe made of rough material that opened wide around his neck, revealing, along with a rosary, a thin cord from which hung a little black bag that was sewn shut. He could see what I was looking at, and, smiling, he answered my unspoken question.

"Some old men gave it to me a long time ago, not far from Jerusalem. . . ."

I felt he didn't want to say any more. A long silence came over us; then Myriam, gathering up a handful of soil that she slowly let slip between her fingers, said:

"Joseph has two older brothers who should get here tomorrow. They're old enough to help his father make the bricks for their house. They are going to live here too; the village is going to grow. . . ."

Joseph got up then, saying that the sun was rising and he had to speak to his father. We watched him draw away calmly, in strong contrast with the restlessness of the other children of the village.

But instead of going toward the house where his parents were staying, we saw him move off into the thorny shrubs of a path that led straight up into the mountains. When he had gone out of sight, Myriam and I couldn't resist following him. Our childish curiosity got the better of our sense of discretion, and we followed him furtively into the stony heights.

Joseph, however, seemed to have disappeared. We soon found ourselves up to our knees in a carpet of red flowers and surrounded only by twisted olive trees. Suddenly, as we were going back, we spied Joseph, little Joseph, lying on the ground with arms outstretched in the form of a cross, his face to the earth.

Zerah suddenly rose up behind us.

"Let him be," he said gravely, "he's speaking to his Father."

CHAPTER · III

THE DEPARTURE

In my father's pottery shed, the wheel was creaking in response to the easy and rhythmic caress of his foot.

"In a little while you will be seven years old," he said, "and soon your life will have to change. I have had long talks with Zerah and some of the others in the village. You see, men are something like the clay that I shape with my hands. They can remain unformed, asleep, or they may be destined to come alive, to serve a special purpose. The difference between men and clay is that a man is also his own potter."

With a brush of his arm, my father swept back the hair that had fallen over his eyes.

"In the past seven years you have gathered the clay you will work throughout your life. All we have done—Zerah, your mother, and I—has been to add a little water, now and then, to make it all hold together. But from now on you will have to become like a bowl, collecting all that our people have gathered for generations and generations. But do not forget: a bowl is not only meant for receiving; half of its content will evaporate if it isn't offered quickly enough to the lips of those who are thirsty."

This he had said without pausing as he concentrated on a cone of clay turning beneath his wet fingers, which were the color of the earth of Galilee. His voice was calm, but could not mask a deep emotion that I was only to understand much later.

I instinctively drew in a deep breath, as if to heave a sigh, thinking I knew what was in store for me, but this was not so.

The clay stored in one corner of the little workshed gave off an acrid odor. To moisten it my father—no doubt through long habit unaware of his action—dipped his hands into a jug of water before adding:

"There is a mountain about two days' journey from here. It rises above the plain of Israel. Long ago, those of the race of Essania built a great school there with the help of the kings of the land of the Red Earth. There, they have stored up all they ever knew, and even more. The others in the village believe it would be good for you to go there, and so do I."

These words shot through me like a clap of thunder. I felt like a sheaf of wheat thrown beneath the stamping feet of the oxen to free the grain.

"But why me? And the others—aren't they going?" I don't know if this cry of revolt actually escaped my lips, or if I managed to bury it deep within myself.

I ran out of the workshed, blinded by the injustice of it all, shattered by what I took to be cold indifference on my father's part, but which I now know was only controlled emotion.

It was early in the morning, one day in Shevat.* A cool breeze swept over the hills and the timid rays of the sun cast a pale glow on the landscape. Where could I go? To Zerah? He too was abandoning me—perhaps the whole thing had been his idea. Perhaps he had known all along. So that was why he had wanted me to spend so much time with him, filling my head with things way beyond a little barefoot Galilean boy.

I had the impression that I was uncovering some awful plot, one that was as fearsome as the flint sickles wielded by the reapers in the autumn fields. I wouldn't get to see the Tiberias waters after Passover, as the Brothers had promised all the children of the village.

---

*Shevat, the eleventh month of the Jewish calendar.

Filled with anger, my eyes streaming with tears and my feet scratched from my heedless flight over the stony paths, I ran unthinking beyond the village walls. I stopped by an immense pomegranate tree, whose scarlet flowers and deep shade had brought me so much comfort in summers past. Perhaps here was a friend who would share my misery? Hadn't the old man of the well told me one day that we could talk to plants and trees too? I wondered just who this Zerah was, after all.

To the horizon, the blues, the grays, and the yellows of the neighboring valley unrolled their solitude. A far-off bleating of sheep and the song of a partridge signaled the existence of a secret life to which, deep within me, a voice advised me to pay heed. Through the hawthorn bushes, I caught a glimpse of someone in a blue linen robe and then recognized Joseph. He often wandered about the nearby hills, and I was not surprised to find him there. He seemed caught up in a dream, and he walked almost straight toward me without appearing to notice me.

What a strange boy Joseph was! They said he was not yet six years old, and he hardly paid any attention to our games. There were days when he was just like any of us, and he ran around, laughing, and played stones* with us, but it never lasted very long before he was off capering among the thistles on the mountainside, peacefully by himself.

For Myriam and me, Joseph was something of an enigma. We couldn't make out whether his eyes reflected infinite sadness or if they already showed something like the serenity of old age. I remember Myriam repeating something Ephram had said to her father as they were picking olives together: "He's an old soul; Joseph has the youth of old souls."

We were always happy to see him even if he was somewhat reserved, and we liked playing with him and talking with him, for what little he did say brought a smile to his lips, or perhaps to his eyes.

I cried out, to attract his attention, "Joseph, I'm going to leave!" But he had seen me anyway and was now running toward me. And

---

*A form of hopscotch played by children in Essene communities.

then I witnessed something I was never to forget; it was one of those moments when time seems to slow down, as if a door were opening and would never be shut again. As he came hopping over the rocks, I saw Joseph suddenly surrounded by a subtle blue glow that lit up the whole landscape. There was a silence, almost crackling in its intensity. Long, pure blue flames were shooting out of him like some sort of life force, to be transformed into twirling smoke that evaporated into thin air. It was as if the sun had come out from behind a cloud, as if the whole mountain were vibrating, resonating in time to the child who was leaping from rock to rock.

Joseph had himself become a sun, a blue sun. . . . I found myself suddenly wishing that I were even smaller than I was and that my sadness would disappear.

"What's the matter, Simon?" As Joseph came closer the enchantment gradually faded, and finally before me stood just a little boy hardly six years old, with a big smile on his face.

"I'm going away, Joseph," I stammered. "My father wants to send me to a very important place, near the sea, where he says I will learn all sorts of things."

"I know, Simon," said Joseph, "I was there when Zerah and the others were talking about it. That's good news, isn't it?"

He sounded so obviously right that I could not argue with the simplicity of his remark, and as we made our way back toward the houses of the village we talked about the preparations for the journey. We didn't take the usual paths; I followed Joseph, who took pleasure in making his own way among the brambles and the hawthorn bushes. In fact, it was as if he had his own paths that nobody else knew about, and following him helped me to calm down. Strangely, he seemed to know a great deal about this big school where I was to be sent. He talked about the place in much detail, but I listened distractedly, still entranced by the vision of Joseph surrounded by flames. Maybe that was the flame Zerah was always talking about. What if I had finally perceived it after so many vague hopes? But then, he had always spoken of one flame, of one light, and here I had seen a hundred of them, or a thousand, or perhaps even more, and it was the whole landscape that had burst into flame as Joseph passed through it.

There was another thing I couldn't understand, and I suddenly blurted out: "Why were you allowed to listen to Zerah and the others?"

By the others, I meant the Brothers, all the "old" people, men and women of twenty years and more, who had earned the right to wear the white linen robes. Every evening when it came time to fill the old earthen lamps with olive oil, I would watch as they filed into the only really big house in the village, in total silence. At the same moment, on the terrace of the gray stone house, someone I never did see would light a fire into which were thrown sweet-smelling resins. . . .

"I was with them the other night," he replied, "I was just lucky."

But I could tell he was trying to get around my question, and that he did not want to say anything more about it. Perhaps he had been told not to.

The following days were spent getting ready for the journey, and I made an effort to appear calm and untroubled. Myriam kept her distance, and I could see she was not very enthusiastic about what was taking on every aspect of an adventure for me, and making me the center of attention among the other children.

We needed two donkeys, which we managed to find in the village. They belonged to Joseph's brothers, two strapping young fellows with weather-beaten faces that already showed the marks of hard labor. I wondered naively how Joseph could have two brothers so much older than he, and with such a young mother. I found out several years later that his father had previously been married to a woman who had died in an accident.

The departure did not take place before the new moon. One of the donkeys was loaded with supplies: dried figs, a cheese, hard wheat cakes and some warm cloaks, in case we would have to sleep out under the stars on the way. At the last moment a heavy trunk was strapped onto the animal's back. This set it to braying, and then the second donkey started up as well.

I had imagined quite a send-off, but there was almost no one by the old well when my father and I set out. The day was just dawning, and only my mother and old Zerah, a staff in his hand, were standing there, wrapped in heavy cloaks.

My mother kissed me quickly and whispered a few words in my ear, then drew off in silence; it was not customary for us to make open show of our sadness.

Zerah held the donkey with a firm hand, while my father mounted briskly; I was hoisted up in front of him, and the animal brayed even louder. By way of farewell my old friend raised his right hand to his heart, his fingers spread wide. And that was all, as the donkeys started off down the narrow path leading to the village walls.

As we rounded one of the last dwellings of the village my attention was captured by the sound of hurried footsteps and the comforting glow of an oil lamp. From a terrace overhead, I caught a faint glimpse of a face—the face of the friend who had sat with me under the lemon tree, little Myriam. I could just make out her slightly forced smile and the beginning of a wave goodbye, but then we moved on and I could see no more through the thick foliage on either side of the path. Both our animals slid down a stony slope and my father held onto me firmly with one hand, while with the other he swished an olive branch through the air, just grazing our donkey's rump. Once we were down on the road to Joppa he pointed at the sky and broke the heavy silence.

"Look," he said, "this is the big morning star. We call it Moon-Sun, or Ishtar.* To our people it spells mystery and light. Remember this name, Simon, it will serve you well. An old legend has it that we owe much to the rays of Moon-Sun. Look how it shines, more than any other star in the sky."

Moon-Sun seemed to wink at me out of the fading darkness of the heavens, and I watched this star until first daylight. Our village was behind us now, and the first camel trains were already on the road after a stop of only a few hours.

My father talked of one thing and another, and tried to speak reassuringly of what I was to do up on the "mountain by the sea," whose name was Krmel.† He told me that I would have much to study, including the traditions of our people and the ancient texts;

---

*Venus.

†This spelling represents the pronunciation as it can be inferred from the Akashic Records. It is presently called Mount Carmel.

I would learn to heal and then, at last, I would be given a task, a task for my whole life.

This didn't sound very exciting to me, but then, all the Brothers had made so much of my great fortune in being singled out to go to the Krmel, perhaps it was true. As if he had had trouble finding his words, my father added, after hugging me closer to him, "You'll have to stay there several years. Your mother and I will not be allowed to visit you, but if the Father wills it, we may find a scroll or two and we will write to you." And with a forced laugh, he added, "You'll see, you will come home wiser than your old friend Zerah!"

The subdued colors of Galilee rolled on, a succession of pink, yellow, and gray pastels, of dry, chalky landscapes where, here and there grew a timid patch of grass. I didn't know whether to cry or to laugh at my good fortune.

The rising sun beat down with such force that soon we had to cover our heads with cloth, and stop now and then to let the animals draw breath. The day passed without incident, other than a few words exchanged with other humble travelers like ourselves whom we crossed on the path. At their approach I couldn't help trying to look dignified, as if to tell them, "I am on the way to the Krmel," but no one paid any attention to me. It was rather my father, with his white robe and his long hair hanging down onto his shoulders, that drew their attention.

We passed through several little ochre-colored villages, all of which smelled of sheep and goats. Dusk came on, lighting the first heavenly constellations sooner than I might have expected. Dismounting, my father urged the donkeys on more quickly than before. The region became more wooded, and soon all around us grew orange, lemon, and olive trees. At the foot of a twisted old tree, the road forked and we headed to the right, to reach the foot of a hill that looked drier than the surrounding area.

There, a big fire was crackling, tended by a number of men and women and a small group of children too. My father told me he knew this place and after waving to those around the fire, he drew the donkeys a little way off toward a low building that seemed imbedded in the rock of the hillside.

The doorway was so low I had to dismount to enter. I found

myself in a vast cavern, lit only by what little light came in through the tiny doorway. Judging from the number of animals bedded there, it appeared to be a sheepfold, or a stable, and the musky smell was suffocating. Some sheep started bleating as soon as we entered. After unloading our donkeys, we tied them to a sort of natural ring carved out of the rock wall.

"Is this a sheepfold?" I asked. I was about to spread my cloak on the hard ground.

"No, it's a bethsaïd," said my father. "That's a sort of lodging that the Brothers have arranged, where sick people may be treated and where travelers like ourselves may stay. Come, and bring your cloak with you; this is not where we are going to sleep."

I was puzzled. All I could see was this one great chamber. Where else did he think we could sleep? My father headed toward the back of the cavern, and there I saw him slip behind a bit of daub wall, I understood there must be a hidden staircase there, as he suddenly disappeared from sight.

Grabbing the rough cloth sack my mother had given me, I followed him and went carefully down the steps carved out of the rock. I didn't have any trouble seeing where I was going, as there were oil lamps in little niches cleverly carved into the wall of the staircase, which led down to a huge room. Here a number of people, men and women of all ages, were busy around a long rectangular wooden table big enough to seat about thirty people. They seemed to be preparing a meal, as a large woven basket was on the table, full of wheat cakes. In one corner of the room two men were sitting before a fireplace, stirring up a fire and blowing on the red embers.

One hand over his heart, my father performed the ritual salutation and each of the people there replied in kind. Then a couple who seemed to know where we were from came forward to embrace us and invited us to make ourselves at home.

"Is there a free corner of the room where we can sleep for the night?" asked my father.

"Of course there is, Joshua," replied the woman, "come with the little one."

And we followed our hosts across the vast room with the respect and discretion as would befit a holy place. In fact, we were not used to such luxury. The dirt floor had given way to great, carefully cut and fitted slabs of stone. In places, care had been taken to shape geometric patterns: a circle, a triangle, a square, made to interlock by the craftsman who had designed them.

But it was especially the ceiling and walls that fascinated me. Over the rock which, judging by the evenness of the angles, had been carved by master craftsmen, a smooth coat of clay had been applied and then painted with motifs in shades of ochre, blue, and red. It was only several years later that I would come to understand the symbols that I saw before me.

There were suns and various shapes of crosses, in patterns whose logic I could only vaguely apprehend. In the spaces between the symbols were inscribed many little passages in a language I had never seen before.*

We followed our guides through one of the many doors along the walls of the great room. In the flickering light of an oil lamp set into a niche we discovered a much smaller room with a large number of mats in a row on the floor.

There was also a honeycomb of cavities in the stone wall, in which humans, or at least children, might lie. My father pointed out that some of these were used as beds, while others were just seats set into the wall. He also drew my attention to a hole carved into the ceiling. He said that holes like this one were to be found in all the rooms, and served as air vents, leading to the hillside above, where they appeared to be but natural crevices.

The evening meal, which followed a sort of litany chanted by all, took place in dead silence around the table. We ate what we had always eaten at home—soup, wheat cakes, and olives. Afterwards, the atmosphere livened up and some people started chatting, trading news, and laughing over their stories, while others, in a more serious mood, made quiet commentaries over written scrolls that they passed from hand to hand.

As for me, exhausted from our long day on the road, I soon slipped off to bed.

•   •   •

*Today these would be called ideograms.

"Io . . . Io, diup! . . ." My father leapt astride the donkey I was already on and whipped the air with his switch. The journey would be easier that day as a fine rain was falling, caressing our faces. Our unpredictable mounts seemed to enjoy it too.

"You will see, Simon," said my father. "The Krmel is not just a school. It's also a sort of monastery, and a truly great temple. The ancient scrolls passed down to us from our ancestors claim that the mountain on which it was built has been sacred since the beginning of our world. Our Father, the Father of us all, sent one of his angels there, a long time ago, and it is said that there you can hear the heart of the Earth beating."

"The Earth has a heart?" I asked.

My father didn't answer right away, but said he'd rather walk alongside the donkey for a while. I felt he needed to think for a moment before giving me a reply.

"I don't know, Simon, I'm not learned enough in these things; the wise men taught me simply to know my own heart, and to use it. I have not studied the hearts of higher beings. You will learn all that yourself. The secret walls of the Krmel will perhaps share with you the mysteries of the realms beyond our own, and of the coming One."

"The coming One?"

"Yes, Simon. You will know all about this, and it will be your life."

In this way the hours passed, and as we went along the landscape changed, and then changed again. Then a slight wind came up and the horizon was revealed. Before us a chain of bluish mountains rose above the others, against the mauve hues of the sky.

"The Krmel!" my father cried out suddenly as we rounded a bend in the path. I searched in the direction of his gaze for what might even vaguely resemble a building, but all I could see was a great mountainous mass, whose shape was heavy and slightly rounded. There were a few ochre-colored spots, but nothing that looked like what had been described to me back in the village. It was only after quite some time on the path that I could make out the enormous stone mass of the Krmel, whose heavy walls soared up into the sky. A certain uneasiness plucked at my heart. I had expected something different. This huge structure looked more like a fortification than a school or a temple. The walls and their square towers did not seem to be vertical and appeared to get thinner as they rose skyward. As we approached, mute with emotion and curiosity, myriad tiny openings in the walls of the structure became visible. Some of these were barred, while others looked so small that one would have had trouble putting one's head through them. As the path led a good part of the way around the monastery, we had time to admire the stonework that was said to be more than ten centuries old. I counted three big wooden doors, which were much taller than they were wide.

"The sea!" I suddenly cried out. I had seen the sea before, but the very sight of it helped calm the anxiety that had begun to grow within me.

And thus it was in that state of mind that for the first time I passed through the heavy doors of the mysterious Krmel, where I was to spend a good part of my childhood. Joseph, who was so calm, and Myriam, who was so wild, were far behind me now, and I would have to learn to live without them here. It would now be the time for questions.

The stones of an immense courtyard rang beneath the hooves of our tired donkeys, and as the sky reddened over our heads, a Brother in white, thin-faced with flashing eyes, appeared suddenly before us.

"You are late!" he declared curtly.

CHAPTER · IV

KRMEL

"The teaching you will receive here is not vouchsafed to all, Simon. It is a great privilege. You must always remind yourself of this, and never complain."

A giant of a man with a ragged beard spoke these words as he wrote on an enormous scroll of woven fibre. His fluid and gentle voice contrasted with the terms he used, and I didn't know whether I should trust him or be on my guard.

As I timidly raised my eyes, I caught what looked like the beginning of a smile aimed my father's way. The tiny room in which we were gathered was filled with scrolls of yellowed paper piled up in the pigeonholes in the walls. I glanced around the room and noticed that by way of furniture there was only the little writing desk made of light-colored wood over which the Brother was bent, hard at work.

I was a little cold, and this sensation was doubtless accentuated by the draft that could be heard whistling behind the door, as it swept down the narrow corridors.

Before arriving at the office of the scribe monk, we had been escorted through an endless meandering labyrinth of passages and seemingly unoccupied rooms, filled with the invigorating odor of burnt wood. Several Brothers accompanying youngsters of about my age had passed us from time to time, in silence, one hand on their chest. I had anxiously examined their gazes and had now and then seemed to make out a smile or a word of welcome. Perhaps it was sheer imagination on my part. Zerah had had so much to say about the good heartedness of those who guarded the Word of our people!

At first, what I could see of the Krmel appeared austere, and yet something within me responded to it. Without really being aware of it I was pleased by the simple combination of wood and stone.

"Are you listening to me, Simon?" asked my father, bringing me out of my reverie.

The giant had sat up and was holding out to me a bit of reed, sharpened to a point.

"Sign your name here!" he said, pointing to a corner of the yellowish paper.

I plucked up my courage and managed to reproduce the few signs that old Zerah had taught me as we sat in his doorway.

My father inscribed his name below mine, and suddenly from behind me appeared one of the Brothers, who asked me to leave the room. So I waited in the long corridor, peering up through a little square opening at the still clear sky above. In the courtyard below our donkeys had started braying again. I could hear men talking around the animals; they were no doubt unloading the trunk we had brought this far, the contents of which had been kept from me. The creak of hinges behind me made me turn around to see my father coming out with the scribe.

"Farewell, Simon," my father said. "You see, this is where we part. I can wait no longer, and the Brother must show you to your room. You know what we expect from you, and when you come back to us. . . ."

He broke off there, and from the folds of his cloak, he took a little package, modestly wrapped in a faded old cloth, from which he extracted a pair of strong leather sandals. Never had I been given such a present! Blushing with pleasure and in a hurry to try them on and show them off, I hardly felt the weight of his hand on the crown of my head, nor did I feel it slowly drawing away. When I looked up again, I was alone with the huge man who put his hand on my shoulder and hurried me over the polished slabs of stone, down the long corridor. And so it was that, quite simply, I entered Krmel. Without comment I was shown into a small cell, probably my room, and a jug of water was set on a sort of low table along with a plate of cold vegetables. The door was closed again. I was alone.

The night passed, but I hadn't managed to sleep soundly; I kept watching for morning, between two waves of memories in which I was tossed in precarious sleep. At last, the first rays of sun began to creep into my room: a fan of white light filtered through the barred window . . . and no one came. They had probably forgotten me; after all, I was but the son of Joshua, the potter, and there must have been many other children there from all over the land. I sat for a long while on my straw mat, hanging on the slightest sound of footsteps, desperately staring at the heavy iron-bound wooden door.

Hours went by, and I wished that I could reach the little window that surely looked out upon the countryside or the sea. I tried jumping up to it, but it was too high and I had to give up. Then I started dreaming of the powdery paths of my village, of the pastel landscapes of Galilee, of the listless plodding of the donkeys, of the secret warmth of the bethsaïd, the sounds and the scents— all this took form within my imagination. I don't know how long this went on, but shadows were beginning to invade my cell when I came face to face with my solitude once more. My sandals, held tightly in my hands, linked me with a world that was gone forever. After a time, strained impatience stirred within me, and soon gave way to nervousness, then to despair. I had no idea whether the door had been locked when I was left there. Even if I had been physically capable of leaving the obstacle was insurmountable for a little seven-year-old Galilean like myself, used to unlimited freedom. The sun was beginning to go down and still I would never have dared call out nor attempted to test the heavy hinges.

Now and then, between two phases of a fear that had begun to gnaw at me, I seemed to hear furtive words rising within me, followed by short melodies that rose and fell. And thus hour followed hour.

Suddenly the sound of a gong, though far off in the distance, made me jump up shivering. I leapt to the door and pulled it violently inwards. It opened with disconcerting ease, and a flood of unknown scents washed into my room. I dried the tears that had begun to flow and let the floating scents guide me.

At the end of a zigzagging corridor, I went down a narrow wooden staircase whose steps were well worn by years of use. I found myself in a little inner courtyard, surrounded by high walls covered with frescoes slightly protected from the weather by wooden gables. I just had time to notice that these gables were held up at regular intervals by enormous tree trunks, forming an ambulatory. A small group of men dressed all in red were chatting there, and I chose to cross the courtyard at top speed through the first open door I happened to come upon. It was already so dark that I stumbled, not having seen the first steps of a staircase that climbed before me. This made me want to run even more, and I sped up the wooden steps. At the top a huge doorway awaited me, and through the open doors spread a yellowish, dancing light. A heavy cloud of burning incense enveloped me.

"Sit down, Simon!" A surprisingly grave voice stopped me in my tracks. "We have been waiting for you since this morning; sit down!"

It felt as if a thousand pairs of eyes were staring at me. A great many men were there, sitting with their backs to the four walls of an immense room that was all draped in blue. At the far end, facing me, one of them stood out from the rest. A square of red cloth, carefully placed on his head, fell smoothly onto his shoulders and hid most of his face from my eyes.

"Well, sit down!"

Stunned, at last I did as I had been told, folding my legs beneath me.

"Not like that, Simon. Now you must learn the position of the triangle.* It is thus that you must sit from now on."

And the voice particularly stressed the words, "from now on."

---

*Essene name for the oriental lotus position.

"We have been waiting here for you since dawn. You will learn that here, nobody gives anyone orders and nobody takes charge of anyone. Each of us must overcome his own barriers and break through his own solitude. We of the Krmel are here to allay our fears and learn to take a step toward others. Consider yourself lucky, Simon: some have taken up to three days to break out of the false prison of their cell and to come up here."

The voice, which I had trouble locating, but which seemed at times to come from the man with the red cloth, suddenly took on a gentler, more paternal tone.

"Relax, Simon, and don't be afraid of our harshness; it is meant to forge souls. Listen now, and learn to know us. All here are not of the race of Essania. Among us there are Brothers of the Red Land, as well as those whom the people outside call Nazarites and Nazarenes. We are many but our heart, our goal is one: to transmit that which was once or is now; to prepare the place of the One who will come, which amounts to the same thing. Have you ever been told of the ancient people of the last Earth?"

"No," I whispered.

"Very good. Be aware that your life as a man begins here and now, and that from now on, nothing of what you see and hear within our walls must part your lips to fall into the gutters of the cities. Nothing!"

There was a long pause, and then began a tale that even the mists of time have not been able to cloud. I remember it now as a long Ariadne's thread that I had to trace into the innermost recesses of my being, there surrounded by the dancing flames of the oil lamps.

"Listen, Simon, son of Joshua. There was a time when the face of the Earth was very different from the one we know, when the continents and the seas were not those of today. The sun and the stars did not show their faces as they do now; it was as if our Father had drawn a great mauve veil over our heads, and the stars rarely deigned to appear. The Nameless One had divided Earth into two parts: the South, which he had made the realm of the mountains that spit fire, and the North, the realm of ice and sleep. From the meeting of these two worlds rose a great mist that veiled the heavenly vault. This lasted for thousands and thousands of years, our years, and the men who lived at that time did not look like us. To you, Simon, they would have appeared horribly frightening, being so big, with low foreheads. As the thick mist that clung tenaciously to the Earth made it impossible for them to see more than a few paces away, they looked within themselves and saw their souls, along with our Father's flame, smouldering in their breast. After they had spent season after season breathing the water that was in suspension in the air, they finally learned to drink the air that was to be found in the water, in far greater abundance than it is now. It was then that the Earth agreed to spit forth its fire less often. The elements separated, and these men were at last able to behold the heavens in all their glory. And there was real day and real night, and they opened their eyes outward on the world, and then their bodies metamorphosed so as to adore the thousand facets of Nature.

"Ages passed, and they forgot their long conversations with the Nameless One who slept in their hearts. You must understand, Simon, that the people who dominated the Earth at that time were called people of Atl, as *atl* meant 'water' in their language. On a vast continent in the middle of the seas, these people had nourished the seeds of seven tribes, and it was when the fifth of these tribes had imposed its law that the changes I have told you about occurred."

At this point the voice paused, and whispered what seemed to be orders. Then I saw that in the four corners of the room, embers were being stirred to life in big bronze vases into which resins and herbs were thrown. Bright flames sprang up and sent shadows dancing over the walls. I could no longer feel my feet, numbed by sitting still so long in the cold, but for the first time since my arrival at the Krmel I felt good and wouldn't have moved for anything in the world, for I wanted to find out what had happened next to the people of Atl. I closed my eyes, and the voice went on.

"This tribe, son of Joshua, was called the people of Sem,* from whom descend all the white-skinned people walking the Earth today. Their civilization was beyond comparison, so magnificent was it, so powerful, and so advanced in its science. Twice already the Earth had shaken its spine, and twice the continent of Atl had

---

*Here we find the origin of the great Semite branch.

been split and quartered and broken into many pieces, and the waters had flooded in. Now listen, Simon, remember this above all else: the wise men of Sem, foreseeing the final catastrophe, went to see the sovereign of the land of the Red Earth to tell him of their fears. Together they decided to build a storehouse for the sum of their most secret truths, one which would be as strong and unshakable as the human mind could conceive, so that their knowledge might be preserved for those who came after them. If the Nameless One allows it, Simon, one day you may see this storehouse; this will be a day when the arms of the sun will warm not only the sand—but hear this now—cruelty and vice had, by that time, invaded the hearts of the people of Sem, and the heads of the seven tribes saw that the moment had come. Six of them fled, with all their people, toward the white, ice-covered lands of the North, while the seventh, with his sons and eleven men of wisdom, chose the torrid heat of the Red Earth. Then, one night, as the Lion advanced to meet the Crab, the stars began to fall from the sky. The land of Atl sank beneath the waves, and our Earth was almost totally laid waste. You know the rest of the tale, Simon, there's no need for us to tell it here. As I have been told, our Brother Zerah has read to you countless times from the scrolls of Moses, among others. The great king who wanted to preserve the wealth of knowledge of Sem was named Zurid, and he lived more than three thousand six hundred months before the invasion of the waters. Those of the land of Israel, Simon, the people of Moses, are the sons of the seventh head of the race of Sem; and those of Essania are the sons of the eleven wise men, priests of the other six tribes, who chose not to follow their people, but to devote themselves to the keeping of the treasure and the sacred flame of Zurid. Here, our task, and your task, is to protect that flame against the winds and the tides until the time comes when it may at last flare out in the light of day.

"Will you accept this task, Simon? Will you accept the linen robe?"

I summoned up all the bravery of my seven years, crouching on the floor in a patched tunic, penetrated by the stares of those who called themselves the children of the One, and acquiesced with a nod of my head. The Brother in the red veil stood up at last and I could see he had a long emaciated face, an ageless face, with a thick white beard and eyes that were clear and bright and to me looked like pearls of kindness. His hair seemed to fall almost to the ground, and in spite of myself my eyes followed its downward flow.

"A yes must be a yes, Simon," I heard him say. "Nothing can replace this sound."

"Yes!" This fragile syllable had just risen from my chest and was echoing in the immensity of the room.

"Come, then!"

Two men approached me, took me easily by the arms and brought me to the one I had supposed was their leader. In one movement they took my tunic off. I heard soft quick footsteps behind me and another Brother, who seemed much younger, came with a carefully folded black linen robe in which I was quickly dressed.

"Lie down."

The voice sounded reassuring, but two strong hands were at once weighing on my shoulders. Instinctively guessing what was expected of me, I lay down on the floor, face to the stone with my arms outstretched in the shape of a cross. This must have caused some surprise, as I heard a murmur spread among the assembled Brothers. From above me there came a slight amused laugh that was only half stifled. I couldn't help lifting my head to see what was going on, and my gaze met the ageless face beneath the red veil and two eyes like diamonds that were staring straight into mine.

At that moment a huge hand was laid on the crown of my head, almost containing the whole of it in its grasp, and my face was pressed down onto the cold slab of stone. This imperative pressure was maintained for a long, long time. All my thoughts vanished and my eyes closed, as if I were about to drink from a well of pure, sweet water. Where the pressure of the hand was applied, I felt a white mist flowing into me, mingling with my very being: a mist that, as it filled me, gradually became light and peace.

In a flash, my past was erased; I was no longer Simon from the village of the Brothers, but a cup into which was poured a flood of pure love.

Suddenly, in the middle of an ocean of immaculate light, a tiny blue spark sprang from the depths of my being, right at the root of my nose, and it grew and grew. It became an azure sun, and the closer it got to me, the brighter it became. I was no longer in the heart of the Krmel, but a hundred leagues, a hundred thousand leagues from there, I didn't know where, standing in, or rather hovering over, a grassy meadow and surrounded by whirling and dancing beings.

Out of the silence rose a soft slow chanting, and then I felt as if my body were being scattered to the four corners of the universe. My eyes opened—only to meet the blackness of the cold stone. I tried to get up, but my stiffened limbs refused to obey, and I found I was holding my breath.

I was instantly seized by two strong hands and set on my feet. The man in the red veil had disappeared, and I was caught spellbound by the chant that rose from the assembly of Brothers like a cloud of incense. They were all still there, immobile, as if made of marble, modulating their voices like a single soul. At last the chanting died out and a hand slipped into mine.

"Simon, you have met the Nameless One with your other self, the self that can behold him. Keep this memory deep in your heart."

The Brother in the red veil was once more beside me and spoke to me as my father would have done.

"This place is a hundred times sacred, son of Joshua. It was chosen for our race by a very great king of the red people,* more than a thousand years ago. Since this time the most wonderful and the most terrifying secrets of all humanity have been stored here; and it is here, by immersing yourself in these secrets, that you may reawaken your sleeping soul."

I felt his hand tighten on mine and he drew me a dozen paces over toward the stone wall. Then with a careful gesture the ageless Brother lifted the corner of a heavy blue drapery. Before me I saw a tall, wide window that revealed the scintillating immensity of the heavens.

"Look!" he exclaimed. "She is the one! Your path will often cross hers. She is the Initiator." And his finger pointed to one particular light in the sky, a light throbbing like a heart, and I recognized Moon-Sun.

---

*An allusion to Pharoah Totmes III.

CHAPTER · V

WORDS OF YESTERDAY AND TOMORROW

I was given another room; it was simple and clean, furnished with sanitary facilities I hadn't even imagined existed. I set out the few things my father had left with me: a bowl or two, a warm blanket and my sandals . . . which were soon taken away from me.

"You won't need them here," I was told. "We all go barefoot. This is the rule. When you call out to the Father, it's your heart that speaks, isn't it? For it's your heart that is closest to where he lives. Well, it is the same with your mother, the Earth. When you speak to her, or when she speaks to you, it is through your feet. Is this not logical?"

It was, of course, and my childish notions of justice and property could not argue with such reasoning. In the days that followed my arrival and my first initiation, I understood that only a few young boys were admitted to the Krmel. In all there were about thirty of us, coming and going in the long corridors, following the teachings given by the Brothers and observing the long hours of communal prayer.

I remember the early phase of my life as a little monk being arduous, exhausting for both body and mind, neither of which was accustomed to such strict discipline. Any idle talk seemed to be against the rules, as I quickly learned, taking the cue from the frowns of my companions if I dared to interrupt their meditations.

The regularity of the daily routine was astounding. Every morning I had to be up at five o'clock. I would hurry to roll my mat in one corner of my cell, and perform rapid ablutions with the water from my jug. Then, I would run down the corridor to meet the older Brothers or companions of my own age in a spacious but sober temple, where we all joined in a long prayer. There was a frugal breakfast afterwards: some dried fruit, a biscuit and a bowl of mildly flavored warm water. Then came the first lesson of the day: one of the Brothers whom I never saw sit down took great pains to teach us, with strict discipline, how to read and write Hebrew and Greek, both of which he said we would all need to use.*

He was followed after about an hour by another Brother, a rather jovial old man who couldn't seem to stop smiling as he inspected us, one after the other, all the while twitching his thick white eyebrows. He made us do mental exercises, designed, at first, to help us control and direct our thought processes. This practice was held to be of the utmost importance, even more important than the study of the sacred texts; and I soon realized that this would be the keystone of our learning. Then came another prayer and another class, in which we were asked to comment on ancient words. And on it went, tirelessly, an alternating pattern of lessons and prayers that lasted until the sun went down. We were allowed hardly more than two hours a day for recreation. At last, the long-awaited gong signaled the main meal of the day, the only real meal, in fact, that we all took together. The same gong sounded again at midnight and then at three in the morning, calling us up from sleep, reminding us of the short prayer we were to recite, lying on the stone floor facing east. This ritual was repeated seven times a day, and three of these prayers, spaced seven hours apart, were accorded special solemnity. And thus was my life ordered as the months went by. There was little time for tearful, nostalgic recollection of a more pleasant time belonging to the past.

---

*For most of us, our mother tongue was Aramaic.

This rhythm was, however, interrupted early one morning as I rushed out of my cell, knowing already I would be late to the temple. A white-robed Brother, who seemed to be waiting for me, seized me by the arm with a firm hand.

"Today will be a special day for you, Simon," he said. "Follow me, and do not worry about your classes; your masters have been told that you will not be present."

With this, he led me through a labyrinth of rooms, corridors, and crumbling stairways that I hadn't imagined existed. I had the feeling that we circled the Krmel ten times, following a mysterious route, the only purpose of which could have been to confuse my sense of direction.

At the foot of a stone stairway worn by centuries of use, my guide pushed open a heavy door that was hidden behind a dusty and faded drapery.

"You must never breathe a word of this, Simon! Never!" he said.

"I promise," I said instantly, delighted by the promise of great mystery, "I sw——"

"No, Simon!" he interrupted. "Those who wear the white robe never swear to anything . . . your word is enough. All through your life, this must be your rule, remember. Let a yes be a yes and a no a no. The children of Abraham know this. They know what the word of a Brother in white is worth, and they will never ask you to swear an oath. Now take this torch, and follow me."

A very steep stairway, carved into the rock itself, seemed to sink endlessly into the bowels of Mount Krmel. My guide took care to shut the heavy door behind him, and we plunged into a darkness so dense that our two torches could barely penetrate it.

Rapidly our eyes grew used to it, and I saw that our progress would be made easier by a succession of little vessels filled with a sticky black substance that we lit as we went, transforming them into blazing lamps.

Clinging to the rock walls as I made my way down, I didn't dare to speak, only too happy to be offered this unexpected adventure. There was a dampness around that seemed to come from everywhere at once, along with a moldy smell, a smell of forgotten centuries that filled the air. Farther down we went, interminably, following the abrupt turns of the stony stairs. Little by little, I felt the walls changing from the rough-hewn rock of above to a smooth polished surface that reflected the light of our torches like marble. It was as if, for mysterious reasons, the walls had been glazed by some unknown force.

As if in answer to my unspoken question, the Brother said, "It was the people of the race of Sem who made these steps, Simon, our ancestors, who knew the art of reading the future and forseeing its needs. As you can see, it was neither with hammer nor chisel, nor even with acids that they worked. Their science gave them the means to melt rock as easily as the sun melts snow. Does this surprise you? The secret has been lost only recently . . . and we must be very blind not to have rediscovered it. You see, Simon, the heat that liquefied this rock is sleeping there, beside you, beside me, beside us. It is fluttering in the air we breathe, and we have only to find a way of harnessing it."

He paused in his explanation for a moment, then resumed, deliberately changing his tone of voice.

"What we must now learn is how to harness old Zerah's flame."

"Zerah!" I cried, "Do you know Zerah?"

"No, son of Joshua, my gaze has not met his on this path, but the flame of which he spoke is the spirit of the Earth, of the universe; it is the soul of your soul, it is your spirit and mine at the same time. How can we not know that which is our self? Not to know is willfully to persevere in our blindness or our indifference. Remember this, Simon: there is but one thing in the universe, but one force—the force—the one that proclaims the 'I' in us, that makes each of us seem to be a multitude. Think of a drop of water, Simon, is it not one with the ice crystals that appear if you chill it? In Nature, all that exists and lives, does so according to this image, and the soul alone is able to take on varying forms, depending on the direction of the focus it chooses to take. It is all so simple, and it is we who make it all seem complicated."

How often had I heard this seemingly unimportant statement repeated? It was perhaps simple, but the child I was then felt more fascinated by this rock wall as smooth as a mirror, which sent back the flickering reflections of our two bodies.

As we progressed downward, I felt a suffocating heat rising out of the depths of the Earth, and breathing became difficult. My guide halted abruptly. Several meters before us his torch revealed a low door, so narrow that it looked as if it had been designed for a child of my age. Long ago it must have been daubed with red paint; there remained three or four faint traces of signs in a script unknown to me and about a hand high.

"What is it?" I asked.

The Brother gave no sign of having heard my question, and seemed to be lost in thought; then he bent down on one knee and turned to me.

"Simon," he said, "here we are going to face a great danger; it is important that you realize this. This door separates us from a realm to which the world of mankind has no right of entry unless granted permission. Numerous forms of life exist on this planet and just as there are impalpable beings in the air we breathe, others live in the womb of the Earth we walk upon. Yes, Simon, we are now going to cross the threshold of the realm of the Earth spirits—but don't look at me like that! I am not speaking the language of superstition, my words are simply those of one who knows because he has learned to see what most refuse to see. The little light that shines in your eyes has helped us to understand, the other Brothers and me, that you are one who is able to look into certain eyes, and face certain presences.

"Look at this door. As soon as we pass through it, myriad strange beings will come to surround us and will perhaps try to slow us down. You should not be afraid. As long as your soul remains pure they will not be able to harm you. Be like a crystal, this is all I can advise you."

With these words the Brother inserted some sort of metallic tongs into a hole in the door and at the same time gave it a strong shove with his shoulder. The heavy postern gave way slowly, and a breath of hot air swept over our faces. A yawning hole, pitch-black, opened before us. My guide entered without hesitation, bending almost to the ground, so low was the doorway.

"Shut the door behind you, Simon," he said, "and put out your torch. One will be enough; there's little air here."

Hardly had I pushed the door shut and extinguished my flame when I was overcome by the distinct feeling of an alien presence in the tunnel. This sent a shiver up my spine. I remember involuntarily gasping. All around me I felt a swirl of strange beings, coming at me from all directions and brushing me as they swerved past.

"Remember what I told you," whispered my guide, "a crystal!"

Before me weaved the pale light of the single torch, flickering in the darkness. My chin tucked nearly to my chest, I tried to walk as quickly as I could, torn between the desire to pause and look around me or just advance with the doors of my soul shut fast. But all over my body I felt a stinging, prickling sensation, and in spite of myself I opened my eyes wide. Then staring into the darkness I saw something like a veil that was imperceptibly disintegrating, as if the obscurity were evolving into a powder of light, into a collection of dense particles spinning in an apparently chaotic dance.

Suddenly I stopped as if frozen. Around me, in the middle of this sea of mysterious living presences there appeared faces, indescribable faces, half-human, half-mineral, at once grimacing and angelic. And then whole beings seemed to leap out of the black light, beings like crystals, like roots, covered with fur as no human being could ever be, agile little creatures with cruel eyes that looked at me contemptuously.

In an instant I found myself amid a crowd of beings from another world who seemed to have decided to escort me. I felt like screaming and running but I couldn't make a sound and my legs were as unresponsive as if they were made of wood, just barely able to support my heavy, numbed body. I kept my eyes riveted on the one thing that tied me to the world I knew: the dancing flame of the torch, just a few paces ahead of me as I lumbered on. Then the torch halted for a moment.

"We have been adopted, Simon," my guide announced. "Did I not tell you so?" He stretched out his hand to me, and I took it at once.

"Every element lives its own life, son of Joshua, and this existence is no more monstrous than our own. Love these beings, for without them you could not live. Without them the flax seed could never germinate, nor its flower blossom. They are a part of the vital body* of the Earth, the essence of the minerals that mankind melts and casts. Look at their long, claylike hands; the Father has them gather all that mankind sows; they work together with the spirits of fire, of water, and of air. Did you know that the people of the furrows and the mountains honor them, though they do not know it, through the hundreds of seemingly insignificant rites they have perpetuated over the ages. There will, however, come a time, Simon, when these same people will have petrified their hearts so much that they will no longer feel the breath of the spirits. The fruits of the Earth will become scarce, and humans will invent a multitude of potions and new soils. This will be a sign, one of the many that will silently proclaim: Times are going to change.

"I tell you, Simon, love these creatures, for, as He has to everything else in the universe and beyond the universe as well, the Nameless One has given them a soul similar to your own, issued from the will of the sun.

"But can you not feel how your body is vibrating? Your heart has slowed its beating and the Father's energy is flowing more slowly through your body. For these reasons, you must not seek after their presence. But you will recognize them, wherever they dwell, and honor them and live in harmony with them. They are on a path toward the same palace of light as we are, but theirs is a different path, remember this. The substance of their bodies is not the same as yours, and this is also true of their souls. Only your vital being is similar to theirs. For this reason, do not try too hard to analyze their profound way of reasoning and judging. It is impenetrable to one who sets foot on the surface of the Earth."

Drinking in these words, my child's mind had ceased to think, the better to look within. Only the drops of sweat beading on my skin as we trod heavily forward brought me back to the reality of my body making its way through the suffocating heat, down the dark passage.

The beings that swarmed around us were emitting a low humming sound that at times rose, then fell, and seemed to fathom

---

*Etheric body.

the depths of our souls. Soon we arrived at a second door, in every way identical to the first. The Brother halted two paces in front of it and planted his torch in a crevice of the glazed stone, undoubtedly designed for this very purpose. I watched as he traced a circle around where he stood with his finger pointing at the floor, all the while counting his steps as he trod in place. Then he launched into a haunting, singsong chant.

Instantly we were surrounded by little streaks of light that sprang up out of nowhere, spinning around us in all directions at incredible speed. Abruptly, our escort seemed to disperse, like a puzzle whose pieces are scattered to the wind. Then all was still, and we were left alone. My guide turned to face the heavy wooden door, and pulled it open.

"This is not magic, Simon," he said, visibly drained by the effort the opening of the door had demanded of him. "You must learn to tell the difference. Magic is never more than a technique that enables any person of strong will to dominate the laws of Nature, laws that are unknown to many. Here at the Krmel we work with the heart, giving expression exclusively to the heart. Let it enlighten and embrace the whole of your being and it will always remain the supreme key, the royal path. All else is but illusion, but a crutch for our still weak souls."

As he uttered these words, a brilliant light invaded our field of vision. I felt as if I were breathing through every pore of my skin, and stepped quickly forward to free myself at last from the narrow tunnel.

It was a fascinating spectacle. We found ourselves in a vast, high-vaulted chamber, flooded in soft white light. It was a haven of serenity and invigorating silence. Everywhere there were scrolls, tablets, books, all stacked to great heights, though it gave me no impression of disorder. On the contrary, everything looked as if it were classified, indexed, and arranged with great care. But it was the spotlessness of the place that most intrigued me. Not the least speck of dust could be seen, not the faintest trace of the passage of time. I could hardly imagine one of the Brothers, not even one of those assigned to the maintenance of the temple, coming here regularly to spend hours dusting shelf after shelf of precious texts with a peacock feather, as was the custom. The Brother who had led me to this astonishing place seemed to radiate in the presence of these ancient scrolls and metal and stone tablets, as he strode lightly around the chamber. I followed his example and found that the beauty of the works stored here, their voluminous and majestic quality, was almost hypnotic. It was almost unthinkable that these pieces of writing had been kept for so long. . . .

"For so long that human memory gets lost in the meanders of time," my guide said, reading my thoughts. "A part of the archives of our Earth and of its peoples is gathered here in safety, Simon. Do you realize how privileged you are? Two whole continents have sunk, have been swallowed by the waters and by the Earth since the first of these scrolls, the first of these stone tablets were inscribed with the patience and precision of a goldsmith. The history and the knowledge of our planet have been stored in that way for nearly one hundred thousand years. Among this multitude of works there are those not composed by human hands, and these still remain a mystery for some of us. May you one day be initiated into their secrets. Others are in the form of picture writing, similar to those used in the land of the great red kings, and date from an age when the very name of the people of Atl meant nothing yet.

"These are the books from the time of Ma, the Earth Mother, a name that that also means "water." It was in these days that those called Elohim by the children of Abraham began traveling regularly about the planet, to guide it in its march forward. Look carefully at these two signs, Simon, they carry the imprints of these great beings."

The Brother held in one hand a little black metal tablet, and pointed to the middle of a tangle of hieroglyphs, where two miniscule drawings were finely engraved. Immediately I recognized one of them as the image of Ishtar, Moon-Sun, which I kept finding everywhere, even in the depths of the most secret of all retreats. The second image was familiar, although I didn't know it as well as the first. It was like a spiral drawn above a cross whose branches were of equal length, all under the protection of a lunar crescent.

"This is one of the symbols of Hrma,* whose glory shines not far from that of the sun. As I have told you, the messengers from

*Mercury.

Moon-Sun and Hrma came frequently to live among human beings in those far-off times. They were acknowledged as guides and legislators, some developing the people's intuition and love, others their precise and secret knowledge of phenomena. They were like the two hands of the Father, opening the eyes of the human race. You must understand that this is not just an image, Simon. The bodies of our ancestors who lived on the land of Ma were still primitive. Their eyes were not like real eyes yet, but simply vague sensitive spots on the surface of their skulls. Their skeletons were soft and could bend at will, and only the radiant forces of the moon, which was still coming to life, forced them to solidify.

"I see your smile," he said, looking at me, "but you must realize that humanity is like a flower that blossoms slowly throughout eternity, according to the seasons of its heart and mind. And so, the human body will not remain forever as it is now.

"Now you may be wondering why I have brought you here. This place must prove to you that the race of Essania is one of the keepers of the Tradition."

"The Tradition?" I asked.

"The knowledge that the true children of the Nameless One have been perpetuating on Earth since the dawn of time. The ages pass, Simon, but since the beginning, there have been colleges of beings who have taken on the mission of maintaining and spreading the Word."

"How long will it go on?"

"Until the opening of the door of the Self of humanity! You will understand these words later."

"Are all those of our religion waiting for this door to open?"

"Our religion?" he repeated. "Never use this term again. What does it mean? That you have come into the world somewhere with a color of skin, habits, beliefs, and hopes? If that is what it is, then it means nothing. We have no religion, Simon, we have no beliefs; we walk without a staff upon the ray of light issued from the Father's mouth . . . and we prepare the advent of Him who is to come."

"Who is he?" I asked.

In answer to my question, the Brother in the white robe smiled broadly, held two fingers to his lips, then brought his right hand to his heart with fingers spread wide like the rays of the sun.

"It is imperative that this library be guarded in this way. For in the hands of those who divide rather than unite it would be far too great a source of power. It is also as a precaution that the location varies. Yesterday these scrolls were preserved beneath the stones of our Dead Sea temple. Tomorrow they will leave our land to find refuge in the country that is waiting beyond the snows, where the sun rises: one of the countries of Assa,* from which the present name of our people comes."

The chamber in which we stood was not the only one in this secret sanctuary of Knowledge: three galleries leading outward revealed many other rooms, smaller, but filled with equally fascinating things. There were small plaques of copper and gold, and voluminous scrolls of parchment and papyrus carefully bound. Occasionally, my attention was drawn to some particular objects, unusually shaped objects, that to my young mind, evoked strange possibilities that, perhaps, were real.

The Brothers who were entrusted with my instruction at the Krmel explained to me, years later, that a number of these objects, carefully placed in the heart of the subterranean library, had specific functions. Some of them were responsible for the lighting of the chambers and enabled us to see as in broad daylight. In fact, the light did not emanate from the objects themselves, but they served as an amplifier for the light that is found in the heart of all things. As the years passed, I came to understand that they could not be limited to a functional purpose, for everything about them urged them to act as living symbols. Let every human being grasp the profound implications of this fact and act accordingly. "We create nothing; we just lift veils, only revealing what already is." Such was one of the key teachings of the Krmel.

There were, of course, other objects whose functions were less sacred. Some were there to maintain an atmospheric equilibrium, renewing the oxygen and checking the purity of the air. I was told that the surprising cleanliness of the place was owing to the exclusively sacred character of the library and its contents. The matter that entered into their composition had been purified, sublimated, by the sacred nature of the texts they contained. These scrolls and tablets

*We leave it up to the reader to meditate on the sonorities and meanings of words such as "Asia," "Essene," "Asgartha," and the "Aces" used in our decks of playing cards.

might be said to have the same qualities as living beings. The clarity of their souls, or of the teachings they perpetuated, sufficed to transmute their bodies, the parchments and tablets, and to render them almost inalterable. Although in the eyes of many this may seem a mere fable, a symbolic way of presenting things, it is not so. It is a fact. All matter conforms to the law of the spirit that inhabits it. Impurity and corruption in a body are always due to a lack of perfection in the force that dwells within, with the exception of one form of aging, which is to be attributed to the vibrations of the planet itself.

Our visit to the sacred library of the Krmel lasted a long time, and the hours passed without complaint on my part. I was in another time, another place, far from the harsh discipline of my daily existence. The Brother went on and on, explaining certain texts he read aloud to me, and drawing my attention to the calligraphy of the most ancient among them.

"There are letters and symbols that are real living beings! Always remember this. Patterns and drawings are forces that exist in the real world. You will one day know how to wield these forces, but be patient. First, you will have to come to understand that a man, or a woman, or even a child, is also a book that may be deciphered, just like the writings you see around you here. People have their codes, their strong points, their ability to understand,* which always send us back thousands and thousands of years. The only difference is that their souls have not yet managed to breathe out the spirit that will dust them off and make their reading easier!"

Did I really grasp the whole meaning of the words said by my guide of that day, whose name I didn't even know? I can hardly say so. It was easier for me to follow the sober, careful movements of his fingers as he selected the scrolls he would read, leading me through the archives of the past. I was, however, particularly attentive to one text that he read to me almost in a whisper. He said it was a text that came from an initiated priest of the Red Land:

"There are worlds: I have, I am, and I become. These are the Father's three costumes. I write this for the peoples who are yet to

---

*See the Koran 10:14–15: "We have tied each man's bird around his neck. On the day of the resurrection, we shall show him a book that he will find open. 'Read in your book,' we shall tell him; 'you will only have to account to yourself today.' "

come, so that they will not seek in vain. He who ignores this condemns himself to come back, again and again. People do not live only once; they will reappear another day. Different worlds and different places await them on their paths that lead them through many lives. Eternity is a circle whose center is the Father, and all the faces of the Father are those of the Great Sun. Learn then, sons of the future. Remember the words of yesterday and of tomorrow."

"You see, Simon," said the Brother, "we have the bad habit of always assuming that people of ancient times were ignorant, super-stitious, and primitive creatures, and that it is only we who see clearly, and make progress. But, then, what is progress? Pride and complacency? No, I tell you, everything that is possible for a human being to know was long ago brought to Earth from the stars by the Lords of the Ten and the Seven. All we may do is preserve and maintain this knowledge and remember it anew, until the day comes when our spirits will be fit to join theirs."

With these words, the Brother meticulously replaced the sheets of papyrus he held in his hands, one on top of another. Then he let a thick wooden cover fall into place over them before returning the text to its allotted space on one of the shelves. I could feel that our journey beneath the Krmel was coming to an end. The little timepiece that each of us has within us told me that up there, on the surface, the sun was beginning to sink into the sea, reddening the horizon.

We took one last look at the secret chambers filled with their precious texts, as if to assure ourselves that our presence had not disturbed their secret life, and then we braved the narrow corridor once more.

We got back up without difficulty. I was exhausted, and I do believe I went up the last few steps in the Brother's arms. I had been looking forward to going to sleep, made drowsy by the heavy clouds of incense and the dull ringing of the gong which echoed once more down the corridors, but a sharp familiar voice brought me out of my dream. It was one of my masters, urging me to the temple.

"Simon! Come on, Simon! To the temple, quick! It's time for the service!"

CHAPTER VI

THE AURA

Never again was I to see my guide of that day who, in the space of a few hours, had curiously warped time, bringing together past, present, and future in the underground heart of the Krmel. I spoke to no one about my discoveries, as I had been asked not to, and no one ever made allusions to the subject. My fellow pupils seemed to have been unaware of my absence. Had they been told not to mention anything? Had they also had the same experience at some time? I was never to know.

Winter came knocking on the doors of the Krmel. I remember gusts of wind sweeping down the corridors and whistling under the doors of our cells. I remember the growing severity of our masters, which seemed to be in keeping with the rhythm of the seasons. I can still remember the sound of our hurried footsteps as we ran barefoot over the stone floors in the temple of lessons. There we would spend endless hours intoning the same texts, penning the same letters in various languages. The lessons we were taught and the precepts that were engraved in our minds became at times real obsessions, so often had our instructors declared they would not bear mediocrity. But there were no reproaches or punishments at the Krmel. Indeed, the masters knew how to find just the right words that would suddenly bring one face to face with one's conscience. And so in less than a year, an impressive number of texts were forever stored in my memory, and it was only when looking back on that time that I could appreciate the effectiveness of such methods. One of the Brothers once explained their purpose in these terms:

"What does it matter to us that you learn the words of the ancient texts written by the peoples of the sun as we insist? Have you not understood? It is your will, and your will alone, that we cultivate in making you strain your memory. We just want to purge the rust from your brains; nothing else matters."

The Brothers insisted on the utmost cleanliness. It was a rule that we were not to wear the same robe more than three days in a row, and every time we would begin another activity we were to wash our faces, hands, and arms. The initial reason for this was simple respect for the activity at hand, which in the eyes of the Brothers was like a living being that was evolving in an invisible world. Much later, we were told that there was another reason for cleansing ourselves so often: we did not dwell in a body of flesh only, far from it; and the activity of our brain, or of our consciousness alone, was enough to soil the surface of another body, easily cleansed by the simple act of washing with water.

In the same way, the few sacred objects that were used daily—triangles, stars, and censers—had to be washed and polished after each use. This was a golden rule we could not break. Furthermore, these objects were to remain strictly personal. We were taught that some of the substance of our vital souls impregnated them little by little and that this made their use even more beneficial. This invisible and almost magical aspect of things intrigued and excited me, and so I always enjoyed the exercises in psychic development that were a major part of our instruction and enabled us to comprehend the more subtle workings of our world.

My first year of study at the Krmel ended with an event that marked a decisive turning point in my life, an event that no cataclysm could ever erase from my memory and whose repercussions I still feel today, like a suspension of time in music, in the interval between one life and the next. One morning in the month of Adar I was awakened by a familiar voice that had long been buried in the inmost recesses of my mind.

"Simon! Simon!" I heard.

A shiver ran through me, and though my eyes were still shut, I finally perceived an unusual brightness in my cell. Perhaps I hadn't heard the big temple bell and the sun was already high, but it wasn't so.

I felt the reality of the moment like a wave of tenderness flowing into my heart. Joseph, little Joseph from the village, was standing there before me, bathed in a ray of white light. He was smiling at me, and his eyes were glowing like two aquamarines. In an instant I sat up on my mat, wondering what was happening.

"Simon! Simon!" His call penetrated me with convincing force, and I saw my friend's lips moving, saw the folds of his robe rippling as if he were dancing towards me. For an instant, I felt a shiver run through me again, as if a wave of springtime had risen from the earth, slowly flowing through me, right up to the crown of my head. Joseph took three steps forward, and I lost contact with my body. I was but a single eye, a single consciousness, spreading wide like a target, offering itself to the first arrow, the initiator.

"Look, Simon . . . look! I am not the memory of a far-gone time. The memory of dear ones is only for those who dream their own deaths, for those who make of their lives an empty breath. Your mother, your father, Myriam, and all the others from the village dwell within you, before you, not like shadows, but in their real bodies. Break the wax that seals the doors of your heart, hear their voices echoing within your being, stretch your will, forget your flesh, and their eyes will meet yours, I can assure you.

"You find your existence hard here, but it is really your own coldness that you perceive. I know this place; there is more warmth here today than anywhere else in the world. This I know, and my knowledge stems from my life in ancient times. The Brothers seem harsh to you, but it is your own selfishness that you feel. I know them; they are like muscles shaped by great effort. But pay no attention to the muscle that works, grasp the will that tightens them. Accept this as your life for a time, Simon, and observe the many faces of love."

Joseph lapsed into silence, then brought his hand to his heart, his left hand, and his whole body began to vibrate, to glow, as if all the force of the sun were locked within him. It was peace, total and absolute beauty, and to me it seemed that the walls of my room were evaporating, vanishing towards infinity.

The faces of all the Brothers in the Krmel drifted before me in a flash, in a torrent of clear soft light, and for the first time, I met their eyes, big as worlds. Yes, you, Samuel; you, Moshab; you, Jacob; I recognize you all. I know what we are doing here. . . . My father, my fathers, Galilee, my loneliness, the cold winters of the Krmel. . . . The Purpose. All became clear. . . . and these seven years, my seven short years. . . .

Then all was erased in a flash. The walls of my room returned at dizzying speed, and, Joseph and his light burst into a thousand splinters. My body was tingling all over, and I could hardly stand up. A thin ray of chilly light told me the day was just dawning. I had a strange, inner conviction. . . and I rushed into the corridor, to the nearest opening that looked down on the inner courtyard.

Below, far below, there was a cluster of a dozen men wrapped in long cloaks, several donkeys stamping their feet with impatience, and at their side a boy whose long auburn curls were flying in the wind. It was Joseph! I held my breath. The sound of slow, steady footsteps made me turn round. It was Moshab, one of the Brothers, coming to find me.

"Come, Simon," he said, "someone is asking for you." He was looking both moved and amused. He threw a fold of his heavy cloak around my shoulders and led me off at once. It was such a curious reunion with Joseph in the little courtyard of the Krmel . . . . There we were, in the dying glow of several oil lamps, as the sun sent its first flaming rays over the high walls.

We murmured a few words. In simple phrases we reinvented the art of speaking, listening to each other between our words. He quickly drew two little parchment scrolls from the folds of his robe. One was from my parents, the other from Myriam.

"I too am going to live here now," he said calmly. "I will have to study for six years."

Six years! This straightforward statement, spoken so naturally, almost knocked me over. Was I also to spend six years here? No one had ever clearly answered this question, which had occurred to me the very first day of my stay at the Krmel. It had to be Joseph. . . .

"After all," he continued, "this is what we wanted. We did say yes to the Father. Everybody in the village is proud of us."

Joseph laughed, as if to get a reaction from me, but there was none. Speechless, I stared at him and at those around us. At regular intervals, I thought I could see little tongues of bluish flame springing from our bodies. It wasn't the first time I had had this fleeting perception, but I had never spoken of it to any one. I could see each of us surrounded by a big white shell, a cocoon, of milky white light, so peaceful and soothing, through which shot blue streaks of flame. I spoke without thinking: "Look! There are little flames everywhere!"

As soon as I uttered these words, the enchantment was broken, and my perception returned to normal.

"Zerah sends his regards," said Joseph suddenly, with a blend of kindness and playfulness in his eyes. This phrase triggered memories of hundreds of things my old friend had said to me. A question welled up in my heart. "There were flames all around you, rising, twirling, dancing—what were they?"

Two hands were laid on my shoulders, two rough hands, with what I felt to be long fingers. A voice behind me said, "Later, Simon, after the long prayer, you must come to see me."

I turned to face the Brother with the red veil, the one who, a year before, had conferred upon me the first sacred breath of the Krmel. That was all. I didn't even have the time to look into his eyes before he was gone, leading Joseph to a little wooden staircase whose access was forbidden to the rest of us.

Within a few minutes, their two figures, as well as those of several other Brothers, were out of sight. I lived through the hour of communal prayer as in a dream, with only the low sonorities of the chants penetrating my being. With my eyes lowered, I absorbed myself in the rereading of the two parchments Joseph had brought me. They carried with them, poor and yellowed as they were, all the sunshine and the scents of the dusty paths of Galilee. One of the Brothers drummed six beats plus one on an enormous wooden drum, signaling the end of the ceremony. Then as we were taught to do, I inhaled deeply through both nostrils, breathing in a lungful of incense smoke which would make my inner being vibrate more closely to the Nameless One.

Overjoyed at the prospect of missing my Greek writing class, I quickly managed to find my way through the maze of corridors leading to the rooms of the Brother in the red veil, in my view the most inaccessible place in the Krmel, receptacle of mysteries.

Every time one of the Brothers tried to intercept me, I repeated proudly, "I am expected." Finally, a huge Brother with thick gray hair let me into a small room whose low door was flanked on either side by an imposing candlestick with eleven burning candles.

Sitting quietly on the floor in a corner of the room, the Venerable One looked as if he had been waiting for me. "How long have you been able to see the flames of beings, Simon?" he asked gently, indicating I was to sit in front of him.

"The flames of beings?" I asked.

"Be still and listen. The fire and water of their souls, the rays of their hearts. I know what you can see, Simon; let me explain. Let me tell you how the Nameless One created mankind, and why contact with a person may warm, or burn you."

The ageless Brother then lifted his gaze and began to tell this story: "Long, long ago, when the Father had been holding his breath for a long time, he awoke. From the center of his single round mouth escaped a long breath that was the breath of the soul of our breath. As this fantastic white emanation traveled further and further from the Father, it fell into an infinite spiral, the colors of the rainbow. And thus it became ether, gas, fire, water, and clay.

"And from that, you see, life was born everywhere throughout the immensity of the heavens. The earth, in the form of shapeless clay, learned to recognize water, and water realized what it was when it perceived fire. Fire and water, which rested on the clay, then created the gases. It was at that moment that mankind was created from the union of the four, revealing the ether, which was sleeping in each of the four elements. But my story does not end there, Simon, the five elements are not the end of my story but the beginning . . . . You will have to discover on your own how it continues and develops.

"We humans have one body of earth, another made of water, another of fire, and so on. Our little human brains can count six of them, plus one more. Now, look, Simon, these bodies are real living beings, each with its own desires and hopes, and they form couples, two by two. In this way, a human being possesses above all three real bodies, each having at once male and female tendencies. As for the last one, the jewel of Sheba, it encompasses all the others and crowns them like one hundred and forty-four thousand diamonds.

"Now this, Simon, is what you may see as thousands of flames when your heart is able to receive without desiring: these three bodies. As for the jewel of Sheba, your eye has caught a glimpse of it only once. It is the numeral four, the base of the pyramid which propels itself towards the single light. This is why the ancients gave four letters to the reflections of the divine names."

The Venerable One paused. I felt he had weighed each of his words, combining the subtlety of their meaning with the impact of the sonorities he imprinted in me. If it had not been for the repeated lessons given me by my masters, I would probably have understood nothing of his message. But today more than ever, I know why my young mind, trained above all to feel, was able to understand the "parable."

"It is now time your will directed what your heart has always apprehended spontaneously. I believe it is necessary to teach you, Simon, something that the mortal eye does not know how to screen out. I say 'I believe,' and I think that my trust will not be betrayed, for what I have to teach you is like a double-edged sword. Either you will use it to detect and to combat evil, or its blade will cause division to grow within you. Can you see the danger? Knowing how to read others' bodies should teach you to know them, to help them, to cure them, not to creep inside them and use them. Do not rejoice, Simon, I am not giving you a power. No one could ever give real power to anyone else. All I can do is offer a method that you may develop, and which may be better suited to you than to your companions, since it seems to be calling you.

"Let me tell you which are the three lamps lighting the body so that you may learn their functions. The problem I set before you is at once simple and arduous, and consists of specific exercises aimed at regaining a faculty that amounts to this: knowing how to look. Does everybody know how to open their eyes and look, Simon? No, far from it—otherwise all would see!

"Listen carefully! To the person who has been able to develop the capacity to perceive the three lamps of mankind, the aura—this is what we call the vision of the three lamps together—appears as a beautiful, large and luminous egg-shaped envelope. It is like a shell of light that surrounds the individual who is like a pit in the heart of a fruit. The Brothers also call this 'radiance.'

"Its nature is extremely subtle.* Or, for lack of better words, so inadequate are human languages in this domain, I am also tempted to speak of exhalation, of patterns of currents† moving according to different rhythms. If one manages to perceive this radiance, he is immediately struck by its gaseous, extremely mobile, fluctuating appearance.

"The whole aura can radiate to a distance of almost three cubits‡ from the body, but beginners in the art of reading the aura, of course, do not perceive the full extent of its radiation. Human radiance is composed of successive, more or less subtle layers that can only be discovered gradually.

"The part of the aura that surrounds the head is often the first to be seen, as it is always much brighter. That seems only logical, doesn't it? Isn't the brain a sort of mechanism, a living fire that feeds the rest of the body? You should know that the egg of light is not perfectly shaped, in that it is extended at its summit by a flamelike projection brighter than the other parts. People from many lands know of this sheaf of light and wear headdresses that are strikingly evocative of it.§ This crestlike flame rising from the crown of our heads is to be understood as a manifestation of our inner fire, of cosmic and divine origin, which burns in thinking creatures endlessly in search of some higher truth. It is the sign of the jewel of Sheba, wherein dwells our supreme human consciousness. When you see it, you will then learn to analyze this strongest of exhalations, which reveals much about its possessor.

---

*Today we would say "electric."

†Or waves.

‡About 137 centimeters (54 inches).

§For example, the Blackfoot and Carajas Indians, as well as the Chinese mandarins, who wore crestlike plumes on their heads.

"You must also know that the brightness and the dimensions of the aura are in no way constant. They depend on a great number of factors and circumstances that I will explain to you. Beforehand, remember this: one's radiance is composed globally of a number of colored waves that mingle with one another, coming from a basic hue. This basic hue is an indication of the very depths of one's personality and aptitudes. Against this background appear colored wave patterns in every direction, and it is these wave patterns that define the aura as something unstable and hard to grasp. These patterns are not, however, as disordered in their motion as you might first have thought."

"I know," I exclaimed, full of confidence, interrupting the Venerable One, whose eyes seemed to have gradually closed as a result of letting the "something" that was shining within express itself. "I've seen them crisscrossing and concentrating in some places."

"That is right," he continued, smiling. "They form swirls, wreaths, in numerous places on the body. They constitute what we call 'vital knots' and a great many of them correspond to the organs on which our lives depend. Our spleen and our heart are such centers of force, as is the root of the nose. You will see, too, that several zones stand out because of the vividly colored spiral turbulences that seem to sink right into the body itself. These spirals indicate the locations of the 'wheels of force', some of them being particularly necessary for maintaining the organism's equilibrium. One of these is at the pit of the stomach,* for example. Furthermore, there are six of these, plus one other, of the utmost importance, which have been known since the time of the people of Atl and in all traditions everywhere on Earth. They are more or less visible from the base of the spine to the crown of the head.

"Our aura, of course, follows the body in its tiniest movements and adapts itself to any position we may take, following even the slightest shift of an arm or even a finger. It may be defined as an amazing field of energy activated by a multitude of vibrations[†] that stem from forces at work in the heart of our physical being and in our consciousness.

*The solar plexus.
[†]Today we would say, "by a strong vibratory activity involving both electromagnetic and psychic frequencies."

"Now listen more closely, Simon, for your will is still too easily distracted. Your intellect thinks it necessary to complicate the simple elements I am explaining to you. These energies I have just mentioned do not issue initially from the 'nervous' or 'vital' centers of our bodies. They are first absorbed from the 'outside' by the wheels of force—that I, as well as your teachers, have alluded to—and only then redistributed. The 'spirals' you have probably seen represent—in a sense—entrances into our bodies.

"But what is the 'outside,' Brother?" I asked.

"That is a good question, Simon," he replied. "It is not the atmosphere, or at least not only the atmosphere. In the air you breathe, in the light you absorb, there is a fabulous energy that our senses, being still too crude, are unable to perceive. Some of the wise priests of the great Temple of Solomon call this the 'living light' or 'od.'* It is at the origin of the ether I spoke of before. If you observe the radiances, you will realize that the healthier a person's physical and emotional life is, the more active his wheels of fire are and the more they breathe in this od. Therefore we all call this energy 'solar' or 'cosmic'—so positive, nutritive, and life-giving is it for our whole being.

"Now what about the three bodies mentioned earlier? They are three envelopes. The first one, in itself, cannot really be called the aura, as the extent of its radiation is so limited. It is, nevertheless, the most visible of the three to a noninitiate, for it appears as the "densest" one of all. This density should lead you to conclude that it is almost material, so close is the nature of its vibration to that of our physical body. Of the three envelopes, the first is the only one that follows the contours of our body exactly, radiating evenly, rarely more than two fingers' width from the surface of the skin. In the Krmel we call it the 'vital body'; it is composed of ether. Some peoples of the Earth believe it to be a form of the soul, but this is a mistake, a confusion due to the close links between the ether and blood."

"Isn't it like incense smoke, Brother?"

"That is right, but it is not so unstable. It is thicker in some places than in others, and is gray-blue in color. But you will see—

---

*This is the "astral light" of certain traditions, the odic light spoken of by the Norse in reference to their god Odin.

later—in the case of some beings whose health is splendid at all levels, that it may become golden-white in color.

"The vital body is in fact the 'aura of health' and we hope you will often have the opportunity to make use of this fact. You will see that it is fed from the spleen. But Simon, the Brothers hope that you will not stop at this point on the path, if you are in the least disposed to follow it. If you want to know more, and to be of service, you will find it necessary to draw from beyond this purely vital body.

"Once we let our heart and our eyes vibrate, then the radiance of our second body shines: our emotional body,* which expresses our desires, our anxiety, our disappointments, our happiness, our natural tendencies, our qualities, and our faults. You can see this radiance a cubit† beyond the vital envelope, and you will soon understand that it is the most unstable layer of the aura, as it follows the rhythm of our thoughts and desires. Its basic color varies from one person to another and changes from one moment to the next, depending on one's emotional activity. You will find that this emotional aura is not constant, as we are never exactly the same from one moment to the next. Few know that this aura also provides a number of indications concerning a person's health, indications that complement what we may learn from studying his health aura. The illnesses of the body, Simon, very often reflect the illnesses of the soul—never forget this—and one's emotional aspect is closely linked to one's purely physical side. The emotional aura is nothing more than the radiance of the ego. But if the Nameless One allows it, you will not stop at this point either. You will try to look beyond this second radiance, to discover a third envelope, clearly egg-shaped, and it will seem much less perturbed than the emotional aura."

"A body of motionless light, Brother?"

"No, Simon; no, nothing is ever motionless. It would be wrong to say that this body is always constant, but you will notice only small rippling movements on its surface, which vary slightly in speed and regularity, according to the individual's mental activity.

"The other peculiarity of this mental aura is to be seen in its

*The astral body.
†About 46 centimeters (18 inches).

basic colors, which vary much less than those of the emotional aura, and which are generally light yellow, blue, or white.

"Now remember this, Simon: The more an individual's personality is correctly developed, sound, and radiant, the stronger and more stable this third body will appear. It is a shell with two uses."

"Two uses?" I asked.

"Everything is double; everything has two sides. The mental aura functions on the one hand, as an emanation into the atmosphere that surrounds a being's personality, with all its inner strength, and on the other, as a protection against all the aggressions of a psychic or mental nature from without. So, you see, this third aura is like a springboard for communication with others, while it acts as a barrier against all that is in disharmony with the being it protects. It goes without saying that it is more highly developed in some people than in others, son of Joshua, so much so that one person alone may seem able to light up a whole assembly, while another may appear dull and extinguished. Unfortunately, for many people the third auric body remains in an embryonic state. These are unstable, impulsive people, whose reactions are often childish and very primitive."

"When will you teach me to see all this clearly, Brother?" I asked.

"You have not understood, Simon. I will not teach you, for I cannot teach you what you have to discover on your own. It is up to me simply to help you avoid making mistakes, to teach you to respect certain details. For example, you must know that atmospheric conditions may make your task easier or more difficult.

"Bright sunlight and very dry weather make seeing this radiance easier, especially the etheric flame, which is always strengthened by the sun's rays falling on the region of the spleen, where they create a small depression. Fog and snow also help this perception.

"You must also realize that extreme humidity, as when the body is immersed in water, or just after a bath, immediately disperses this etheric body and then, to a lesser extent, the emotional aura. Now, Simon, it is of the utmost importance to know that when one's body is suddenly plunged under water, the etheric body is completely expelled from the organism for a fraction of a second.

When an etheric body is projected from its physical support, one loses consciousness for as short a time as a flash of lightning, but still long enough for certain things to happen on a more subtle level. You will see; there will come a day when you will clearly understand the importance of this detail.

"Since you now know about some causes and their effects, you will avoid reading the three bodies of one just coming out of the water before that person is thoroughly dry.

"Now do not think this is just a fantasy dreamed up by the Brothers! All during the day, and even at night, organic wastes, and other wastes too, are accumulated on the surface of the skin. These wastes possess their own radiance. It is important then that a body be cleansed, so that its aura may be clear and unpolluted."

With these words, the Venerable One opened wide his blue eyes, and looked deeply into my own. The sensation was strange, my heart can still feel it now. It was like a bridge spanning our two beings. Were it not for the candor that goes with childhood, I would probably not have been able to bear this searching gaze. Several seconds passed in this way, when the Brother in the red veil slowly rose and crossed the little room toward a thick drapery of dark blue linen.

"Now follow me, Simon." he said. "I still have some help to offer you."

With one arm, he swept aside the heavy drapery, revealing a narrow corridor, and nudged me forward. We turned immediately to the right, and I found myself in a room about four meters square. Two of the walls had been painted white, and the other two black. The Brother drew my attention to a circular opening in the ceiling through which soft daylight penetrated indirectly, evenly bathing the four walls. I saw that at the base of the walls, on the floor of the room, there were many earthen oil lamps that were spaced at perfectly even intervals. Thus it seemed that the walls of the room could also be lit from below, if necessary. Even more strangely, there was also a large wooden board, exactly as long as one of the walls and about ten centimeters wide. I was told that if one sat on the floor facing one of the walls, this board might be used to mask the light of the lamps that were lit at its base.

"This room, Simon," the Venerable One told me, "was so designed for a number of reasons, the most important being the learning of very precise aura reading for medical purposes. But let me tell you again that you must not expect any sort of recipe, neither from me nor from the design of this room. To make progress, you will essentially have to modify your mental approach to the world.

"You already know that becoming aware of the limits of one's senses is the first step. If you want your path to be a beautiful one, you must go far beyond mere intellectual comprehension of facts. You must open yourself up to a reflection of a spiritual nature, unique to each of us. This should allow you to discover the world and its people beyond the too frequently opaque veil of appearances. You will work with your heart, Simon, nothing but your heart! You will think with it and through it! If you know this deep within, I have nothing more to reveal to you.

"You will cultivate two essential qualities: willpower and patience. Learn how to want something with constancy, firmness, and regularity rather than stubbornness, as blind obstinacy raises unconscious walls that are insurmountable. Let your gentleness be firm, and your will untiring. In this way you will not become rigid in your work. And thus you will make real progress if only you do not seek to use the sword of your thoughts to test what passes before your eyes, but rather seek to understand it and to love it.

"From now on, I ask you to make the analysis of the light of beings a regular practice. You know the Brothers have devoted the better part of their lives to healing work. May you one day make your contribution to this work.

"The exercises I am now going to show you should be practiced daily, as often as you can. Before you begin anything at all, you will have to spend a few minutes developing calmness and silence within you. In order to do this, find a bare room, whose colors are neutral. Avoid rooms where the colors are bright or whose walls are heavily patterned. In the Krmel, the choice is yours. Make no mistake; this is of the utmost importance. Next, this is what you will have to do: watch me closely."

The Venerable One then raised the sleeve of his white robe to his upper arm, and stretched his hand out toward the white wall, his fingers spread wide, without stiffness.

"At the beginning, it is not white or black that matters, Simon, as long as you choose a uniform background. Make sure that no detail of the wall—or even of your hand, such as a ring—might draw your attention. Now look at what I am doing: I am looking at my hand without focusing on it; I am looking at it, without seeing it; I am looking far beyond it.* Do what I am doing: you should see only the vague outline of your hand. Let your mind be totally absorbed by the blurred image of your splayed fingers.

"Try this at first for a few seconds, then try it again a little longer. Very quickly, you should be able to see a very thin halo, like an opalescent glove, around your fingers."

"That is true, Brother, but I have already seen this first lamp of the body many times."

"Do as if you knew nothing, Simon. Even the simplest exercises have their usefulness. You may think you know, but until now you have only had the briefest of glimpses.

"No, Simon, no, that is exactly what you must not do. You must avoid the irresistible desire to fix your gaze on your hand. It is a reflex, and your perception has just escaped you. Move your hand, slowly bring your thumb to meet your forefinger; your body's ether will reappear. Keep it up, and wait for me for a moment."

Slowly, with a smile on his lips, the Brother went to a corner of the room, took one of the many oil lamps and hung it from a hook fixed in the ceiling. He went out, and I was left alone, wondering at my fortune in being instructed privately by the Venerable One of the Krmel. I felt curiously sad: Why should I be here alone, while the others were studying together? And Joseph, whom I had seen, and Myriam, whose letter I had read . . . . My anxiety fled quickly as the soft noise of the Venerable One's footsteps made me raise my eyes. He had just returned carrying a thick crackling wick. At once, a warm glow spread from the hanging lamp, and the familiar smell of resin filled my nostrils.

"Let me show you a second exercise, Simon," he said. "Stand up straight here, beneath the lamp, and with your eyes shut tightly, lift your face toward the light. You will perceive a yellowish or whitish luminous fog. Now do not let the light limit you, rather try

---

*To borrow a photographer's term, one could say that one should focus not on the outstretched hand but on some imaginary object far beyond it.

to look far beyond it, with your eyes still shut, but relaxed. Focus mentally on the root of your nose, right between your eyes, or slightly higher, whichever seems right to you. Gradually, then, bring your head down to the horizontal."

I obediently followed these instructions, and what I saw inwardly gave me immense pleasure. As my gaze fell toward the horizontal, all the colors of the rainbow passed slowly before me. I lifted my face once more to the fog of light, and once more came slowly down. As I returned to the exercise, my attention was drawn by blue and violet ribbons of light and then, by a spot of light of a deeper blue which was coming forth in the center of my field of vision.

"Can you see the veil of Isis, son of Joshua? It's that little blue sphere of light that should grow until it completely absorbs you. One day it will be so big that you will dive right into it. This is your one eye. Some say it is the third eye, although it deserves to be called the first. Its importance is fundamental and its development, among other things, will enable you to perceive the three auras.

"This second exercise should not last long, Simon, and you should know that it is not good to repeat it too often. Three or four times a week should be quite enough. It will enable you, if you feel the need, to become aware of the inner gaze possessed by everyone.

"This eye, you understand, has no material existence anymore. It is, all the same, very real, and on the physical plane its action stems from the simultaneous working of two little bodies located in the human brain.* Only a real desire to work on an inner plane, to unite with your inner being, will give this exercise any lasting value. You see, in the moments of concentration and of seeking after peace that your masters require of you, the first of these two little bodies exerts a force that comes to influence the second one, giving birth to the veil of Isis.† But I must warn you, Simon, do not concentrate your will on the perception of the one eye, for as you surely know, the reflection of a light must not be mistaken for the light itself. And this is the mistake, alas, that we humans always tend to make.

"Now that you know these things, the third stage of your

*The pituitary and pineal glands.
†Today we would say that the pituitary gland triggers a magnetic phenomenon that stimulates the pineal gland and gives rise to the third eye.

investigation will consist in finding out against what kind of background it is easiest for you to see the etheric flame. This you will discover quickly, after a few trials, by comparison. Some people perceive the body's lights more clearly against a light background, while for others, a dark background is better. We advise you to choose the extremes, that is, white or black, as, to a certain extent, the intermediate tones can influence the vision you may acquire. Now come closer to the wall and consider the lighting of the room. The sunlight falling from the ceiling, combined with the light from this line of oil lamps is just enough to cast a soft surface glow on the chosen wall. Herein lies the secret of the last step to good training.*

"When you come here to practice by looking at one of the Brothers, ask him to stand at about a distance of one hand from the screen you have chosen. Go back about four strides from him, and stare at him, as I have shown you. In the beginning of your training, it may be better if you squint a bit, so as not to be attracted by the lighter and darker parts of his body. In this way the contrasts are reduced and do not distract your attention.

"Above all, never open your eyes wide when you attempt this, for you will get no results at all. If you follow all these instructions very carefully, your perception will expand progressively until it encompasses all three bodies. But do not be impatient. It may take you long months to grasp the whole range of colors. Little does it matter, as time does not count when one is at work on oneself; for make no mistake, this is what it is all about. It is only by taking the path of self-metamorphosis that you will come to be of real help to others.

"Before you leave me, Simon, I must warn you of one other thing: any clothing we wear gives off its own aura. So be careful not to mistake the clothing's aura for that of the person whose aura you are attempting to read. Remember that a clean and naked body always offers the clearest vision of its aura.† This is not a mere detail.

---

*A modern adaptation of this procedure may be obtained by using a deep black sheet or a movie screen. Lighting may be provided, especially if the background is white, by two neon tubes placed in close proximity to the screen, one on the floor, the other fixed to the ceiling. Ideal lighting is soft and skims the background surface.
†Nowadays we should expressly avoid synthetic clothing and underclothing, as well as colored fabrics.

Only in this way will your reading be untainted, and will you easily be able to identify which of a person's organs are unhealthy, owing to the specific coloring—often gray or brownish—that they give off."

Then the Venerable One led me back to the room where he had welcomed me initially. He paused to point to a small alcove two steps below, which could be filled with water, so that one might wash one's body before the "reading of the three lamps."

I was surprised to find so many washing places in the Krmel, even more than in our village, where the cool flow of the spring played such a sacred role in most of our daily acts. Water seemed here to be vital to everything we did, almost as much so as the air we breathed. This blood of the Earth, as it was sometimes referred to by our instructors, was to be used whenever possible, between each of our daily occupations.

"So now, Simon," he said, "your presence here will be encouraged for half an hour each day. You will be excused from the text translation class, if you wish."

I found myself at the doorstep of the Venerable One's apartments, and a soft cool wind swept under my black robe. I failed to catch my instructor's parting gaze, as his long hair hid from me part of his face, but I felt the warm squeeze of one of his hands on my shoulder.

"One last thing, son of Joshua," I heard him say, just as I was getting ready to run down the cold flagstones of the corridor. "Remember this: Purify your heart before reading someone's lamp. Beware, for if you are not as pure as crystal, you will look at another through the veil of your own darkness."

The heavy door closed softly behind me, and I rushed off over the stones, drawn by the litanies that were already rising from the temple like ripples of peace.

CHAPTER VII

THE SOFT VOICE

I n the following days, I spent my free hours searching for a trace of Joseph in the courtyards and classrooms of the Krmel where I was allowed to go. But the Krmel was enormous and I could still get lost at times.

Was it possible that his arrival among us had taken place only in my imagination? Had I just personified my desire to break out of my solitude? No one seemed to know of my friend, and in the silence of the corridors of the monastery, I hardly dared pronounce the syllables of his name, which the walls seemed to enjoy echoing back to me even louder.

I was distracted from my daily habits in this way for nearly a week. The Brothers who had seen me talk with Joseph seemed themselves to have disappeared. I at last caught sight of one of them, coming away from a long group meditation, in which most of the inhabitants of the Krmel were expected to participate.

"Joseph?" he asked. "I don't know of anyone by the name of Joseph, Simon, who are you talking about?" But I did notice, nonetheless, a hint of playfulness in his voice, and with great aplomb, I tried to search his gaze. The Brother then let out a thundering burst of laughter, and quickly drew me aside, into a little recessed courtyard, where we might speak more freely.

"Listen to me, Simon," he said. "There is no one called Joseph here any more. Those who brought your friend here ten days ago did not register him under that name. So Joseph doesn't exist any longer. As for his new name, the Venerable One hasn't seen fit to reveal it now. You see, Simon, disclosing someone's name gives people a certain hold over him. The Father has asked your friend to be born anew, totally free. This is why he is within these walls, to become transparent, freed from his past, freed from the walls of his village, and from the dusty valleys of Galilee. But don't worry, you'll meet again. Some of the Brothers who have traveled through far-off lands need to have long talks with him. You must understand this and not forget the work you have been given, Simon."

With this, the Brother pressed his forefinger against the center of my chest, and with a faint smile, left me. Without really knowing why, perhaps out of shame at having given way to a feeling of impatience that I had been enjoined to subdue above all else, I felt compelled to look down at the ground. I only caught a glimpse of the Brother's ample robe as he was drawing away.

But I did see Joseph again. He began participating regularly in the hours of prayer and group meditation, but once these were over, he always left quickly, alone or at the side of a very aged Brother, whose baldness made my companions and me smile. We had always been taught that long hair was a distinctive sign of our people.

Joseph would sometimes come to find me during our free time, and we always shared the communal meal at sundown. He told me that three masters, not always the same ones, were instructing him privately, and that this sometimes weighed heavily upon him. From what I gathered, he was being given the same teachings as the rest of us, though with subtleties or depths unrevealed to us. This could not but reinforce what had always seemed to me his strange and rather fascinating side.

Joseph, whose name I no longer dared breathe, did not, however, grow distant from me. Only his gaze would wander further and further into a distance he seemed to perceive beyond the massive stone and earthen walls of the Krmel. He, too, enjoyed speaking about the village, and we would recall those who had been close to us both, Myriam, old Zerah, and others. The serious side of his personality often provided a striking contrast with the playfulness he could sometimes display. I was somewhat at a loss, never knowing whether he wanted to make some joke or to contemplate the Nameless One, as he liked to say.

My life in the Krmel, shared in part with him who was no longer Joseph, went on in this way for two more years, at the end of which the teachings I received took a new turn. I was asked at this time to share in the work in the fields that provided part of the community's subsistence.

"Every man should know the Earth," said one of the Brothers who was breaking us into his hard work. "The Earth is not just a collection of red or black dust we walk on; the Earth is a ferment, a whole world, a multitude of tiny beings that mirror the life of the Father, a manifestation of life that exists and thinks because it is created for us by His will and His thought at every instant across the ages. With our feet on the ground, in the very clay itself, we, the Brothers of Essania, must learn to speak to each grain of life in each grain of life and so on, infinitely; and this in order to forget what we know of our bodies, to mold ourselves anew as little or as big as this particle of life. This grain of life is the One and we are the children of the One. This is why we must try to identify ourselves with the tiniest speck of dust that the wind blows into our eyes. This identification is the key to compassion, and compassion is the key to the Father, the key to humankind."

I could not have imagined that going out of the Krmel for the first time after many years would be so difficult. It meant beginning to face, at the age of ten, a world I had often been told was painful to the Brothers, because it was a world where people knew only how to live in their own dreams. Nonetheless, I was deeply moved when I saw once more the pastel hues of the countryside, the timid green of the olive trees, the vivid color of the almond trees in blossom.

From that time on, our instructors would take us out onto the mountain slopes facing the sea for our lessons. We worked in small groups of six or seven, and I then understood the "secret" kept by my older companions, whom I had often seen heading out beyond the walls of the Krmel with one of the elders. Outside like this, studying, or meditating according to given methods was easier, more attractive, but I soon found out that this was a sort of trap.

The Brother who was overseeing us at these times seemed to keep a close eye on how we behaved, how we reacted, and accordingly, our groups were sometimes reformed. We had to overcome the temptation to let ourselves be distracted, as life out in Nature is not always as calm as one might expect; there is always some leaf falling from a tree, some cocoon ready to open, some insect devouring another one. During our work, whatever it might be, silence was still the golden rule. Only the measured voices of the white-robed Brothers, who were doing their best to complete our knowledge and enrich our souls, were to be heard on the hillsides and in the orchards where we studied.

In a way, I rediscovered the gentle sweetness of life I had known in my parents' village; my masters seemed to be less austere than they had been before. Had they wanted to try us, to harden us, to mold us according to certain rhythms, right from our arrival at the Krmel? I was to learn much later that a certain harshness during the first years of study was one of the educative principles of the great Essene and Nazarene center. I recall very clearly one lesson from this less rigorous time in and around the Krmel, a lesson which was taught us one day as we were tending the grape vines. One of the Brothers, who was very tall and thin, came to speak to us about the art of the "soft voice" or the "voice of milk" for which, according to some, our people were renowned throughout the land and beyond. He insisted that we go on with our manual work as he spoke, as did many of our masters. He told us the Brothers of ancient times had noticed that, while the hands worked, the doors of the mind and the memory were opened wide. The teachings received at these times were thus better understood and retained. Whenever possible, this method was respected, unless a visiting instructor of very high rank had come to teach us. This notion of high rank was, anyway, only relatively important. All the Brothers ignored any consideration of hierarchy amongst themselves; they only respected, as far as possible, the customs of the land, and accorded greater deference to a few beings who were really advanced on the path.

"Every phrase that leaves your lips is a universe that you create," declared the tall, thin Brother in the white linen robe. Then he paused for a long time, hoping perhaps for a response, for some look of recognition in our eyes. But nothing happened. We saw nothing really unusual in what he had said. We were all used to understanding the value of symbols, and his words appeared highly symbolic.

At length, he spoke again: "I am not speaking in images," he said.

This time, as he had perhaps hoped, we raised our eyes, and our work slowed down.

"Every articulated sentence is a universe; every spoken word is a world along with its sun, and every sound you make is a planet, an earth full of life. Be aware that, in truth, you are a god to the words that you utter. They create and support worlds that you cannot even imagine, but that you may no longer ignore. The most ancient texts known on our Earth proclaim that everything came from a sound emitted by the Father. This is not a vain statement. Vibration is the most original of all conceivable lives. If you want to follow the way of the Nameless One, do not let your words fall from your lips, but let them flow softly like a milk of life. Do not let them spring forth like a torrent, but let them wash peacefully like a cooling wave. Other Brothers have taught you the art and principles of analogy, so receive my words today in this spirit. From now on, you will try to see a solar system in each word, whose core you will imbibe as a central fire, and whose every syllable, every sound, will be to you like so many planets.

"Let me tell you that these sounds are matter on a plane that your eyes and your minds cannot yet apprehend. Remember that matter is a force. You will have to learn how to control it with your heart, for like any other energy, it is two-sided and may prove either vivifying or devastating. Its action will depend on the exactness of your pronunciation and on the warmth you will be able to impart to it with the vibrations of your heart."

I felt like putting aside the little piece of pliant wood I had been using to coat the bases of the grape vines with a sticky, rust-colored substance. But each of us had been entrusted with a specific task, to be accomplished before the next communal prayer. We were granted complete trust that we could not possibly betray.

Striding up and down the long rows of gnarled vines which clung as best they could to the mountainside, the Brother went on with his lesson.

"Let me tell you that in our language, and in our way of being, there are three sacred sounds that you must know how to modulate to perfection. Upon their exact pronunciation and mastery will depend a number of things that many of you will accomplish, and which will be perceived by others as miraculous. These sounds are the *A*, the *M* and the *N*. You may notice that I do not pronounce them with my nose, or with my throat; these sounds, when correctly shaped, come from a point in the center of my chest, right from my physical heart, from the very root of my breath. Our exercise will consist in trying to make them resonate within you as close as possible to this point, so that the whole thoracic cage becomes like a drum, like a sound box. If you do this correctly, when you close your eyes, your whole being should vibrate.

"Only when you have mastered the pronunciation of these three sounds will you be capable and worthy of singing them together. Be aware, children of the One, that at this precise moment, when you reach this stage, you will set off a chain reaction within yourselves that will cause all the cells in your body to vibrate in unison. For one brief moment, your flesh, and your energy, will be transmuted so that you may accomplish the wonders that are sometimes required in order to help others. Follow me now, in the modulation of each of these sonorities. Take a deep breath, filling first the depths of your lungs, so that the whole mountain will hum to the song of our *A*. I say 'the song,' for too often you tend to forget, though you have been told many times, that your speech should be brought forth like a soft melody, rather than like a chain of separate sounds."

We were then allowed to sit down, our backs straight, and in the first cool rays of the sun we attempted our first correct utterance of the *A* of ancient times. Under our instructor's guidance, the sound that gushed forth from our breasts was so deep that my whole spine tingled. Very quickly our chant soared out over the valley, mingling with the bleating of the ewes grazing below. With my eyes closed, as the instructor had suggested, images of light splashed over the screen of my mind. I saw the sea with its sparkling waves. I saw camels that merchants were relieving of their heavy ochre and purple burdens. I saw half-naked men rolling heavy jars over the ground. At last, I felt a veil of intense blue light drawing over my inner being. Then came a calm, perfect silence. It seemed to me that with our chant dying out, the surrounding world of Nature had gone to sleep. In the following days, we repeated this exercise many times, in exactly the same conditions. This went on for nearly a full cycle of the moon, then we learned the *M,* and its force, and at last the *N.* Practicing these exercises brought me great calm, and in this healing silence, like a balm soothing my ten-year-old's soul, came the whys and the hows of life. Our instructor in the art of the "soft voice" stayed nearly a year with us, which was exceptional on the part of a "passing master."

Contrary to what we had thought, we came quickly to understand that we would need years—four, perhaps five, or even more—before we could expect to blend correctly the three sacred sonorities into a single, continuous flow. Our guide in this field reminded us often that we had to form these sounds in our minds and in our hearts before attempting to utter them. This was sometimes hard to achieve, and our thoracic cages didn't always obey our wishes, which was often discouraging.

Some Brothers had taught us that the science of the ancient peoples of the Earth had forever associated an immutable number to each letter, and thus to each sound. We were told, moreover, that the numbers corresponding to *M* and *N* were of particular importance.

"Numbers," as the Venerable One himself had taught us, "on this Earth are but a pale reflection of what they represent in eternity. In the planes of existence near the Father, they exist as distinct beings to whom the Nameless One has entrusted the ordering of all things in the universe. Regard them as great intermediate spirits between the infinite and the creatures, spirits without which there would be no measure, no balance, and no rhythm. When you speak, or when you count, although you may not be aware of it, you set the extensions of their forces into action. You must understand now how you may improve your lives as well as those of others, by working consciously and harmoniously with numbers. A right understanding of cause and effect gives rise to right thought, which will naturally be reflected in right speech and right measure.

"You are still, children of the One, like the leaves on the Tree of Life that are dimly aware of the twig on which they have budded, and that have only the vaguest inkling of the branch from which this twig grows, and do not even suspect that this branch springs from a central trunk that leads down to the roots that nourish the tree. This must change through right understanding and right speech. You must let your being flow into the trunk of life, you must become Man, and not just men among men!

"To help in your work, in your solitary prayers and in your daily meditations, mentally recite the alphabet of our language. Stop at each letter, or each sound, and try to send a thought of love to the spirit that presides at its source. Visualize its immaculate egg of light.

"If you can only keep a pure heart, this practice, along with our usual meditations, our purifications, and our prayers to the divine central fire, will make your words flow from your lips like honey, like the milk of the pure.

"Let your words be yourselves; let the perfection of your terms and of your pronunciation not be calculated, rather let it be an outward manifestation of the impulses coming from your heart."

The latter part of my childhood was filled with these precepts. The practice of the vocal exercises in which our masters put such faith even became a sort of game to me. The little boy whom I still saw as Joseph often came to join me in my exercises in vocalization in one of the courtyards, in the shade of a fig tree, which must have grown there as if by some magic spell. It soon became clear that I was just a beginner compared to him. It seemed to me that he chanted the sounds and words as would one of the oldest Brothers of the Krmel. It happened more than once that the depth of the sonorities he managed to produce out of his little chest made one of the elders pause in passing, and stare over at us.

I was stimulated by Joseph's self-assurance and the progress he was making, but I understood at the same time the difference there was between us, and the reasons why he was one who was given private lessons, one of whom I had been told, "Brothers who have traveled through far-off lands, need to have long talks with him."

His face, at times sad, at others radiant, eventually became an enigma . . . and sometimes frightened me.

CHAPTER · VIII

AT OLD JACOB'S

The observance of the Day of Atonement was approaching.* In the Krmel, it was not customary to observe this holy day, as none of us lived according to the rhythms of the Jewish people. Nonetheless, some of the atmosphere rubbed off onto us all, and we would stare off into the distance towards the sea, and at the red and white terraces of the neighboring village. If the wind was coming from the right direction, we could catch the sound of the trumpets blaring out their message of imminent celebration, and this filled us with joy. Those Brothers who had attended the "Great Pardon" in the past took pleasure in reliving the ceremonies for us in great detail, ceremonies that were, in fact, of a sober nature. Through their stories we would imagine interminable processions of rabbis, the light playing over their long, blue-fringed robes; the silent devotion of the crowd and the solemn gestures of the high priest entering the Holy of Holies in the temple in order to expiate his own sins, along with those of all his people.

*Yom Kippur.

We all no doubt secretly wished we could attend such an occasion one day. Perhaps one day—later—the Krmel would open wide its heavy doors for us, onto the vast world. We weren't moved by curiosity nor by the desire to experience ways of life different from our own; rather, it was simply the desire to know, to understand. We were encouraged in this by the elders, who wanted us to have a perfect knowledge of the law of Moses. We were told that unfortunately, as a whole, the people of Palestine did not see things this way. Indeed several of our masters had been refused access to the temples many a time and had been forbidden to participate in even lesser celebrations.

One morning, as we were clustered at the outer wall, where a narrow, latticed opening made it easier for us to hear the plaintive sounds of the trumpets rising from the valley, one of the Brothers silently approached us.

"We must go out today," he said abruptly. "Late last night a merchant arrived from town, asking for our help." Slowly he went on to explain that for some time some kind of epidemic had been raging through the valleys, now causing people to die in the streets of the town. The merchant had come late at night, fearing reproach from the townspeople, and had begged the Brothers to keep his plea for help a secret.

A murmur of approval, almost of joy, spread through our little group. We were to go down to the town! Then one laconic phrase fell from the lips of the Brother, who now seemed quite impressive: "The black of your robes suits you perfectly this morning!" That was all.

One of us whispered a word or two, then a heavy silence fell over us, interrupted by the braying of donkeys waiting in the sunny courtyard. The Brother went a few steps away, then turned around and came back.

"Does your happiness only stem from the suffering of others? In two years, according to the law of Moses, you will be adults. If you become like leavening in the art of selfishness, of what value will have been your hours spent in prayer here? Today you will not only heal others, but yourselves as well. Keep this in mind: The origin and the growth of all the body's ailments rise solely from the negativity that emanates from the human heart, your own hearts included, even if the Father has called you to the Krmel! Break out of your shells! How long will it take you to get rid of your black robes, given to you when you entered here as a symbol for the rotting of your selfishness?"

We went soberly to our cells to get our cloaks. Only eight or nine of us had been told this news whereas there were many more of the Brothers in white when we all assembled silently in a corner of the big courtyard beneath an old fig tree. Our first task was to load the donkeys with small red earthenware jugs and strongly scented baskets, in which I recognized the herbs we had had to gather at the past two solstices. These herbs smelt of the sun and the moon, and I thanked the Nameless One for the chance of perhaps learning exactly how they were used.

Next, we prepared our own provisions, as we had no way of knowing how long we would have to stay away. The cloth bags we carried over our shoulders were filled with barley bread and flatcakes.

One of the heavy monastery gates creaked on its hinges, and our company, about forty of us in all, set out. We were at once staggered by the heat, which was extreme, even for the season. We had been taught breathing exercises to better resist the heat, but as I labored over the rocky paths leading down into the valley, it was not easy to call them back to mind.

For a while we passed through our terraced vineyards, then came to a beautiful forest of holm oaks which appeared to stretch all the way to the sea. We spoke little, but the atmosphere created by the elders remained light and gay. One of them even started up a chant we had heard occasionally at night, drifting down the corridors of the Krmel; then in a flash I felt how strongly I was attached to my existence as a young monk, and to the heavy stone and earthen walls of the Krmel, this depository of ancient lore. The chant was like an indecipherable reminder, like a thread leading me back through the labyrinth of my memory.

Towards the end of the morning, we came in sight of the first dwellings, on whose terraces fish and vegetables lay drying in the sun. As we entered the village, we were struck by the presence of a large flock of sheep, apparently waiting for a sign, or a command, from the shepherd.

Many of them bore crude red or black markings on their foreheads. I had no idea what this might mean, but guessed that these were perhaps animals which were fated to be sacrificed in the penitence rites. My heart beat faster, and I felt an emotion that came from far away. It was a long time since I had last walked in the streets of a little village. All the commotion that had fascinated me then, now frightened me a little. This village, however, was quite unlike Joppa, being at first nothing but a few small streets bleached by the sun and swept by the sea breezes, lined with makeshift little shops. Only the intersection of two streets that seemed to be used as a marketplace showed any real animation. The fishermen's catch of the day was displayed there, along with some fresh vegetables, in the midst of an indescribable chaos caused by the passage of a camel train and a flock of goats, both trailing after them the dust from the roads.

Looking around I realized that our group had split. Having failed to notice the others' departure, I found myself accompanied only by a little monk of about my age and four of the Brothers. The breaking up of our group had probably occurred as we had entered the village so as not to attract attention to ourselves. Brother Moshab seemed to have resolutely taken the head of our little group and was leading us with confidence to a place perhaps known to him alone. As we were threading our way through the crowd I noticed that all the people who were gathered there, simple peasants, merchants, and rabbis alike, were casting furtive glances at us. I had been told repeatedly that in their heart of hearts, the people of Galilee held the white-robed Brothers in deep esteem and for the most part recognized their honesty and their righteousness. Nonetheless, I felt a certain uneasiness at being looked at like this, and measured in a glance. We finally left the little square, heading into a narrow, almost deserted alleyway, whose houses were sometimes linked by heavy stone archways. In most of these dwellings there was an upstairs room and there, through the opening of a tiny window, we glimpsed the face of an old man wearing a square of brown material on his head.

"Here we are," was all Brother Moshab said, and we all stepped single file through the doorway of the house. It took a while before our eyes became accustomed to the darkness within. As in most of the houses we knew, there was but a single room lit only by the narrow grated openings set into two of the walls. One corner of the room was slightly elevated, and we could just make out some carefully rolled sleeping mats and cooking utensils the color of earth and fire. Then, the old man whose face we had just seen descended a narrow and visibly shaky ladder that led to the upstairs room.

"May the All-Highest bless you," he murmured timidly, pushing aside some bundles of wood piled at the foot of the ladder. "I did not think you would be here so soon . . . bless you."

"May you too be blessed, old Jacob," said Moshab. "But tell us, where is your son?"

"He is up there, follow me."

And with an agility which amazed us all, the old man made his way up the ladder and disappeared above. Brother Moshab followed him, and so did we, one after the other. The upper room differed very little from the one below. Here again was the same austerity, the same colors of earth and stone, and again a ladder, leading this time to a terrace above. After a moment, we saw in the darkest corner of the room a rope bed, the only furniture to be found in the house. A vague figure lay huddled up there, closely wrapped in a woolen cloak.

"You see," whispered the old man, as he approached, "here is my son. He hasn't been able to get up for more than ten days. He has a fever and he is suffering from pains in his belly—and there are many more like him in the village, and all over!"

The son turned his face towards us, and in the semidarkness we could see just two feverish eyes, those of a man in his forties, who was shaken now and then by a succession of frequent tremors.

"We do not know what it is," said old Jacob, nervously passing one hand over his cheeks. "Nobody has ever seen anything like this. No doubt we will have to make many offerings and pray to the All-Highest."

With a sure and gentle hand, Brother Moshab removed the heavy woolen cloak wrapped around the ailing man and laid it carefully at the foot of the bed. The man, who wore only a soiled, crudely fashioned loincloth, was curled up almost into a ball, shivering with cold in spite of the suffocating heat that filled the house. In the dimness I tried to meet the gaze of my comrade, or more reassuring, that of one of the Brothers. Two of the others then went out, saying they would unload the donkey and prepare some herbs. I then looked at Brother Moshab, who knelt slowly at the side of the ill son and held his two wrists, then his ankles. The Brother was breathing slowly and deeply, more heavily on each expiration, as if he were filtering, rejecting, an exhausted force.

"Simon," he murmured suddenly, "make yourself useful now." I approached the bed, at once flattered and anxious at what might be asked from me.

"No, take a few steps back instead. Now is the time for you to put into practice what we have taught you. Look carefully at this man and try, if you can, to see his three lamps."

I was almost paralyzed. This was the first time I had been asked to do such a thing—such a thing in public—and for a person who was really ill. For a few seconds I doubted my own ability, and I wanted to make him understand that I could not, that it was not possible. But I couldn't find the words to tell him, and as I hadn't moved, one of the Brothers placed firm hands on my shoulders and backed me off several paces from the man lying there trembling on the bed.

There was no excuse to be found. The small group moved away from me a little, and I searched deep within for a spark of calm, a little spark that I would have to breathe into life, so as to be able to see.

Old Jacob's son had shut his eyes and seemed to have stopped expecting anything any more. Quickly I saw him surrounded by a dim, yellowish gray halo, shot with dirty brown streaks. A sort of whirling depression could be clearly seen in the upper part of his belly. It looked as if the energies that would otherwise be drawn into this place were instead swirling around, finally to evaporate. His etheric flame was weak and seemed almost extinguished.

"Brother," I said with sudden self-confidence, "I think the little sun* is ill." As I said these words, I looked up from old Jacob's son to see the long white profile of one of the Brothers who was evidently checking my work.

"That is good, Simon," said this Brother, as if he were giving his verdict. "It is indeed the little sun that has failed. It no longer

*The Essene name for the spleen.

absorbs the energies from the Father, and has left the body defense-
less."

At the other end of the room, the old man sat in a ray of dusty
light, his forehead on his knees, mumbling a litany of incomprehensible words. He was praying. Without consulting each other, Moshab
and the others approached the bedside of the ailing man. They stood
with their feet together, raised the ample sleeves of their robes, and
as one, stretched their arms out over his body. I could feel that they
gradually tuned their breathing to his, as I had so often been taught
to do.

"You see, Simon," I could still hear my master's words within
me, "the first key mislaid by man on this Earth goes by the name
of compassion. Compassion alone will open the door to helping
others totally, absolutely totally, without ifs, ands, or buts! If a being
is suffering, find out what he is suffering from and then take his
disharmony into yourself, by identifying with him. To do this you
must breathe and vibrate in rhythm with his being; in this way you
will tap precisely into the source of his suffering, and divert it, by
guiding your body of light into contact with his own. All you have
to do is want this with all the strength in the world, Simon, want
it and know the proper techniques, a few simple gestures, so simple
they will one day make charlatans and "lovers of stone"* smile. For
one who can make his heart vibrate like a drum, Simon, all instru-
ments seem dull, all potions evaporate, and all suffering becomes a
grindstone on which to polish the bodies of compassion. Warm
your heart, let your hands radiate and no spiral of pain will be able
to grow, no web of suffering will be woven. Understand too,
Simon, that one does not destroy a pain that exists in and of itself,
as it is the weakness of our own soul that has enabled it to form its
nucleus. In each fraction of our inner time, we create worlds! Had
you forgotten this? Learn to be a father to these worlds, rather than
a demon through insufficient love."

The Brothers stood around the son of old Jacob for a long time.
Little by little, their breathing became imperceptible. It was as if they
were absorbing life through every pore of their bodies, as if they
were breathing through their souls, as if they were emitting rays like

*Hypocrites.

flames from their outspread fingers and the palms of their hands. Below them, the man was still sweating heavily, but his trembling had stopped, and he looked now as if he were simply asleep. Following a brief exchange of glances, the Brothers lowered their arms and hands closer to the surface of his body, taking care not to touch each other. With their hands still outstretched, they began to make little vertical, then circular, movements, to establish, as they would always do, a firm link with the vital body of the ailing man.

At this point, my comrade and I were invited to join the group, and the Brothers, half bent over the man, made room for us. My hands were over the man's chest, and for the first time, I noticed little pink spots there and then on his belly. Behind us the two Brothers who had retired earlier came back, and judging from the noises I heard, I guessed they had brought up some metallic vessels from the floor below. There was a sudden glow in the room, a crackling, then a strong scent of burning herbs rose about us. It was not the smell of incense that I knew so well but something acrid and stronger that filled the room, penetrating everything. Then I heard the measured footsteps of the two Brothers who came and went, placing little earthen and copper cups full of the burning herbs all along the walls. At the same time, very quickly, the narrow windows were stuffed with old bits of coarse cloth. I had the impression that the ensuing obscurity, so thick as to be almost felt, brought us all closer—so close that we became a single body, a single energy, striving to convert any energy other than itself. The alchemy of our hearts was at work . . . .

At that point there was only one goal, one fundamental reason for the present moment that stretched infinitely: healing. With all the strength of my soul I began shutting the doors of my senses. I had to forget about the weight of the tunic on my shoulders, my hands outstretched over the man's body, and the contact of my feet on the wooden floor. I still had to relegate my body to a lower plane; to visualize a little ball of non-light, racked with fever, and to transmute it into a shining new sun. I was lifted by the wave of love force emanating from the Brothers and forgot about myself as well as about the passing of time. Only an acute tingling in the palms of my hands managed, little by little, to break the spell. The air seemed suddenly almost unbreathable. I felt as if a thick dense cloud, saturated with the disagreeably intensified smells of the highlands, was suffocating us all. Unexpectedly, the clear voice of Brother Moshab cut through the darkness. It was time, he said, to move back from the bed. Then the silence was broken only by the sounds of soft footsteps and the swishing of our robes. Someone approached with an oil lamp whose bright glow finally brought me out of my numb state.

Brother Moshab ordered that the windows should remain stuffed until the next day, then he went back alone to the sleeping man and knelt by his side. With his fingers together, he placed his right hand slowly over the man's spleen, then over his lungs. The rest of us stood in silence for a moment, letting Moshab, who was the most experienced among us, act alone; then we climbed down to where we hoped we would be able to breathe more freely. It was in vain, for at the foot of the ladder also, a considerable quantity of herbs was still smoldering.

We went outside quickly. Old Jacob was already there, and we found him in the alleyway leaning against a wall and nervously chewing on a few grains of wheat. He did not dare to look at us, undoubtedly fearing the worst for his son. One of us went to him and asked him to burn all his son's clothes, as well as any objects he had used, or was still using. The old man gave no answer, simply nodding his head in consent.

"Jacob," said another of the Brothers, approaching him, "tonight we will pray to the Eternal One for the healing of your son and of the others. Believe in the Father's assistance as you believe in the rising of the sun each morning, and no illness will prevail."

I heard a door open and shut behind us, and Brother Moshab came out of the house to join us. He looked exhausted and held his hand over his eyes to shield them from the glare of daylight. It was time to get back to some of the others who had come down from the Krmel. We twisted and turned through the maze of village streets, and I let the others choose the way without attempting to understand the logic of their path. We had once more to cross the village square, which was now calmer. The animals had gone, and only a few lingering passersby and a merchant or two, busy repacking their goods, were still there, reminding us of the chaotic activity that had filled the place some time before.

Our growing thirst drove us into a little shop outside which oranges and lemons were displayed. There, we were surprised to meet a traveler, one of our people, who was not staying at the Krmel. He had come up from the South, where our Masters also taught regularly,* and had decided to remain longer in the village because of the epidemic. According to him, the disease had already claimed many victims, and he had stopped counting the number of linen cloths he had to knot around the heads of the deceased, as was the custom. Even so, he said, life was going on in the village as ever, as most of the inhabitants expected their salvation to come with the observance of the Day of Atonement, its offerings, the high priests' penitence, and the ensuing sacrifices.

The oxen and the lambs had already been chosen, and even the poorest of the inhabitants wanted to offer up something, if only a bird, to the holocaust. Although we respected the ways of thinking of the people of Israel and agreed with their fundamental tenets, for us things were not so simple. We had always been taught that man held his own existence, and his own fate, in his two hands, and that he had to find his own strength within himself, in harmony with the Father, rather than to expect everything from him. We had always been told that this was one of the conditions essential to the growth of our inner beings.

Night fell quickly, spreading its purple mantle high over our heads. We had rejoined the others outside of town, and we made ready to spend the night, some of us on some flat stones, still warm from the sun, others on a thin patch of grass. I looked up, avidly searching the night sky. It seemed quite a long time since I had been able to contemplate Moon-Sun in total peace, and this thought brought back memories that were buried beneath what appeared to me like years of experience.

The star was there, faithfully, and I stared up at it, measuring its trajectory and the intensity of its brightness. Around me the atmosphere was cheerful, although some of us were worried by the seriousness of the epidemic. As decided previously, we settled down to our long, almost endless prayers, litanies which seemed as if they would drone on until dawn. Then, very late in the night, two of the

---

* Probably at Qumran.

Brothers rose to announce that those of us who felt the desire would take it in turns to pray throughout the night. We decided that this would be done in groups of three and also that three Brothers would fast and pray until the epidemic had been eradicated. I later came to understand that their work, on planes of existence I knew nothing about then, could greatly help the apparently more tangible healing work of the others. I, too, decided to keep this vigil. My first contact with the face of a certain reality, and the role I had been called upon to play, gave me some feeling of importance. My training at the Krmel was at last bearing fruit. I guessed I was just beginning to put my finger on something I couldn't name, and, late that night it was with indescribable happiness that I felt the litanies flowing through me.

The days that followed were in every way similar to the first. We went our separate ways into the village and into the surrounding countryside, healing and counseling the people. Only rarely did I see the Brothers advise the use of potions; they preferred working with the warmth of their hands and their hearts, their faith, and their intimate knowledge of the techniques they had learnt from their fathers. Three days went by, then came the the Day of Atonement. The priests filed through the crooked, narrow streets, enveloped in the clouds of incense that poured forth from all the houses. We heard that, on the morning after our visit, the son of old Jacob had got up and had asked for food. As for Jacob himself, he did not reappear. Rapidly the disease lost ground. Not only were there no more new victims, but the Brothers had obtained spectacular results in the space of a few hours. For some, this was due to the power of the holy day; while others, on the contrary, felt that we were responsible, and wanted to pay us. Yet our rule was to accept no more than a meal, and this only when our work made our presence necessary for a whole day. We had to stay on for five more days following the celebration, five exhausting days during which the Brothers gave all they possibly could.

Even today, while reliving these moments, I cannot help but see your eyes before me—Moshab, Jude and all the others—your eyes, light or dark, in which so much light was to be found; your eyes that would not grow dim, even in two thousand years.

CHAPTER · IX

THE LABYRINTH

M y twelfth birthday arrived at last. Life in the Krmel, so harsh at the beginning, though much less so later on, was to leave an indelible mark on my mind. The endless vigils spent in prayer, the long solitary meditations and the rites that punctuated each hour of day and night, could only lead to two opposite reactions from the soul consciousness: either they unbalanced and shattered it, through an excess of rigidity; or they molded and transcended it, by making it capable of facing any difficulty of living.

Within the framework of the Brothers' strict demands, in the scrupulous respect for their way of life, and sustained by the warmth of their being in even the least of my troubles, I was happy to develop the abilities and the toughness expected of me. I didn't know where I was heading, but I had finally understood I had to go there, wherever it was, and that it was exactly what I had wanted long ago—in the worlds where the soul forges its future life. Nazarites, Nazarenes, and Essenes alike believed in the multiple births of the soul. Reincarnation was not just an empty word for them. For these men it was more than a doctrine to follow, it was

89

an everyday reality, supported by proofs that continually came to them. Moreover the notion of proof, in a purely metaphysical realm, was an empty one. Each of us had a feeling for the order of things through senses that today have been dulled.

This worldview did not isolate the Brothers in white robes from the majority of the people of Palestine. Even among those who followed the law of Moses strictly, many of the faithful believed that the soul furthered its evolution from one body to the next. For me, this was an obvious truth, and it never came to my mind to question the Brothers about it.

One day I was told the Venerable One wished to see me, along with several others my age. Both impatient and a little nervous, the five of us went together to the door of the ageless Brother's apartments. As always, we found him sitting on a simple mat, his back to the wall, with his eyes half shut.

The room seemed smaller than it had before, but was just as simply furnished as ever. Two heavy, faded blue draperies barely managed to warm the walls. In a broad beam of sunlight, on the wall over the Venerable One's head, I saw an eight-sided star, a triangle whose summit pointed upward, and a single point, all painted with great finesse.

"Come closer," we heard him say quietly, "come closer and be blessed."

We replied with a slight bow, our arms crossed over our chests, as was the custom.

"Sit down and have a little of this milk I have requested for you," he said.

We obeyed without a word, passing around a heavy jar of red clay filled with creamy milk.

"Your time here with us is coming to an end now," he said in a louder voice, and smiled calmly through the long locks of the silver hair that fell on either side of his face. We could see his eyes shining like pearls. He went on: "As you have come to know, your work here has not always been easy. We have asked much of you, but we only ask it of those who can give much! Let this fact burn like a flame for you in your new lives.

"If we have taken much from you, it was to give you even more. It is up to you now to do more than keep the embryos of treasures we have deposited in your crucibles. Stir them up, make them boil, make them blossom into scarlet flowers that you will scatter all around you! But do not let the seeds you sow sail with the wind. There is earth wherein seeds may germinate, but they will merely dry out on earth which has not felt the touch of the plowshare for a long time. You have been told this a thousand times. Soon your fathers will come to take you away, and you will go forth over the roads of the land. There is perhaps one of you who imagines that the image of the Krmel will be erased from his soul as soon as he finds himself at home among his people. This is a mistake, for your people are as much here as in your villages, and your hearts are forever filled with the essence distilled by the Nameless One.

"For eight years you will have to continue your work at home in your villages. More than ever, you will grow up making the way of life of the children of Sdech* your own. You will remain students of our Brotherhood until your twenty-first year, when you will be authorized to wear our white linen robe. Only then will you be assigned a task, a mission, like the rest of our people, a mission that the Father will ask you to fulfill to the end, even if it means sacrificing your life. My words will no doubt shock you, but that's what I truly wish for you all, in these times. It will mean that you will have taken part in the Great Work which is unfolding on this Earth, and the final armor will be forged on your souls, that of the ruby and the swan, of the one desire and of total love."

At that moment I saw in the eyes of the Venerable One a glow I had not known before. It was at once a fire, a wave, a mist, and a breathing out, propelling itself far, far out into the future.

The one we sometimes referred to as the Just among the Just then picked up a handful of sand out of a bowl beside him, and gently moving his hand over the floor before him, drew a wide, thin circle with the grains of sand. He continued his gesture and the four equal branches of a cross appeared beneath his hand, four branches made for as many arcs of the circle, which gave to the whole a feeling of movement. He finished his drawing by tracing two letters of the Hebrew alphabet. In the Krmel, this alphabet was not used

*Another name for the Essenes.

in our studies, but its knowledge was compulsory nonetheless, and had even to be regarded with a certain veneration. To the right and left of his drawing, I could read the letters Heth and Qoph.* In doing so, the Venerable One seemed to have woven about himself a tangible veil of silence, isolating him from the rest of the world. None of us, at that moment, would have dared to break the subtle spell that he had just cast with a few simple gestures. We sat in silence, and watched as he moved his forefinger through the meanders of the circle, the cross, and the letters. It was clear he found some meaning in these symbols, a meaning we could not even glimpse with our still meager knowledge. At last he looked up and blinked once, slowly, as he nodded his head. This meant that our interview was over. As one, we approached him, our heads bowed, our arms folded over our chests in sign of respect, and in turn, each of us felt the warm, enveloping touch of his hands on the crown of our head. I felt curiously that a page of my life had been turned over, and still today it seems that in these magic moments, my child's soul grew several years more mature.

We left the Venerable One's apartments, our eyes interrogating the cold stone floor, as if some heavy truth, some terrible sentence, had just been pronounced concerning us. Behind us we heard the creaking of the doors being shut by one of the Brothers.

My departure would take place in only two or three weeks' time, but in my heart had opened the cold wound of those who have had to leave all behind them. Suddenly a firm hand seized my arm, and turning around, I saw an old man whom I had met occasionally in the corridors of the Krmel, and whose joviality amused me a great deal. He pulled me away from my companions.

"The Just One has given me a message for you, Simon," he said, leading me down a stairway that gave onto an inner courtyard. "You are well aware," he went on, in a decided tone of voice, "that we have done everything we could to develop certain capacities in you. We have repeatedly tested you, in order to know on which path the Father was waiting for you. Now we believe we have the answer, and as it will soon be time for you to leave, we must submit you to trials in keeping with what is awakening within you. Do you understand me?"

---

*The numerical values of these two letters are 8 and 100.

I found no meaning in the Brother's words; what I wanted most was to be able to sit on the ground in a corner of the courtyard beneath the scorching sun.

"You must develop your clairvoyance, Simon," the old man said, patting my head, "and also your willpower. When the Nameless One bestows a gift in the heart of a newborn baby, it is in the hope that this gift will not lie forever buried beneath the dusts of time. An unexploited possibility is like rich earth that is left to the weeds, like a scorned treasure. What would you think of a man whose family was hungry but who was too lazy to stoop down and pick up the gold that the Eternal Force put beneath his feet at every turn of his path?"

I still failed to see what the old man was getting at, except that I absolutely had to cultivate some abilities I had hardly suspected were mine.

"Every being exists for a special purpose, Simon," he went on. "The purpose of everyone here is, first, to acquire a dimension that should make of us neither hunters nor prey, but rather balance beams, points of equilibrium. Secondly, we are asked to master phenomena which seem to deprive common mortals of any real freedom. This happens first through the germination, the flowering of the fifth element of our being. Why is this? It is to be able to stop talking, Simon, and to start singing! To teach people to sing the melody that the stars and the Father have written within them.

"To do this, Brother, you will be given three days . . . ."

I still had no idea of what the old man was trying to tell me, and at that moment, I didn't really care. It was the first time anyone had ever addressed me as "Brother," and this was enough to capture my whole attention. I welcomed the name proudly, like an initiation, like a promise of coming nobility. Yet once more, the fateful words struck my ears:

"We will leave you for three days, three days in a place unknown to you, in total darkness. Your task, little Simon, will be this: find your way out. But you will also have to find your way out of your fears, of your little role as a monk; you will have to find the stone of light. You will understand my words better when the time is right! Now, take this."

The aged Brother, whose little eyes—nearly without eyelashes—were now looking at me through thin horizontal slits, opened his hand and placed a round gray stone in my palm. I turned it over in my fingers, and saw that a deep groove divided the stone into two equal hemispheres, each of which was crisscrossed with many slashes, seeming to form some kind of intentional pattern. I traced these lines with my fingernails for a moment, then looked up once more.

Beside the Brother stood Joseph, smiling at me. The two of them, standing there staring at me, looked a bit like accomplices. My face must have reflected my dumb confusion, or my astonishment, perhaps, for they both immediately burst into laughter.

That night, the owls that flew their nightly rounds over the Krmel might have observed two silhouettes making their way across the great courtyard. A Brother, who was much younger than the old man who had told me about the nature of my test, led me to a part of the monastery where we rarely went: a tiny room full of ancient manuscripts that breathed an old and friendly odor of dust, one of those odors that almost seemed about to talk. The door, which had been securely locked by means of an enormous though rudimentary padlock, was just as securely shut behind us by the Brother as soon as we were in.

In one corner of the room, beneath a wooden trunk that we slid to one side, there appeared a slab of stone bigger than the other ones. The Brother took a metal hook from his belt and inserted the point into a notch in the slab and lifted it, revealing a trapdoor. I must not have realized at that moment what was happening, or towards what ordeal I was headed, as the sight of the gaping, utterly black hole that had opened at my feet inspired in me curiosity rather than anxiety. Had I really understood I was to spend three whole days in there, several meters below the ground, trying to solve a problem the scope of which I could only dimly grasp? I don't think so.

The Brother uncoiled a long rope he had brought with him, and wedged one end of it tightly under the slab of stone we had lifted and paid the rest of it out into the hole. This done, he gently held my head between his two hands.

"Three days, Simon," he said, looking into my eyes, "is the most that will be asked of you. Before this time is over, may you find the way out of this underground place and gain the open air on your own."

He then uttered a quiet prayer, and hugged me close to him in his arms, as only my parents had ever done. Once again, he took the end of the rope in his hands, and I understood I was to slide down into the dark opening in the earth, where my secret being was likely to be revealed. My mind was hazy as I penetrated into the womb of the Krmel that night. It seemed a long way down, although the depth was probably not more than the height of three or four men. My bare feet finally came into contact with the damp earth, and I let the rope go. I heard the Brother asking me if I had reached the ground, then came the scraping of the stone slab on the floor above. . . .

Suddenly, there came a dull sound whose merciless echo was thrown back by the walls of my underground prison; the trapdoor had been irremediably shut behind me. Instinctively I felt at my left side, where hung the water skin and the barley loaf I had been given. I cannot say exactly what I did during the first few moments, but I suddenly came to realize the full meaning, the thick black density of the word *solitude*. It was not so much the darkness that bothered me, as the fact of being face to face with myself, suspended somewhere between who I thought I was and who I wanted to be. The Brothers had taught us to breathe deeply in times of confusion but I didn't even grasp that I was confused. I had to understand it all, right away, to prove my strength by finding my way out, as fast as possible; besides the air smelt so dank, tasted so musty.

My first resolution was to find a wall, any wall, which I could follow, and whose slightest irregularity I would have to picture in my mind, so as to draw a mental map of the place. The ground seemed perfectly flat, and I began moving about in the dark like a sleepwalker. Soon my hands met a rough, damp wall, which aroused a pungent feeling within me. I walked forward with great caution, trailing my fingers along the wall. I came to a first corner, then a second, and a third, and finally a fourth; I deduced that I was probably back about where I had started. A clear image of the chamber formed in my mind. This was a room about five paces on each side. I felt like crying out, hoping that the echo would confirm the vision I had of my surroundings. It was not one cry that rose from my chest, but ten, twenty, a multitude of little whimpers that were transformed into as many proofs of my own existence, an existence that I wanted to be absolutely tangible. They were so many buoys I was throwing out to myself. I might have grabbed onto them, and regained my calm, whose flight had been masked by a sort of self-hypnosis, but a horrible suspicion overcame me. What if I were imprisoned there, in a vault which would not be opened before three days? What if the possibility of getting out was no more than a lie, and the whole thing was only to test my nerves and my perseverance? Such an idea was almost unbearable. For after all, what were they expecting from a twelve-year-old, if not endless waiting?

How feeble they sounded, those beautiful speeches about the practice of calling out to the Father in times of anguish, times when the heart freezes. There I was, and my heart was really frozen. Would there always be such an abyss between words and acts, such a gap between the idea and its tangible realization? Instinctively, I wrapped myself more tightly in my cloak, and in my only pocket, my fingers touched the little stone sphere given to me by the old Brother. It felt warm, and at the bottom of this ocean of darkness, I tried to visualize its contours. I had at times heard some of the Brothers talk of a substance they sometimes used, with which they coated an object in order to increase its radiance, so they could more clearly see its ether. Perhaps this too was a fable, just like finding a way out of this dungeon! I sat down on the ground, my back to the wall, and I think I began shivering.

Several hours must have passed by that way. Behind me, I only felt twelve years of emptiness. The proud little monk who thought he was already one of the Brothers could hardly cope with the first blows when put to the test. The image I had of myself was disintegrating bit by bit. My willpower had abandoned me; I had felt it escaping through my fingertips as it had been described to me, a vital substance regaining its own world, loaded with my fears.

"Be someone who wants, be someone who tries," they had often repeated in the temples where we studied. "Every time you give up, your vital energy escapes you, takes to its wings and rejoins a common force, going the way of all human failures, poisoning the

Earth just a little bit more and locking you tighter and tighter into your own negativity. Despair is an inverted pyramid that undermines the worlds. The more complex a thing is, the more easily it breaks down. So be simple, and get rid of all that makes you say, as you roll up your mat every morning, 'I am me.' Throw off your armor of vain, icy strength; make yourself small enough to slip into the mesh of the wind . . . make yourself so small . . . ."

I was rolling the strange stone sphere between my fingers. It felt as if it had just acquired the power to link me back to my masters . . . as if through this stone, their voices might whisper forgotten truths into my ears. "Make yourself so small . . . ." In a flash, an idea sprang to my mind.

"The door to a temple is always low," we had also been taught, "and one must always bow below one's pride in order to enter. But do not think it is the Father who demands that we bow before him; he leaves his children free. It is they who realize one day that they have grown up prematurely, and that the heaviness of their bodies is stifling the flames of their hearts."

I thought I could guess. The Brothers had forever thrown bridges between symbols and matter. They were aware that great beings of light could communicate with souls through images. I stood up again, and tried once more to walk around the room, but this time, I let my fingers trail along the wall at the height of my knees. I came to the first corner, then to the second, then suddenly I felt an abrupt angle, a space in the wall. Yes, there was a way out, a tiny one, so tiny I had to double over to go through. My perception of the surroundings changed immediately. Judging from the walls I felt on either side, I was walking along a sort of tunnel that slanted slightly upward. Then something felt different again. The walls no longer echoed my breathing with the same intensity. I had probably entered a second chamber. Immediately I held my breath . . . there was something, there was something alive in there. There was a continuous shrillish murmur, an unexpected coolness. At once I thought of water, and located a little spring, a thin trickle of water running just in front of me, on the right. I straightened up. Once more I decided to try to form a clear picture of the chamber. I counted six hard stone walls, rough to the touch. My recent success had somewhat cheered me up, and I went in search for a way out, following the same method as before. I found not one, but three openings, apparently equal in size.

Once more I felt myself trapped. It seemed that some perverse intelligence had decided to make fun of me. I would probably have to overcome one problem after another, all the way to the end. It was the practical aspect of the riddles I had been trying to solve for the past hours that puzzled me most. Could it be possible that someone in the Krmel had conceived of such an incredible circuit just to challenge the shrewdness and the tenacity of young monks?

My mind was drained. Was I to rush headfirst into one of the galleries that opened close to the ground, only to retrace my steps if need be? If so, then why did the Brothers take such pride in teaching us the "patience of the watching cat"? And what was there to watch, to observe anyway, since I was all alone down there? Then I started to pray, and pray again, with all my might, with all my unfaltering willpower. I repeated hundreds of prayers, at first consciously, then mechanically, hoping for some miraculous manifestation of salvation. My lips articulated words, whole sentences even, and my mind grew less and less aware of what I was saying. I was like a spring that unwinds, unfolding its spiral until its axis is finally free from the tension.

My liberation came in the form of sleep. I plunged into big luminous triangles, and swam through them. When I awoke, my lips were still forming the same words. I had no idea of how much time had passed, but my mind was full of a sensation of intense activity. Without thinking, I wrapped myself in my cloak and rushed into the middle gallery. Something told me it might represent the balance beam so sought after by the Brothers. At the end of the gallery was another chamber. I can still remember its ten walls, smooth this time, and warm, and the poignant feeling of suffocation there. It was the same story all over again. My barley loaf somehow seemed absurd, and I left it behind. Three more chambers followed, one after the other, connected by tunnels of various sorts, the details of which I do not recall.

Each of the chambers I discovered was made up of more walls than the last. In the third I counted ten; in the fourth, twelve; then sixteen, then strangely enough came a little room whose irregular shape I didn't manage to grasp mentally. I left this room through a wide and certainly very high door opening directly onto a vast chamber that appeared to be circular. Its walls were polished to perfection, and presented innumerable facets a little more than two hands wide.

I was tired, tired of all these problems and of all these solutions that led nowhere. Was I really meant to live like this for three whole days ? I thought I might just as well stop here. Once more, sleep, an empty sleep, overtook me. I had the persistent impression that the apparent absence of life down there was gradually taking me over, and opening an abyss in the deepest levels of my being. I thought I was no longer heading for a way out but for a sort of inner funeral. This state of sluggishness, which gave way to unconsciousness, must have lasted for quite a while.

Nevertheless, when I woke up, something had changed. For a moment I thought I could see in the darkness and I even had the feeling I was at home. With astonishing acuity, the steps I had taken thus far passed through my mind, and I was able to review my progress up until then. I had discovered seven chambers, each one different from the others in dimension, shape, atmosphere, warmth; everything had been planned differently. Suddenly it hit me that I had journeyed through symbols of human consciousness. Could it be that these seven chambers symbolized humanity's seven wheels of fire spoken of by the Venerable One? Could the three galleries, which so often led from one room to the next, represent the triple flame of the Earth Mother, the serpentine flame rising through the center of our spine? It appeared clear to me that I was most likely at the summit of humanity's tree of life, whose image had been built underground by the Brothers of ancient times. Was it their hope that each time a chamber was entered, a new level of consciousness would open? If so, I concluded, their experiment was a miserable failure. I had found my way as some rat might have done, not by using the inner flame that I had been promised. I had been digging a hole in myself, not filling myself with a new strength.

Suddenly, three words struck me with unbelievable violence: "Who are you?"

The voice had come both from within and from without, and sounded neither friendly nor hostile.

"A rat! a rat!" I felt like screaming, and then an answer, a mere breath, slipped into me, lightly, peacefully, and with perfect clarity.

"Simon, Simon, you speak of a hole, as of an abyss, but is it not necessary to dig a hole before you may fill one? Remember the temple chants: 'Empty, empty your soul, and it will be filled with the Eternal.' The rat is an image of the promise of times to come and strikes the hour of the being who plunges into the labyrinth of his own skull, into the meanders of his own brain, and goes all the way back to his origin. Its name is written in the heavens, next to the One where the prodigal children drink from the cup of the Father. The rat comes from the point where the sun rises. It shines, like the promise of the inner star.* It is the center of the target you must aim for, the heart of the tree; cast off the layers of bark, don't let yourself be drawn into their eternal magnetic round. Slow your pace! Rejoin your axis!"

I leaped to my feet and, unthinking, I rushed to where I supposed the center of the chamber to be. After about twenty steps I had the curious sensation that I was sinking into the ground. There was a steep slope and I was undoubtedly swept into a spiral, quickly confirmed by the stone walls closing in on my right and left. Then my feet met even ground again and groping around, I realized that before me there opened a slightly arched gallery. It seemed to have been dug right out of the bedrock, and I could walk upright without any difficulty.

Abruptly the path became more puzzling. The gallery slanted to the right, to the left, back and forth in seemingly infinite alternation. What happened next made me panic again; once more my self-assurance deserted me. One, two, three, four galleries opened to the right and left, unevenly spaced, challenging the instinct that only moments before had armed me with blind faith in myself. I took the first on the right, or on the left, I don't remember, but without a second's reflection. This gallery split in turn into four new ones. The one I took, with just as little hesitation as before, led me into a wide, circular trajectory, like all the others I followed subse-

---

*We offer these apparently enigmatic words to the meditation of the reader. In terms of symbols as well as sonorities, the reader may direct his research toward the words *ram*, *ra*, and *rate*, the latter being the French term for the spleen, a fundamentally solar organ.

quently. I quickly understood that I was indeed in the grip of a labyrinth and that I could indefinitely be made to circle around my goal.

I almost ran down the tunnels, as if my speed alone could bring me closer to the light, which once again, drew further and further away. Something brushed by me, I was certain of it! This brought to mind the subterranean beings I had come upon once when accompanied under the earth by one of the Brothers. So I was not alone! I could not be alone, anyway, that seemed obvious, and I had not been right from the beginning. Solitude, I had been taught, is the trap into which fall those who shut their eyes.

"When you close the shutters of your heart, you can see only yourself, and when you can see only yourself, you do nothing but look at yourself. So you love yourself, or you hate yourself, but you pick at yourself, and take yourself apart, and cut yourself up, you scatter your being, and you become less than ever able to grasp the union, the ultimate oneness of things. A hermit is never alone. He grasps the life that vibrates even in the air he breathes, and grasping it, he makes it even more intense, and then releases it into the sphere of the universe." Thus spoke the Brothers.

I stopped in my tracks and burst into tears. It was clear that they were forcing me to turn inward, though I wasn't sure I could do it.

What happened then remains in my soul with the tenacious strength of some reality escaped from another world. As I let myself slide to the ground, a hand was laid softly on my head. Startled, I looked up to see Joseph standing there in a halo of magnificent shining blue light. He was smiling and his eyes, filled with unimaginable clarity, gave me more strength than even the wisest of sayings. They unfolded a ribbon of enchanted words in my soul, none of which I could ever reproduce.

The vision, or rather the presence, faded away quickly but was enough to change me into a rock of serenity, filled with a silence capable of building worlds.

Where Joseph had stood there rose an enormous, stark-black cubical stone against a background of shining, absolutely pure white light. It stood like some colossal temple, at the top of a flight of steps. Behind it I could sense the warm presence of some incredible and indescribable power, with which I knew I was in intimate communion. Then I heard a voice calling my name, once, then a second time. The voice seemed to come from behind the gigantic cube of stone. I felt it was at once a supplication, an order, and an encouragement.

Then I had the strange feeling that my arms were turning into heavy wings that I couldn't manage to lift. I felt a lump in my throat and I perhaps burst into tears again—I really don't know, as the consciousness I had of my body was completely altered. In fact I was no longer a body; I was encased in a carcass, an assembly of organs that were total strangers to me. I felt as if I were very small, inside clothes that were far too big for me, so small that I could easily move about within them. I traveled slowly around my body, visiting one organ after another. I saw my muscles tightening and relaxing, my blood running through my arteries, my stomach secreting digestive fluids, my heart beating doggedly. I felt emotionally detached from all this. My inner eye brought me to the center of my skull. There I saw an inextricable network of phosphorescent fibres shot through with little tremors. An impalpable energy was flowing through this circuit, on perpetual alert, according to its own logical patterns. I could see, or feel, the thread of my life as it wound its way through the maze of my brain. The little grooved stone. . . . It was child's play, a pathway whose every turn, every starlike center, every dead end, was there for a purpose and seemed to portray in a single entity, the joys and hardships, the failures and the victories of my being.

Abruptly all this vanished. Before me I could only see the form of a twelve-year-old boy who seemed to be asleep, lying on his side, at the intersection of two galleries. I was no more than a pair of eyes that my consciousness followed in their wanderings. I didn't understand immediately that this was my body that lay before me, and it seemed like a stranger to me. Perhaps that was what death was like. Little did it matter, as a wind of freedom shook the reins of my being, and this alone was important to me.

I felt an invisible force drawing me through the narrow arched tunnels of the stone labyrinth. The darkness had given way to a crackling white and blue light, and I saw the endless succession of corridors as clearly as if they had been out in broad daylight.

Soon, my gaze, which at times wanted to embrace the whole of the labyrinth, met an enormous block of gray stone, partially closing off a hole in the wall. A cold light, crackling with life, was shining from behind the stone. Somehow I found myself on the other side of the stone, and to my total amazement, below me as far as I could see, stretched vast forests of holm oaks and carpets of yellow and mauve flowers. Far, far off on the horizon I saw the infinite blue line of the sea. I was overcome with joy before so much beauty, so much unexpected freshness. I felt as though I was floating in the air and without having to turn around I perceived behind me the great mass of the Krmel, along with the smaller buildings that huddled at the foot of its walls. It seemed I saw all this through a white sphere, or rather a translucent egg, an egg of peace, of deep tranquility.

These moments of ecstasy, of infinite freedom, lasted for some time, and then I felt that someone or something drew a black veil over the eyes of my soul. Once more I was imprisoned beneath the earth, and painfully I raised my numbed body. But I was no longer the same Simon who was enclosed within a labyrinth beneath the Krmel; I was a being who had at last understood the real meaning of the word *prison,* and I felt I was awakening from a dream that had lasted twelve years. From that moment on, finding the way out was child's play. I found I possessed a sort of inner compass and all I had to do was to let myself be guided, without trying to decide rationally where to go. In no time, I was before the heavy block of stone that my inner eye had managed to find a few minutes earlier. A bright shaft of light streamed through a small gap in that final wall and, following it, I only had to struggle through a water hole downward to vanish into the oak forest.

Later, once I was back within the Krmel, my instructors told me that the pathway I had had to take followed a line of force that the initiates of old had managed to locate with precision and to channel to their own ends. They taught me that this practice was not uncommon, and that the seven chambers through which I had passed were so many energy foci, designed to activate the seven sacred centers of the human body.

"There are two primordial forces," the elders told me: "that of
the Earth Mother and that of the Cosmic Father." I had undergone
the initiation of the first of these two forces, governing matter and
germination energies. It was also called the Initiation of the Virgin
Earth. Its object was to awaken all the deepest instincts of a human
being, to expel a certain number of impurities of the soul through
knowledge of the inner self, and ultimately, through self-judgment.
One who underwent this initiation could not help but go deep
within and clean out all that was not really oneself. One was stripped
naked and could find no possible excuse for even the slightest
weakness. Such an initiation took the form of a sort of death, but
like any other death it carried within it the seeds of resurrection.
This was the symbol as well as the power of the number seven, of
the Sheba* of the hidden tradition of Moses and the Brothers.

"Many men and women," Brother Moshab told me, during
our final interview, "imagine that they may scorn the Earth Mother
who nourishes them. Her force, however, cannot be dissociated
from the celestial force. Each of us must assimilate and master all the
energies of the original Virgin, who is the black matrix, before we
may stand as we truly are before the Father. Thus there are two
energies on the plane of fleshly beings such as we are, which may
stupidly become good or evil, if we do not understand them. If the
Mother comes before the Father on the upward path, however, her
force can but slumber if he doesn't come as her beloved to pull her
from her dream. A current of love must descend so that the other
one may rise to join it at the source. Total force is born of this
unceasing exchange and takes concrete form as a single fire, mag-
nified, that stands between the two: the fire of the Nameless One.
Forever it remains the fruit of the supreme initiation, the scepter of
Thoth of our Brothers from the Red Land. Forever it remains the
straight path of the true initiate who has made his way up the thirty-
three rungs of the serpentine ladder.† The Initiation of the Father
bears the sacred name of Noah. It will now be up to you to search

---

*This may be compared to the Hindu deity Shiva, who is also a symbol of death and
resurrection.
†The scepter of Thoth is a symbol of initiatic knowledge. The thirty-three rungs on the
serpentine ladder represent the thirty-two vertebrae plus the thirty-third, which is one
with the thirty-second.

for it. You have only eaten a piece of bread; now you need the wine!"

My last days at the Krmel were somewhat sullen. For the first time a real flame had been lit in my heart, and I was to be torn away from the place and the beings who had brought about my metamorphosis.

I decided to look for Joseph to show him my affection and to confide to him the secret of my anxieties and hopes. The Brothers told me that I was not allowed to meet him. He was not to be seen for a while. I had to accept it.

One morning as I was beginning my ritual ablutions, a Brother entered my room and announced the arrival of my father. Reunions such as this one cannot be described. Six years weigh heavy in the life of a young boy and I wasn't sure whether it was joy or fear that cast a veil over my eyes. Few words were exchanged when we met; we had too much to tell each other. Donkeys were waiting in the courtyard, this was the only thing we knew.

So for the last time, I heard the sound of my bare feet on the stone floors of the Krmel, for the last time my gaze embraced its enormous mass. The road to Jerusalem was a long one, and we had to go.

CHAPTER · X

JERUSALEM

"Hamla! Hamla!"

Before us on the side of the dusty road, two water vendors were haranguing small groups of pilgrims and merchants who were treading heavily onwards toward Jerusalem. At this time of year, when the sun was already shining hot, meeting a water vendor was a sort of blessing. They provided a pretext to dismount, to let the donkeys graze for a while, and to chat with those who, like ourselves, were traveling. There was quite a crowd on the road that ran straight across Galilee, coming to an end at the doors of the High Temple of Solomon. Passover was approaching; it was about the tenth day of the first month, according to the calendar of the priests of Jerusalem. When we had set out, my father had told me that we would not be able to stop at the village, as it would have meant a long detour. The law required that all children should be presented at the temple on the Passover preceding their thirteenth birthday. I could not disobey this law, even though its value was not recognized by our faith. At most, we were excused from attending the ceremonies of the first two days of the celebration. For my part, I had no objections to accomplishing this duty. Going into Jerusalem, where I could see the rich dwellings, palaces, and temples, had all the charm of a dream. The road was long, but I took great pleasure in getting to know my father again. He was just as before, with his big calloused hands, his warm, quiet voice, and the reassuring strength of his personality. There were only a few more wrinkles running across his forehead. These details brought the past back and I delighted in visualizing my mother's face, the faces of Myriam and so many others I had left behind long ago, behind a wall atop a hill. What changes, I wondered, had the years wrought in their faces? I was also happy to discover the countryside we passed through, known to me only from the accounts of traveling merchants. It was a melody in greens and yellows; as far as I could see there were valleys full of trees in flower. Here and there a cluster of cypress trees raised their dark figures to the sky, whereas the olive trees seemed to prefer remaining knotted to the earth itself.

As we approached Jerusalem the landscape was transformed. In less than half a day the lush valleys gave way to a succession of parched hills where large flocks of sheep grazed on the scanty tufts of grass. We passed through several villages—little white and ochre splashes on the barren hillsides or in the heart of an olive grove. There were already signs of celebration here: the streets were filled with the strident song of flutes, and groups of exuberant pilgrims were gathering. Apart from one night when we found lodging at a bethsaïd, we slept out under the stars, warmly wrapped in our cloaks.

Finally one morning, which must have been the fourth since our departure, we sighted the high walls of Jerusalem silhouetted against the bright azure of the sky. It was even more beautiful than I had imagined. The city was set into the mountain; it looked as if it had absorbed all the mountain's majesty, all its austerity, and also all its warmth. I saw it as a single construction, a single force, the color of rock. It was concentrated around a block, the temple, gray and ochre, like the shepherds' land. But that morning, an attentive observer discerned a mosaic of multicolored fabrics, veils, tapestries, some of which fluttered in the wind, overhanging the walls of Jerusalem. Patches of verdant meadows lay at the foot of the mountain. There, a noisy crowd of people was gathering, threading their way among the nomads' tents and a few humble dwellings. We were soon part of this crowd and we struggled to make our way through, pulling at our donkeys who were terrified by the long processions of camels and the shouting merchants.

My father was intent on reaching a cluster of grayish houses a short distance from the walls. It was a sort of bethsaïd, a group of shelters erected by those of Essania as a stopping place for the Brothers, a place where the ill might be treated or the needy provided for. Everyone was welcome and no money was asked from those who sought shelter or treatment there. The goodwill of a few travelers and the work of the community of Brothers in Jerusalem were all that was needed to maintain it and keep it functioning. There were many women who delivered their babies in this bethsaïd, and the poor and the needy came there to claim what they had come to regard as their due. My father told me that this hospitality and generosity had never been abused by the people up to that time. If they were not appreciated by all—far from it!—the white-robed Brothers were at least accorded general respect. Their reputation for honesty surrounded them like a sort of aura, which protected them.

I was aware that we had several relatives in this bethsaïd and so we were hoping to find a room there, which would certainly have been impossible within the walls of the city. But Passover had begun the day before, and despite the warm greeting we received, all they could offer us was a corner of the stable, which, in a way, was not to my displeasure as nights would surely be warmer there than elsewhere. The Brother who greeted us assured us that the census formalities were planned for the next day. In front of priests and scholars I would have to announce that I was born of Joshua, potter in a little village in the center of Galilee, that I believed in the Eternal One, and that I followed his law. Without a doubt, my father had added, I would also have to answer a few more precise questions concerning my faith and my duties. In no way was I to mention my stay at the Krmel, which would certainly have provoked the anger of the priests and doctors. My father was a potter and I would be a potter and this information would be sufficient; my hair and my face would declare loudly enough that I was, as they said, a Nazarene. I should be inconspicuous and satisfy them with some knowledge of religious practices. The Brothers had patiently prepared me for this interview, and there was no doubt that, like many of our people,

I knew the sacred texts better than most of the faithful who went daily to the temple. We ourselves, moreover, honored the word of Moses and that of the great guides who had followed him. We knew perfectly well that some of them had been of the race of Essania,* although this was not to be proclaimed, for we would have been stoned. In our eyes, their words, however sacred, were nonetheless not the only ones to be honored and studied. In our view they presented one aspect of the Father's progressive revelation; they were only just one page of the immense book that the stars had been writing since time immemorial, one page that could be read on many levels and which contained much more than the meaning of its simple letters.

After leaving our donkeys and a few belongings in the keeping of the Brothers we undertook to go to the temple. Once more we had to join the crowd of pilgrims. There was a direct access to the temple from the valley; we only had to go around the city walls a little way and to climb an impressively steep stairway, fortunately surrounded with pleasant verdure. Above us there loomed the overwhelming mass of the house of the Lord, with its titanic walls and its blue and white banderoles streaming in the wind. A little way off to the left I glimpsed the corners of other buildings, apparently vast in size, although much less so than the temple itself. My father explained that over there was a military stronghold, a real fortress,[†] from which orders could be quickly issued to the far reaches of the land. As we climbed, with the resounding blare of the trumpets in our ears, I noticed below a well-defined road that seemed to lead from one of the temple gates to a pleasant looking mountain covered with olive trees. We could see many towering arcades standing amid the clumps of vegetation and the great variety of traveling merchants' stands. At last, now half-suffocated by the moist exhalations coming from the throngs of those who had left the mountains, we entered an immense porch. This crowd was both overexcited and exhausted, having journeyed so long to proclaim their faith in song.

Then before us we discovered a vast courtyard. It seemed to

*Among others, Ezekiel and Elijah.
†Probably this was the famous Antonia fortress.

stretch as far as the eye could see to the right and to the left, with a double row of marble columns rising all around the enclosed space. Between some of these columns cords had been tied up, making temporary enclosures where animals were waiting, trampling their fodder. We could see donkeys, sheep, rams, with their heads painted in red or blue. And among the swarm of animals, I could even make out the proud silhouette of a camel. Then all that disappeared behind the languorous dance of the spirals of incense smoke arising from everywhere. To the right, regularly hidden by the tall figure of my father, I could see a massive tower that shot skyward. Much later I learned that the priests went there each morning at sunrise to make astronomical observations and sometimes, though not so frequently, to prophesy;* from there we flowed along with the teeming crowd into a second courtyard, much smaller than the first, but higher, and we had to go up a few steps whose stones, deeply worn in the middle, bore witness to the age of the place.

My instructors had at times spoken to us about the conception of the Great Temple of Jerusalem and searching my memory, I thought I could recognize the courtyard of the great Sanhedrin. In Aramaic, this meant it was the place where it was customary for eminent Sadducees and Pharisees to proclaim their judgments in important judicial and religious matters. There were many fewer columns and I immediately noticed that the pavement was patterned with big, alternating light and dark slabs of stone. I had been well trained in this kind of symbolism and I knew its meaning in such a place. Such a representation of the forces of light and darkness indicated the origin of those who had built the sanctuary. Traditionally, the high priests cursed with vehemence any religion other than their own. They were unaware, or pretended to be, that King Solomon had called on the sages of Babylon and of the land of Sheba for the realization of his work. The priests execrated Thoth and Zoroaster, but I knew that these were among the representatives of the Father, and that from time immemorial they had united their voices. Trying not to lose sight of my father, I remembered that the number of the stones was planned, and that each one, according to

---

*This tower is traditionally called the Pinnacle Tower.

its location and its color, symbolized one of humanity's tendencies. As we penetrated closer to the heart of the temple, I thought that the agitation of the crowd would decrease, but this was far from the case.

We had to go up other steps then pass through a wide entrance, whose wooden doors were heavily reinforced with iron bars. I had the sudden feeling we were in one of the squares of Joppa; a motley crowd, coming and going around a fragrant fire, was in the grip of an intense agitation. Soon, all I could make out were bales of hay, bundles of rich fabrics, and mountains of fruits. We were accosted by one beggar and then by two more, and I could see no more, I could understand no more. I was no more than a little dot, lost, isolated from the rest of the world, shut within a shell, assailed by a thousand noises and colors, penetrated by all the mingled smells of life and death. The citrus fruits spread their acrid scent, the merchants shouted out their bargains to the pilgrims who were chanting their prayers, lost in their thoughts. This world was not mine; the Galilean gentleness had given way to the bitterness of Judaea. My father, for his part, moved easily through the crowd in the middle of all the uproar and the mad activity. I knew from the few words he had said that he hardly appreciated it all, but the torrents of words and of propositions that flowed over him seemed to flow off immediately, without affecting him. I tried to look at the faces, the eyes, the mouths—where I read astonishment, or scorn, or elsewhere a mocking joke. My father was quiet and smiling, but I understood how difficult it was to be dressed in white linen where men were made of lead.

At the far side of the courtyard I saw another door—higher than it was wide—flanked by two enormous pillars of pink marble; it was not quite opposite the previous one, and its access was ostensibly guarded by several impressive men. I couldn't tell whether they were priests or guards. They had the venerable bearing of the former, with the muscles and the bestial gaze of the latter. It was such a strange combination of gray, respectable beards, long blue-and-white-fringed robes, and all the metal trappings worthy of a provincial governor. They were waiting there, about twenty paces from me at the top of some steps, bearing both the heavy lances carried by soldiers and the gold star worn by doctors, sewn on their chests. We came to a halt at their feet.

I let myself be guided by my father; he knew that we were formally forbidden access to the other courtyards and to the temple chambers. According to the law, Essenes, Nazarenes, Nazarites and others were beings too impure to enjoy this privilege. From what I gathered listening to those around us, I understood it was here in this courtyard that I was to come the following day to be submitted to the census tests. In the face of such a chaos of bodies and souls, I felt a certain unease, a blending of curiosity and dread. My father most probably felt my discomfort, for our first visit to the temple was of short duration. I was unable to say whether I was enthusiastic or disappointed, so different was all this from anything I had ever experienced up until then. We did not have to return directly to the bethsaïd, however; we were in no hurry, and the streets of Jerusalem had so often filled my dreams. . . .

We entered within the walls of the city by way of a gigantic wooden porch. A great number of soldiers, who seemed foreign to our race, were posted there. I didn't know whom they represented, nor did I care; the Krmel had remained silent about a certain aspect of the world that I would undoubtedly have to discover myself. An island is never just an island even if it is a peaceful one, and the time ultimately comes when its inhabitants see the waves coming from the far-off horizons.

I saw my father take a few coins out of his bag and hand them to a man with a surly face, and once more there was tumult around us, the frenzied agitation of merchants and buyers. Odors of food, of flowers, and of burning wood blended in strange combinations, but I was especially captivated by the beauty and the fragrance of the spice stands. There, I saw so many things I had never needed and which, one day perhaps, would seem necessary! Many years later, I learned that there was little merit to being a sage among sages; real greatness belongs rather to whoever is able to remain awake among those who sleep. Jerusalem was a trap, a whirlwind that could make a sleepwalker of me, and this became clear to me in the days preceding Passover. I should probably be thankful for this salutary feeling, which helped me to remain faithful to those who were preparing the path.

Many were the detachments of soldiers we met in the tortuous little streets of the city. We found a number of them in the shelter of a great stone arch at the top of a hill, engaged in conversation with some civilians who did not seem at all put out by their presence. Jerusalem thus appeared to me as an astonishing stronghold where the authority was shared by an odd mixture of priests, soldiers, and merchants; a place where light, blood, and gold had arrived at some kind of compromise. We lingered in front of a palace or two, owned by powerful foreigners or rich Sadducees, and we came upon the strangest temples. How had all the credos of the earth, as well as all its superstitions, managed to come together on these few poor acres of an arid mountainside?

When we got back to the bethsaïd, my father left me alone in the corner of the stable where we were to sleep; he had to contact some Brothers whose work was related to the great Temple of Helios.

I had just sat down on the straw, my back to the daub wall, when something happened that gave meaning to the hours spent in Jerusalem with its atmosphere of both truth and pretense. In the ray of light that shone through the door that had been left ajar, stood a man, a man I knew, a man who had once been slightly bent with age but who now stood tall and proud as a cypress tree. It was Zerah, old Zerah, with his long gray beard, in a poor but beautiful white linen robe that sang of purity. Out of his parchmentlike face, his light eyes were smiling at me as they had long ago. The old man who lived in the house by the old well stepped forward, and I was unable to breathe a word, so overcome was I with astonishment, love, and gratitude.

"Simon," he said softly, approaching, "Simon stay where you are; you do not have to get up. Our hearts are touching already, can you not feel this?"

I made an effort to speak, but my throat was like a knot, and I felt a pleasant coolness penetrating my body.

"Simon," he said a third time, "I have been watching over you for nearly seven years now. Tomorrow the laws of men will make an adult of you. I know that you wonder whether the law of the Father will ever prevail over this tumult of greedy appetites. Let me guide you once more, one last time. Do not let your heart question,

Brother! Truly, in the society of men, beyond all the mountains on this Earth, there is no law of the Father. The temples will never be able to offer anything but the law of the shadow of the Father. The only law, the only real law is not a law at all but an understanding, a harmony, an inbreath and an outbreath which make a being one cell of the Divine. Tomorrow, when you enter the temple, for many men Passover will be all the slaughtered lambs and a whole flood of devotions laid at the feet of the Eternal One. The vital force of the spilled blood will return to its original dwelling, the ether, regenerating the physical nature of the land of Moses.

"As for you, you must know that the day of Passover, above all days, is the one when the human may surge forth from the embryo. This day reminds those who hear with their soul that they must become the masters of the chariot of David. The Nameless One created the first day of today's Earth under the sign of the ox.* On the day of Passover, He yoked seven oxen to pull the chariot of the men and women to come, to remind them of the White Land. But you, Simon, will you see the meaning of these seven forces? Will you see the death that calls out to life? Ponder the significance of my words, and bury them in the depths of your heart. Look at the chariot of David; see the five gold nails that adorn its cubic nature. They express the quintessence of the Being, the Force that absorbs and includes the four elementary forces. This is the place, Simon, this is the moment when spirit sublimates matter. Indeed I say the place, Simon, as the five is a point in your body, it is the mouth through which you absorb the ether, a step on the way leading to the seven. Tomorrow you will receive the Passover like a crown on the top of your head, like a dawn between death and life, like a phoenix. The nameless fire never demands sacrifices, but quickens the Alliance through giving."

As he said this, Zerah took a few more steps forward, and I saw that a fringe of iridescent light enveloped his body. It was the depths

*Certain hermetists situate the moment of the Earth's creation under the astrological sign of the ox, or the bull, Taurus. (Compare the Hebrew word *eleph*, the ox, with the letters aleph and alpha, the first letters of the Hebrew and Greek alphabets. In the Phoenician alphabet, eleph has the form of a bovine head.) This also evokes the symbolism of the septentrion (Latin for "the seven oxen"), and refers to the Ursa Major, the Motherland of the White people.

of his being, all his goodness and warmth that he seemed to be offering me in that way.

"Do you know what is within the High Temple, Simon? In the depths of its innermost sanctuary—in the Holy of Holies—is sleeping, and shining as well, the fundamental Rock, the point of departure of many a civilization, past and future. A double force, both concrete and abstract, it enables some men to build pyramids of peoples and to build themselves. It seals one of the orifices through which one may see the beating heart of the Earth Mother, a doorway to planes of being which support our elementary life. This is not an image; you must understand that it is the square base of the pyramid of the human body, while it is as well the cubic stone of an edifice that is continually being constructed.

"There are one hundred and nineteen of you, one hundred and nineteen who are waiting, as you are, for the moment when they may add their brick—made of clay, of bronze, or of gold; little does it matter, it will be their brick, a world in the making which will help the Mother-Stone to open, then to unfold in the four directions."

The old man's phrase hung in the air and he hesitated, as if he feared he would say too much. His little eyes crinkled in a last smile, then with a humble little wave of his hand he turned around, walked through the ray of sunlight that filtered through the doorway and disappeared into the courtyard. Before me, there was no more than a cloud of countless specks of dust swirling in the last beam of orange sunlight, and a silence that seemed so thick it was almost palpable.

With one hand my father pushed the creaking stable door open and entered carrying a heavy bundle of cloth. With a sigh that he tried to make sound funny, he struggled to catch his breath.

"Father," I said, without getting up, "Zerah has just left."

"Zerah?" he asked.

Once again, that silence. Very slowly my father put down his bundle at the feet of the donkeys, and looked far away as if to penetrate the world, or on the contrary, as if he wanted to cut himself off from it. I rose at last, surprised that my father had so little to say. After a moment we spoke of various things, and only late in the evening, after we had shared the communal meal, did he make reference to what I had said.

"It is strange," he said, "Zerah is certainly gone."

The following day was an exhausting one. As planned, we went to the temple, where my father left me for several long hours with a group of adolescents my age. He only reappeared just at the moment when I was to present myself before a dozen priests, whose venerable bearing impressed the assembled crowd, surprisingly quiet in a courtyard usually filled with the tumult of merchants. I myself was a bit frightened by the eyes of the priest-doctors, which reflected a curious blend of uncompromising hardness and gentleness. Most of these men were sitting on wide, sculpted wooden seats, though behind them others stood waiting, seeming to scrutinize the crowd. All were dressed in rich brocades, a flaming spill of white, blue, purple, and gold. Wearing a tall cylindrical hat heavily encrusted with jewels, one of them began my interrogation. What I had expected to be an examination proved to be nothing more than a quick formality. He limited his questioning to a brief checking of my knowledge concerning the fathers of the people of Palestine, and then asked me to enumerate the daily and yearly duties to be performed before the Eternal One.

I noticed, however, that this was not the case for all of us. Some were asked to give precise details about the Sabbath and its real purpose. For my part, I was only too happy with my good fortune.

We lost no time in leaving the temple and then Jerusalem, where the air, saturated with incense smoke and various other essences, had become unbreathable in places. Passover and the bread rites were to last for five more days, during which time the doctors would go into the streets and squares in order to teach the people, unrolling their impressive parchments and commenting on ancient words and laws.

The path we took out of the city led to the northwest up a long, parched hill. As we reached its crest a soft morning mist was rising over the rocks, in keeping with the languorous music of the conch shells coming from within the city walls. I felt as if I were throwing off a cloak that was too warm, too heavy for me. This land was too full of turmoil; too many opposites were clashing there for me, not yet thirteen years old. With a tug on their reins, we led our donkeys toward the greener landscape of Galilee.

CHAPTER XI

THE RAISED STONES

My heart was singing and dancing to the jolting rhythm of our path. Little splashes of white and gray light, the pastel brightness of the almond and fig trees, a mosaic of ancient stones clinging to the hillside: I could feel the village, my village, not far off. I dismounted from my donkey, and felt the familiar pebbles rolling beneath my feet at each step. A slender silhouette, hazy in the distance, as if hastily sketched, appeared in the shade of the fig trees where the path reached the little stone wall. I stepped up my pace; the silhouette began to run toward us, then two others did the same, like supple white, blue, and pink ribbons leaping over the stones. In a flash I recognized Myriam followed by two of my former playmates.

Myriam! Her silhouette was metamorphosed as she ran closer, transforming the old images engraved in my mind; the little red-haired girl from my childhood was almost a woman now, and almost a stranger. Ten times, a hundred times I had visualized this reunion, imagining it in all its detail. I had dreamed it would take place by old Zerah's well, but here we were, simply on the edge of the path. I had dreamed I would look at Myriam and smile at her, but here I was as if blind, and now incapable of smiling. The only similarity between my vision and the reality of the moment was that her presence overshadowed all others. I remember answering her questions evasively and having to force myself to meet her gaze, or even to look into her face.

My mother rushed up almost at once and the same emotion overwhelmed me. Without a word, it was she who made the first move and took me in her arms. I stood immobile, unable to speak. Adolescence brings out some sort of hardness that is merely a form of awkwardness, and the heart behaves as if it were paralysed. I searched for an excuse to laugh, which seemed to be the best remedy for my clumsiness. My mother, who had carried a water jug with her, then began washing my face, my hands, and my feet in the sign of welcome. As was the custom I had to reply by touching my lips to the crown of her head, which I held in my hands. Unfortunately our mood was to change all too quickly. As my mother and my old friends were fussing over me, I saw Myriam step up to my father and speak to him gravely. The news was quick to reach my ears: Zerah had died two days earlier and was now laid on the floor of his home. My father did not look in the least surprised to learn of his old friend's passing; as for myself, strangely enough, I did not feel sorrow. I now fully understood the importance and the meaning of my first teacher's sudden apparition in Jerusalem. I had not really thought about it until that moment, but now the reason for that event seemed very clear. The old man had offered me one last form of initiation. Even though the *teachings* of the Krmel were exhaustive, they could not offer everything to those who were entrusted to its care.

When we had spoken of other universes of life, I had only imagined them to be wonderful stories that we were to believe in. I knew that by exercising one's thought, willpower, and love, a living being was able to project his body of light far away. Joseph had proved this astonishing fact to me, which I kept deep within me. But beyond death I had only theory to go by—up until now. In the future I would never look tragically upon the frontiers of our world and I would no longer rely on mere words. Zerah had come to me from a world that was real beyond any doubt, and I understood that I had been right to believe in the teachings of the Brothers.

"Happy will be the one who, at a turn of his path, will receive the sublime image coming from another universe. He will be able to say that he has seen, and he will be able to give real strength to his words. You must learn that beings who have departed from our world adopt two ways of manifesting themselves to us, two ways they may use depending on the progress made by their hearts. The first enables them to form a body, or rather what appears to be a body, drawing on the vital energy of the living beings to whom they choose to manifest themselves. But those who have managed to make the sun rise within themselves are aware of how artificial this phenomenon is. It relies on primary external forces that are essentially physical. You must realize that the presence of such a luminous body often gives rise to unpleasant sensations of cold; also it is not advisable to come into contact with the being who is thus manifested as he may involuntarily cause a considerable loss in the vital flame of the one who has touched him, a disorganization of the currents of life that flow in specific patterns throughout his body. Give your blessing to the second way, Brothers, in which the body of the deceased is resuscitated by his own solar willpower, and blossoms before your eyes. Then, and only then, will you be able to say, 'Here is a great being, who exists not by virtue of his human soul but by his transcendental soul.* He knows how to command the divine fire that burns within him, whose every ray is a building block of love on which he may build as he chooses. He knows how to combine the germs of life† found in the universe either at will or depending on the need at hand, in the pure spirit of giving!'"

After unloading the donkeys and receiving myriad signs of friendship from the whole village, we hurried to our little house, whose walls still resembled the earth of Galilee but which now seemed hidden beneath an abundant tumble of vegetation. There were new trees in our patch of garden that were bursting into flower

---

*The Spirit that exists beyond the ego; the ego is still nourished by dense matter, even in its astral or etheric guise.
†The concept of the atom was well known to the Essenes. They also distinguished more subtle kinds of bodies within the atom.

wherever I looked. This was a form of wealth, perhaps the form in our little world to which we were most attached, as to a symbol, a haven of light and of peace in the heart of a sacred enclosure. On the doorstep, in its same place, I saw our age-old water jug reserved for the ritual purifications, and then, in the cool half-light of the single low room on one of the walls where it had always been, my gaze caressed the little eight-pointed wicker star.

Nothing had changed; here was poverty made noble, the simple life, a life lived on the very Earth itself—and perhaps because of this, so far from the Earth and so close to the Beyond. As was the custom I lay on the ground, my arms outstretched, and I kissed the Earth seven times. This for me was no longer a routine gesture, as it once had been, performed in imitation of my parents.

I knew we received energy from the Earth on which we lived, that the Earth nourishes us not only through what she produces, but also through a constant flow of energy arising from her depths. I had learned from the Brothers of the Krmel that our feet were like mobile roots of our body-tree, and were constantly absorbing a sort of secret sap, maternal in its polarity, the transmuted reflection of the solar sap. Our ancestors had not settled their villages, nor had they built their houses just anywhere, as it pleased them, but where, according to precise methods, they knew the vital energy of the Earth flowed freely.* In the heart of every village one spot was reserved as a sort of temple, a place for assemblies, for prayers, or for our communal meals. This was the spot where the Earth force was rising most strongly from the ground. This communion with the terrestrial energies, which we knew to be necessary, motivated the whole Brotherhood in its almost total refusal to wear sandals except in particular circumstances. In this way the Earth spoke to us and we listened to her voice. We knew well that every one of the cells in our bodies, right down to those in the soles of our feet, contained the embryo of all our organs, of all our senses, and of our heart of light.

Having completed the ritual gesture I left the low room.

---

*There were no water diviners, strictly speaking, among the Essenes. Human beings, as they were more sensitive to certain energies than we are today, needed no amplifying devices to locate the lines of force nor to use them to advantage.

Myriam and my parents were waiting for me outside to pay a last visit to Zerah. Myriam led us over the twisting paths to the old sage's home. Outside the stone dwelling, at each of the four corners, there was a white-robed Brother totally absorbed in prayer, chanting in deep tones a prayer whose words I could not catch.

"They are helping Zerah," Myriam whispered into my ear. "You will not understand the chants however. Brothers on their way back from the land of the Red Earth taught them to a few people in the village shortly after you left. It was our Brothers from the banks of the great river who composed them in their own tongue. But I do know that not all of the words have precise meanings, even in their language. It is the way they echo in our hearts and against the walls of the village that helps Zerah to return to the land of his soul. But I doubt that Zerah needs all this, Simon. Two days ago, just after he had slipped into the sleep of death, he came to me by the old pomegranate tree. He waited until I was alone, then he came near me, shining brighter than the moon, and I experienced such an incredible feeling."

"He came to you too, Myriam?" From that moment I no longer doubted that Myriam too had received a message from the old sage. I dared not share my thoughts with her for there was something about her, about the way she looked at me, perhaps, that intimidated me. I thought she would probably tell me more when the time was right for her; after all, wasn't she the one who had initiated me to the "little flame" long ago?

Bowing our heads as a sign of humility to cross the threshold, we entered the stone house and found Zerah in his long white robe lying on the ground, his arms crossed over his heart. He had been there like that for two days, but he looked as if he were sleeping. Only his discolored lips and his big eyes, closed as if he were saying a long prayer, made me think of death. Between the wrinkles of his neck hung a grayish object that I had not seen him wear in the past: the cross of abundance of the red kings.* I felt a need to kneel by my old master to see him better, for the air of the single room was very thick with incense smoke. This enabled me to see that his body was thinly covered with a fine brown powder used by the Essene

*The Egyptian crux ansata.

communities to slow down the decomposition of the organs. It was a rule among the Brothers that no body should be buried, or even touched, before three whole days had passed following the moment of death. The laws of Essania were in general very flexible, but in such a case they were nonetheless imperative. Here, less than ever, did they leave room for the arbitrary. Those who wore the robe of white linen were aware that it took three days for the vital body to be released, organ by organ, from its support of flesh. I lost all sensation of time for a while, then I was brought out of my meditation by the touch of Myriam's long robe and the languorous chanting outside, which suddenly became louder.

We went out in silence. A cool breeze had risen and the mountains in the distance had faded to a soft blue. Evening was approaching and we parted. Myriam and a few friends who had joined us in the meantime returned to their respective homes, in front of which fires were crackling into life. The evening air was filled with the smell of burning wood, a smell that I loved, that I had longed for a hundred times, and that I at last found again. It was like a backdrop against which I could see tall figures in linen robes passing, leading a donkey or carrying a water jug. These white forms, enveloped in smoke, were for me like a sketch of one world that was at once the extension and the shadow of another, of a world of consolation toward which these forms resolutely directed their steps. It was beautiful, quite simply beautiful.

I had to wait until the following evening before I could see Myriam again. She had her work in the fields and with the animals and I had mine. I had been given no indication as to what the future had in store for me, and it seemed the wisest thing to become once more involved in the activities of the village. Life there had changed since I had left. Everyone seemed truly poor, and not simply humble. Several bad harvests had impoverished the Brothers and even more difficult times were expected in the years to come. My father told me that the priests from the Temple of Helios in Jerusalem had predicted the passage of a number of fireballs through the heavens, upsetting the rhythms of Nature as well as those of the human race as a whole.

Even my father had taken to working in the fields; his pottery was no longer sufficient as a means of exchange, and the merchants from town rarely came now to buy his wares. A lot of foreigners walked the roads of the land and traditional trade had been altered.

The sun was going down and I was sitting with my back against the stone wall that circled the village, my gaze turned toward the broken line of the distant mountains, when Myriam came to join me. It was perhaps that evening that I really saw her for the first time. I was fascinated by her long face, framed by her auburn hair falling in wild locks down to her waist. Her nose was straight and fine, and her deep clear eyes were shining like sea-green emeralds. They had so much to say, those eyes—they said they wanted to tell of our early life, of years gone by. Myriam immediately begged me to tell her of the Krmel, how we lived there, all about the mysterious place that I could still feel vibrating within me. I had hardly been taught to be talkative, however, and I was an awkward storyteller, perhaps especially in the company of my old childhood companion, considering what she had become. I talked to her of Joseph, and she held her breath as if she knew the beginning of a secret.

"Joseph!" she said in turn. "His whole family lives here now. They built a bigger house, behind ours, there are so many of them. It's strange, I have never seen such a silent family, nor one so respected. Very often, wealthy men from distant countries, come all the way to see them after meeting the Venerable Brother of the village. I think that some of them know—but the reason for all that hasn't fallen into little Myriam's ears, Simon!" And she burst into infectious laughter that sang to me of the mountains of Galilee. Quickly then, she recovered her self-composure and in a clear voice, began a long tale.

"You know, Simon, almost seven years ago, very soon after you had left us, Joseph's other brothers and sisters who were older than he was came to join us here. Another child has been born since, he's four years old now. Each time one of them arrived in the village grave disturbances occurred in the whole country, as far away as Jerusalem, and they say even farther to the south, where the mountains are very high and where it is drier and hotter.* Three times, foreign soldiers climbed all the way up here. We counted fifty of them, all dressed in purple and leather. I was frightened. The

*This may be the present day region of Massada or (perhaps) even the Sinai.

Brothers waited on their thresholds while the soldiers searched for who knows what. They said nothing, and those who were working in the fields did not even bother to come home. I didn't like that, but now I know they were right. The soldiers came and went like a storm, but you cannot fight the wind, you can only wait until it passes, then you stand up stronger while the wind itself is exhausted. But the wind has its purpose too.

"But I didn't really understand all that until one day when Zerah—it was always Zerah—came alone to talk to my parents for a long time. I never knew what was said, but the next day he took me far into the mountain to a place where there is a huge rock to which the ages have given the massive form of a bull. Nature leaves nothing to chance and what we often take for whims are, in fact, well thought-out manifestations motivated by very profound laws. I realized this very quickly. Now what I have to tell you must not escape from your lips, even if it means your life, Simon. It would be easier to remain silent about the following story but I must tell it to you as I have been asked to do so.

"When we reached a fold in the ground on the side of the mountain shaped like a bull's face, we came upon a row of three or four tombs. They were ordinary sepulchres, simple cavities over which a round stone had been placed. Nevertheless, the place intrigued me, and I had a feeling that their origin went back to the beginnings of time. The work was crude and the tombs were covered with abundant gray and yellow lichen. All around us the valleys were absolutely deserted and the bleating of the sheep we had encountered earlier on the path had long been silenced in the distance. We were alone; there was not a ruin, not even some improvised shepherd's camp.

"Zerah, who had not told me where we were going or why, suddenly started to busy himself in a strange way. He asked me to sit down nearby, then with three old branches he found lying on the ground there he made a triangle in front of what looked like the most important of the tombs. Then he stood in the centre of the triangle and with his finger traced a big circle on the ground, all around the triangle. Then he sat down where he was and became absorbed in a long, silent prayer—or at least that's what I understood he was doing. Suddenly, he got up and walked straight to the nearest and biggest of the tombstones and with the light pressure of just one hand he rolled it aside, revealing a gaping hole much bigger than those commonly dug to bury the deceased.

"'Come quickly,' he said, turning around. 'We will get in and then close the rock over us.'

"I cannot say how he managed to move the huge stone back again, but in a moment we were engulfed in the darkness. The bottom of the hole sloped slightly downward and I felt as if I were in a mouth that was ready to swallow us up. There was a scratching noise, then we were flooded in light. I turned around and I saw the old Brother holding a big torch that gave off a thick brown smoke. He was showing me the way, a large smile on his lips. He immediately tried to reassure me by taking my hand; yet, as long as I was with him, I didn't feel at all worried and to tell the truth, what I regarded as an adventure aroused more curiosity than fear in me. We walked for a while, carefully, holding our breath as much as we could because the torch gave off such an acrid smell. I assailed Zerah with questions as to where we were going and where he had suddenly found the torch he was holding, but to no avail; he remained evasive and amused. All of a sudden a very soft white flow of light appeared about fifty paces ahead of us. We walked forward quickly and in a few moments we came upon a place, Simon, so beautiful I will never forget it. To my amazement I discovered a huge hexagonal room filled with such an immaculate light that my eyes had trouble getting used to it. That light was like life, Simon, so beautiful, so pure, I felt it right in my heart like a soothing, nourishing fire, like a river of peace that even today moves me to tears of joy. Can you understand this? Zerah took me by the shoulders and pushed me forward. Before me there were twelve men sitting cross-legged on the ground and all dressed in white. I couldn't see their faces well as they were partly hidden beneath red veils, but they did not seem very old. I don't know why, but they reminded me of statues of light, whose features had been frozen for all eternity. One of them, however, made a slight gesture and Zerah brought me to the center of the room, facing them, in the middle of a square of blue cloth. Having done this he lay down on the stones of the floor in the ritual position, then he got up and I heard his steps retreating behind me. Four of the twelve Brothers then moved forward together, all at the same serene pace.

"'Don't be afraid, little Myriam,' said one of them in a voice that echoed strangely. 'You have been brought here to be told about certain things whose existence is suspected by few. First we must warn you: what you will see today is not generally offered to beings of your age, for what we call the bodies of light* are not yet fully developed in them. The clarity and strength of your soul is already quite obvious to us. This is the reason why you've been accepted here among us. But do not let your ears imprint these words in your heart as a compliment linked with privilege. Of course, perhaps it is a matter of privilege, Myriam, but also, and especially, of duty, the duty to go forward on the path without turning back and the even greater duty to lead in your wake the thousands of beings who are begging to know. It may be a ball and chain that we shackle to your feet or it may be a pair of wings that we fix to your heels. It is your own will that is to decide this and it is our hope that you will not disappoint our expectations.'

"While the four Brothers were sitting around me on the edge of the blue carpet, a fifth Brother, whose long hair identified him quite probably as one of our people, came toward me. He immediately suspended a sort of jewel before my eyes. It was perhaps just a rock crystal, but it was marvelously cut. Its beauty fascinated me so much that all my thoughts vanished in an instant. I think the other Brothers sent up a very low chant, but my memory of this is rather confused. I heard a whisper in my ear: 'Breathe . . . breathe deeply. . . .'

"Then I felt as if an enormous hole had been opened in the center of my head and the image of the sparkling little stone was blurred. I don't know exactly what happened, but I had the sensation I was floating in the midst of a milky white mist. I had no means of getting my bearings; I couldn't tell which way was up or down. The beautiful luminous room had vanished along with the twelve Brothers and Zerah. For a long moment I felt as if I were falling into

---

*A reference here to astral and mental bodies, developed at about fourteen and twenty-one years of age respectively.

a sort of nothingness and my whole body froze. Then from out of nowhere, a forest grew around me, full of very tall, thorny trees, just like those I have seen since in the north of our country. The air was heavy with dampness and it was so real I felt I could touch it. In the distance I heard shouts that sounded like orders, and I could tell they were coming my way. Then a group of men and women appeared through the scaly trees. It was the strangest of sights! It looked as if about twenty men had been reduced to the state of slavery at the hands of seven or eight women. They were struggling to pull huge wagons, piled high with wood. They looked like animals, half naked, wearing only loincloths made of badly tanned leather. Their feet and ankles were wrapped in ragged makeshift bandages tied with thongs. As for the women, believe me, they were commanding the maneuvers with considerable authority. They were armed with long whips, short spears, and all sorts of other weapons I had never seen before, and they were extremely cruel, whipping and striking the men as they pleased. Two of them especially attracted my attention; bare-breasted and only half clad in white and red veils, they were giving all the orders. They were unarmed, but were wearing many splendid jewels that looked heavy. The only man who was free walked behind them, dressed loosely in an ample brown robe. They went right by me, shouting away, and didn't even notice me. I thought this strange experience was at an end but, Simon, it was only beginning. I felt as if I were imprisoned in a body that no longer obeyed me, as I realized when my legs, acting of their own accord, made me follow the group of men and women to the edge of a village, an odd gathering of huts located on the shores of a lake. I was struck by the bustle which prevailed there. It was a sizable village where life seemed to focus around fishing and hunting, judging by the clothes worn by those I encountered. There too the women seemed in command. Almost all of them carried weapons whereas the men, though not as oppressed as those I had seen in the forest, were clearly in an inferior position. Going where my legs happened to lead me I saw there were no real streets in the village, as the huts had been built wherever it suited their inhabitants, and without any apparent logic—sometimes near a thicket, or sometimes even on pilings in the middle of a tiny black pond. From the distribution of tasks and the different sorts of clothing I immediately realized that the population was divided into three castes. Although I could not understand the language of these beings, which was an amazing blend of rolling and dry sounds, I could clearly understand what they were talking about. It was not my intuition at all, Simon, but an immediate knowledge, an understanding of their speech that was as intimate as it was involuntary. Within me I found an unknown capacity to translate; it was as if the simple vibrations of their words conveyed obvious meaning to my soul. But that was not the only thing that astonished me: from somewhere buried deep within me a voice began talking to me, so fast that for a moment I feared I would not be able to retain what was being said. It was a friendly and humorous voice, perhaps, and I now think it was the voice of one of the Brothers who had drawn me into this experience.

"'Eight thousand years, Myriam,' it said, 'these scenes are eight thousand years old. Be aware that you are no more than a little point suspended outside time. You are just a light, reading in the long memory of the Earth. You have opened its book and you now know that the past may also be present for one who understands the illusion of the passing moment. Only later will you fully understand the meaning of these words. For the moment, be open to this world, and to the word-vibrations that we are engraving in you . . . that we are engraving in you, for the will of the Nameless One is expressed at once by one thousand and one mouths of peace and knowledge.

"'Eight thousand years ago, far north of Galilee and over a good part of the Earth, men and women lived in this way. Woman oppressed man and man stifled his own cry. The law of universes is analogous to that of a stone suspended from a cord, swinging back and forth, from right to left and from left to right. It is the law of justice and of forces tending toward equilibrium. It is the law of worlds that are beating like a heart on their way toward the universe of the Father, the ultimate point, the first impulse, the inbreath and the outbreath of everything. This oppression will continue to pass from one to the other, Myriam, as long as men and women fail to understand that they are like the right and left hands of the man Kadmon, the shadow of Iev, the Source. Since the work of the great white ram that future generations will know by the name of Rem,* the world has not been as you see it here.

"'The divine pendulum has swung and it will swing again. The karma of the sexes, or of polarities, remains an active force. The wives of the sons of Moses, whose very souls the men of today refuse to acknowledge, know this all too well. Those of Essania know the truth, but as long as this earth shelters them they will have to suffer the law of the winds, and pretend to submit to it. Therefore you will find that the women of Essania are not officially allowed to benefit from the secret teachings that the Father has set forth in his masculine aspect, for and by men. But do not be misled by this, your presence among us is a sign. We will now tell you a secret, a secret upon which you will meditate for many long years. From your universe the fish is now rising, and this fish is born of the sea,† and this fish is double faceted. He will bear the face that speaks to the masculine soul, to the metal of its reason; and he will take on as well the face that speaks to the feminine soul, to the innermost recesses of its heart. Your gaze will fall on the latter and this is why you are living these instants, so that you will know the why of man and woman, the law of polarities and of the pendulum, that of the first sound which splits into two. When you hear the song of the flute, little Myriam, you need two ears to fully capture and appreciate its melody. It is split in two as it enters your body then returned to its original unity to make its appeal to your spirit. The Nameless One blows through the worlds like the player of the flute, splitting the wave of his presence within each of us.‡ There are those of us who are deaf, however, and those of us who listen with only half an ear. Do not be among these, but learn the law of the Moon-Sun vibration,§ then the unique law of the Eternal. To this end turn now the

---

*Ram, or Rama.

†The name Mary is related to the Latin word *mare*, from which comes the French word *mer*, the sea.

‡Is this not how we should understand the deity Pan, the image of creative Nature bequeathed to us by the ancient Greeks and providing us with the image of a primary force playing a double flute?

§The law of the Moon-Sun vibration is the law of unconditional love.

eyes of your soul toward these beings of old, for without knowing
it their minds were closer to the flute than your own can be today.'

"I felt the voice fading within me and once more I turned my
attention to the scene that was unfolding before my eyes. It seemed
I had been wandering around for some time when I came upon a
wooden paling against which leaned a great number of staffs, or
rather stakes, that were blackish, and most certainly made of metal,
judging by the way they were sharpened. Of its own free will, one
of my arms grabbed one stake firmly and my legs led me briskly to
a big clearing a little way off from the clusters of huts. A crowd of
men and women were already gathered there. Each one, chin up
and feet placed steadily on the ground, held in one hand a stake just
like mine, planted firmly in the earth. With a quick thrust my arm
drove my stake into the ground like the others. I stood there for a
long time looking through the eyes of my soul and I had the
impression that something was going on not far from me, where the
crowd was gathering most densely. Indeed, suddenly a woman's cry
rang out. As if in echo we all sent up a humming sound, a pure low
note that each of us nourished, it seemed, with the breath of his or
her heart. At the same time, several of the women burst into a long,
shrill wail; a sound which, combined with the deep humming,
became almost unbearable. I could feel it stirring the petals of our
souls and making our bodies quiver. Just then, something amazing
occurred, Simon. Before me, I saw an enormous gray stone rising
into the air in the middle of the gathering. It seemed to obey some
unknown will and it was surrounded by a white halo, a sort of
delicate and intensely alive cloud of mist. The chant, the wail, the
cry—how to describe it?—went on, getting louder and louder, as
if to nourish the prodigious force at work. Then as the flow of
vibrations reaching my being began to subside, the big stone, whose
rough shape was rather elongated, sank slowly back toward the
ground. It passed just over us and then I heard a thud as it hit the
earth, barely missing the crowd. Silence hung over us all for quite
a while as each one of us seemed to savor the feeling of inner
emptiness and release. At last everyone came back to life and the
stakes were all pulled out of the ground at the same time. The crowd
dispersed slowly and I was surprised to find the body I was in
walking up to the tall grayish stone, which was planted in the earth

and surrounded by a multitude of many-colored flower petals. I didn't have time to take a closer look, nor to draw any conclusions, as I felt myself suddenly and violently pulled backward. In a flash I caught a glimpse of a woman in a red veil fleeing beneath me, then all this vanished. I felt a slight nausea, and once again I found myself within the heart of the mountain among the twelve Brothers. You can imagine it took me a while to understand what had happened to me, Simon. Although I had been standing at the beginning of the experience I now found myself lying on the cloth surrounded by the first four Brothers. They were vigorously rubbing my arms and legs, as if to bring warmth back into them. When I was able to get up again they offered me an aromatic drink, which brought my strength back to me. The Brothers, whose faces I still could not see very well, asked me to sit up and they told me that I would also have to learn how to use the force of the sound, not as the beings I had just witnessed, but in another manner more suited to the needs of our times. They gave me to understand that as the voice is nothing but a manifestation of the breath, at once subtle and concrete, I should have to develop the quality of my breathing. I can remember their words exactly:

" 'The breath is the most divine element that can be conceived. You must have as much regard for your outbreath as you have for your inbreath. It is a deep and total cleansing of the human being, not only of the body of flesh but of the successive bodies of light. Many of the Brothers of Essania who practice the true breathing and who sometimes go profoundly into the most subtle techniques always feel surprised that their material body does not enjoy better health. How can this be, they wonder, since they purify themselves through their breathing? It is important that you know why so that your courage will not fail you on the path that we are opening before you today. The air you breathe is an element that is more immaterial than it is concrete. Its essence contains the substance of all life, the deep seeds of fire, water, earth, and of a thousand other things. You must see it as a support, as the dwelling of the primordial spark. Therefore you must understand, Myriam, that before acting in the material world it works on the plane of origins, that is of the spirit.

" 'Everything exists according to the will of the Nameless One;

the transcendental soul is never born out of a body of flesh, on the contrary, it builds a body of flesh and then settles within this body. But first it must create and elaborate its lower constituents: the human soul and its seven little flames that are superimposed. Purification through breathing, though it improves the envelope of flesh, acts first upon the invisible realms. This means that it cleanses the successive bodies of a being, starting with the least material of them.

"'Thus, little sister, the sublimation of the cruder bodies is the last to take place. The vital breath energy acts with greater ease in the realms where it is already the undisputed master. These words should teach your heart the reason why a great many beings whose souls are clean and whose lives are noble do not enjoy bodily perfection. The cleansing of one of their little flames is not yet totally accomplished, and this is why the complete transmutation of their body of flesh may not occur. You must know that this transmutation will always remain one of the hardest tasks for a human being. If a breath alone is enough to shape the spirit, it takes a solar wind to regenerate a dense body. Now, you must strive for this tempest of the Father's rays, Myriam.

"'The master, in the heart of the Eternal One, will be he who will blend the grains of life of the divine breath with the atoms of his flesh. He will become as light as the wind at the dawning of our Earth, as transparent as a jewel, and his body will cast no shadow on the ground for he will have awakened the sun within him. Do not take these words for symbols; there are none more concrete.

"'But until the age when all the beings composing the human melody let the master speak within themselves, we must use the sound force of the breath to calm their wounds. If your eyes say yes, you will receive teaching, daughter of Sdech, the teaching that will give you mastery over sound.

"'A song rising from the throat like milk or like a honeyed drink is a healing dressing to a wound, a balm which may relieve even blinding pain. This you will learn.'

"When the Brothers had finished speaking I understood that their words would echo long within me. Their way of pronouncing them was such that it was as if they had created a host of little beings that were still dancing around my soul. Even today, it still seems that their words were a warm and living force that I might have been able to reach out and touch. One of the twelve, at last, signaled me to stand up and they all filed before me placing their fatherly hands on my head. I think I did not speak even once during the whole experience, Simon. They also told me that before each Sabbath, someone would come to teach me the secrets of the sound that heals, in the silence of the mountains. "That's what happened, Simon, and even today a Brother with long blond hair comes to instruct me in the art of speaking and singing according to the winds of the Great Sun.

"Now listen to me just a moment longer for if my own story is over, there is one little phrase that still runs through my mind like a refrain. It was our old friend who impressed this upon me as we left the strange sepulchre to which he had taken me:

"'You should realize that you,* too, will have stones to raise.' What did he mean by this 'you'? My heart has spent many nights trying to understand its meaning, Simon."

I was unable to answer her question and Myriam, who seemed somewhat disappointed, ended her long tale there.

The night was black and the cry of an owl, keeping vigil in the young acacia bushes growing along our little wall, reminded us that it was late. We had to go back to our families, happy but with our heads full of questions. How many years, how many centuries have passed since that instant when for the first time we communed with the same force, with the same impulse? So many centuries, and yet. . . . In our hearts there still shines the glow of the little oil lamps placed here and there that showed us the way to our homes. It was the ritual call from the Brothers to the heavens, the signal that their souls were watching.

The third day was devoted to Zerah's funeral. On that occasion Myriam and I understood that there were differences of opinion on this, even in the heart of our community. We realized that some Brothers refused to touch our friend's body. We were told they felt that an organism whose flame had escaped forever became impure,

*In the original French text, the plural form of "you" is used here.

for it was reclaimed by the low and heavy forces of this world. The majority of the village did not share this opinion that prevailed much more among the Nazarites than among the Brothers of Essania.* Zerah's body, in spite of our poverty, was anointed with aromatic oils and according to custom, his head was bound with a triple band of linen as a sign of final purification. It was Joseph's mother who took most of these tasks upon herself and it was also she who sewed the immaculate shroud in which the old man's body was enveloped. For the first time I was able to admire the nobility and the purity of this woman's features. She was still very young, and it was said she had been a dove in our people's high temple. We were well aware of what this meant in the way of knowledge and wisdom and we admired all the more the humble work of her long fingers as she sewed away at the broad sheet of linen.

Zerah was not buried in the communal grave as we were all indebted to him for so much of our knowledge. Somewhere on the mountain a gap had been located in a rock wall. We formed the funeral procession and carried the body there. The sepulcher was blocked up with stones sealed by clay. Zerah had wanted no weeping women, although that custom was often still observed among our community. He had wanted his soul to fly away in peace. Everything was respected.

Yet this last detail brought a rain of stones down on us as our little procession crossed the road to Joppa. Those from town did not like people being openly different from them, and our sobriety shocked them. On that occasion too, stones had been raised.

*In Numbers 6:5–7, the Nazarite vow (which is a special vow of temporary consecration of oneself to Yahweh, the Eternal One) exacts of the Nazirite abstention from cutting or shaving the hair of the head, and forbids him or her to approach a dead person.

CHAPTER · XII

THE ZEALOTS

T he months went by, bringing back the scorching heat of summer. For the first time in many years I enjoyed the sight of scarlet and white flowers falling in clusters from the terraces of our houses and along the paths of the village. I learned the secrets of making pottery, and then Myriam and my mother, who was still so quiet, initiated me into work with linen. From their tireless hands, on the rudimentary loom, arose the robe of the Brothers that I dreamed of wearing one day. The tradition was that the robe should be woven in a single piece, with no seams whatsoever, to be one, in the image of the Brotherhood's ideal. This characteristic was said to confer upon the robe an undeniable etheric force during rituals and in the solitude of meditation. It seemed as if life was to flow on in this way, humbly but with serenity. If it had not been for the long hours of prayer and the daily purifications to which I compelled myself, the austerity and the discipline of the Krmel might have slowly slipped from my memory. The vague promises of a task for the future that had been made to me—or rather to us—might also have sunk into the numbing depths of the forgotten had it not been for the unexpected arrival in the village of a Brother from the outside world.

His agitation, so uncommon among those sharing our ethics, caused everybody in the village to gather by the old well. He seemed to have walked for most of the day to come to tell us in a trembling voice that heavy rioting had broken out two days before, farther to the north, in the region of the Sea of Galilee. There were already many victims. According to the Brother the disturbances were due to the excessive tributes demanded of the inhabitants.

For Myriam and myself, and probably for many of the adolescents in the village, this event marked the beginning of a growing awareness of the world. We knew our land was occupied by foreign forces; we had many times been confronted with this oppressive reality, Myriam there in the village, and I beneath the arches of Jerusalem. Never though, had we come upon the aggression and the revolt arising from this state of affairs. In all innocence, from the top of our mountains scorched by the sun we had looked upon the few soldiers we had encountered as quite peaceful occupants rather than as violent invaders. This might be explained by the fact that many of the Sadducees who formed in some way the nobility of our land had long ago sided with them, having common interests. The Pharisee priests themselves, in spite of their intransigence in keeping the Hebrew laws intact, seemed to have become accustomed to this situation. It is true that their opulence, which they never hesitated to display, proceeded to a great extent from their close ties with the foreigners. Their silence and their tolerance in regard to the purple legions had been bought. They were to answer for the keeping of a peace which, in fact, was very uncertain. The people of Palestine were thus under a double yoke and they kept paying their taxes without any end in sight.

When the Brother had finished his account of the causes for the revolt we noticed that he had been wounded in the side. This wound, although not serious, aroused our indignation. It was thus that we came to understand the ambiguity of the situation as well as the weight of one name that until then had been seldom mentioned: Rome.

It was Brother Joab, a robust old man with ebony hair, who

took it upon himself to calm our troubled minds. His words, full of the wisdom of our people's writings, went straight to our hearts.

"Do not think," he began, peacefully sitting on what remained of the well, "do not think that all this is not allowed by the Father. It is allowed by the Divine, my Brothers, because the time is coming, and we will soon have to turn the page of our own history. This is tolerated because human strength is often no better than animal strength. Unfortunately, only when exhausted from tripping and falling may a child be brought to pause for reflection. But you, my Brothers, you who flee the towns and their luxury, you who seek the pure word, do not lose yourselves in the cycle of appearances. Thank the Nameless One for giving you the opportunity to restrain your passion, a passion that would lead you into armed struggle. For years we have been waiting, this I know, for the day when our freedom will flower. But do not the holy scriptures promise us divine help? Your hearts know that iron is for him whose soul is as a spearhead. Let your hearts speak for you."

The gathering broke up at these words, and we returned to our vines and our fields, attempting to let the flower of meditation blossom within us, according to our ancestral prescriptions. I had been taught in the Krmel that the black forces of attraction love to be hated; this makes them even stronger, so they may gnaw away at the energies of the white light.

What then was the meaning of the words said by the eldest among us? Were we not confusing peace and submission? A doubt was creeping into me, into us, a doubt which had perhaps been developing for quite a long time. What was this peace, this love of the Divine, this respect for our Brotherhood and for the ancient promises that we had been taught? Was it just a simple moral code, the code of those who are waiting for the manna that never comes? Was it weakness they wanted to instill in our veins? What was, in fact, the dream of Essania? We were not yet fifteen years old and our hearts were full of questions.

At the dawn of the second day after this event the young Brother who served as scribe within our community went to all the houses, imperatively announcing what we traditionally called a council of elders. Exceptionally, it was held outdoors, so that all might attend. We began with the usual rituals of protection, a short prayer, and purification by water. Then eleven elders, their shoulders covered with wide, blue linen stoles, opened the council. A pastoral note was added when a few sheep that we had not had time to take care of began wandering over toward us. Sitting on the ground in concentric circles, the Brothers were brief and to the point. The situation near Gennesaret was explained clearly, with more detail than it had been two days earlier but without any attempt to spare our feelings. We heard for certain that a small unrestrained band of men were inciting and leading the people to revolt in the region where the disturbances had broken out. For nearly forty years they had proclaimed themselves the enemies of the Roman legions. Their aim was to stir the fires of insurrection wherever possible in the hope of a massive uprising on the part of the people of Palestine. Deep within ourselves we understood them; they were pure in their behavior, convinced that the submission to foreign armies was a form of infidelity toward the Eternal One. It was decided that some of us would be delegated without further delay to the shores of Galilee, in reply to a request coming from a mysterious assembly of Brothers about whom I had sometimes wondered if they weren't purely mythical. Our aim would be threefold: we would treat the wounded, calm the people's spirits, and spread among them the principles of our cause, in so far as this was possible. The secret council of the Brotherhood thus reaffirmed its existence and asked us to undertake a revival of our action throughout Palestine. Many times we had played an important role in history, for we possessed our own teachings that were handed down directly from Moses, and we had always acted according to cycles of dormancy and concrete action, while we remained ever present and active underground.

Something of which we were only dimly aware was happening in the crucible of the human race. It was time for us to come out in the open and act. As we hoped, Myriam and I were among those authorized to take the road to Gennesaret. We had to leave without delay and to keep off major roads where we would have run the risk of encountering armed troops that the prevailing atmosphere and our unexpected presence might render aggressive. Several donkeys were hastily saddled and after short farewells, we set out, cutting straight across the hills through the mosaic of olive groves, vineyards, and already-harvested barley fields. The two solid days' walk we faced left a lasting impression on us, so rugged was the terrain. The sun seemed stubbornly bent on staying high in the sky and our legs were endlessly scratched by the hawthorn bushes and thistles, so we could not stop to rest as often as we would have liked. Here and there we caught a glimpse of shepherds' fires, or the white splash of a little village with clouds of incense escaping from its synagogue. All seemed a harmonious monochrome of shades of green, yellow, and ochre. Even the warm breeze was reluctant to spread the tension from Gennesaret.

It was not until we arrived on the shores of the lake that we saw the first signs of the revolt. We had to bury several abandoned bodies over which the vultures were already fighting. At last we arrived at Gennesaret, which we found devastated. Most of the houses set along the shores of the lake were broken open. They had been pillaged and their few remaining occupants were busy wearily trying to salvage what they could. Hemp fishing nets and ropes lay abandoned here and there, and in the little harbor itself were nothing but shreds of burnt sails and boats dismasted by human hatred. Our arrival immediately attracted the attention of a group of armed men who were scouring the streets and who looked like militiamen. Their poor crude clothing identified them as Hebrews. We recognized them immediately as the fierce partisans of the bloody revolt, the Zealots, a few of whose leaders were said to be fanatics.

Our initial reaction was that of distrust, for the Brother who had taken the lead in our group of fifty souls had informed us that among the partisans were a certain number of outlaws. The only thing that counted for the Zealots was their ideal and they recruited strong and determined men wherever they could, so their forces combined mystical partisans of armed struggle and common criminals. We expected an aggressive reception from them, but we were to be ashamed of this attitude. Standing there in front of us, they were just human beings who were suffering.

It was clear that we could not return to our village before the passage of many days—and with all our hearts we longed to see once more the gentle cloud of peace within the warm solitude of the mountains. Their eyes spoke louder than their clumsy words, and in some of them we could recognize Brothers whose hearts had only learned to vibrate in a different way from ours. It was the same force that moved them, but its action was tearing apart, dispersing, and disuniting rather than consoling. Weary of fighting and aware of the Essenes' reputation as healers, they greeted us with a joy that they tried to contain. We had come to care for their wounded. We learned that the legion had retreated to the west and that the rich partisans of Rome had been massacred.

As the Brothers were questioning the men we had encountered, our hearts suddenly leaped up. There, only a few meters away, among the group of Zealots stood a boy about my age, whose hair fell in long locks from beneath a crudely wrapped turban. He was looking the other way.

"Joseph!" we cried out in unison, and the young boy turned his head and pierced us with his flaming eyes.

No, I sighed within myself, this is not Joseph, it cannot be Joseph. The eyes reflect the soul and there is no mistake possible. We held our breath. The boy's resemblance to our friend was striking and even his name was the same. He who had responded to our cry, this other Joseph, stared at us both with eyes like glowing coals. Then he approached and asked if we knew him. The sound of his voice came as a relief; it was the harsh voice of a young warrior's little heart. Little heart? Was it really so little as that? Indeed, in the few hours that we spent in his company we became aware of a strange presence that emanated from him. It was like some brute force lurking beneath an outward calm, a veiled passion, in short, a force of dislocation. The Zealots themselves made much of him and curiously enough, considering his youth, he was often consulted. It was only much later that we understood the singular nature of this being, his resemblance to our friend, and his brief and disconcerting destiny.

We decided to split up into groups to be able to care for those living in what was left of the little town and on the shores of the lake. As for ourselves, it was decided that we should stay in Gennesaret in the company of about ten Brothers. There we set up a little camp, sheltered by an old fisherman's shack and only a few steps from the water. We did not know then that we would stay there until winter cold set in. The population, wounded in both body and soul, readily entrusted themselves to us. For the two of us, who were just over thirteen, this was a hard apprenticeship. We were as unfamiliar with this sort of wound as with this sort of rebellious being. At first we acted as aides to our elders, brewing herbs or mixing them with mud, especially myrtle, which was of great value for healing. Then, little by little, as we got used to this sort of work, our elders called upon our capacities as healers. For the first time I saw Myriam using the astonishing technique that had been transmitted to her.

"Weakened souls are like lodestones, Simon," she told me, "they attract bodies of low vibrations, the 'beings of illness.'* Each organ emits a subtle musical note and all the organs together transform the body to a harmony from which emanates one basic note that leads all the others. When one organ is consumed or wounded its music is immediately altered and out of tune, and the melody of the body becomes discordant. The Brother who lives alone on the mountain taught me each day to shut the doors of my body and to open the ear of my heart in order to hear the basic note of any given organism. To do this, with the person lying on his back, I hold my hand a cubit away from the hollow of his belly, over the fourth wheel of light. If peace prevails in my soul, my inner silence gives way to a little persistent note that is the base of the person's pyramid of life. Then I sweep my hand over his whole body, but this time only a span† away from his skin, without losing contact with the basic note. If one part of the body is suffering, the note I hear in my heart changes when my hand passes over the ailing organ. The technique is at once simple and arduous, Simon, the hard part being to release one's preconceptions, one's judgment, and what the Brother called the reasoning reason, which engenders an illusory logic.

"Only then may the person be treated. From deep within me

---

*The Essenes regarded illnesses as etheric beings feeding on the vital force of an organ—or of a whole body—and acting on a vibratory plane different from our own.
†About 23 centimeters (9 inches). A span is half a cubit.

I must sound the exact note that my heart hears. In this way my whole being will vibrate in tune to the life of the one who is suffering and my song, though composed of just a single note, will be a balm for the organ whose music is out of tune. The eyes of my soul will then see rays of light coming out of my left palm and this will reharmonize whatever is out of tune. At this point weariness invades my whole being, but only if my love and my will have managed to break through all the barriers. In many cases the person is healed after two or three treatments.

"So many people are still unaware that they are one note on the musical scale of the Father. So few know that all of us together form a perpetual song, a song from which the notes of hatred, and even worse, indifference, must be removed."

We then set about caring for the ill and wounded as we had been taught to do with the help of the Brothers, who guided our as yet inexperienced hands. And we who, just out of childhood, had thought we were invested with great secret skills, found that our elders could handle the light and the music of their souls with a power and a confidence of which we were not yet capable. They were no longer the humble Brothers of some unknown village; their calloused hands were ready to become a source of radiating force whenever and wherever a heart called out to them. Occasionally, as the council of elders had asked them to do, they spoke officially with groups of men and women about their own knowledge of the Nameless One. The people of Galilee feeling wary, however, they knew they had to be careful about the words they chose. The Brothers wished to calm these people and instill in them the hope that their prayers would be answered by the Almighty rather than by warfare.

We spent the evenings together sitting around a fire, casting grains of incense onto the burning wood. The lapping of the waves not far off and the soft sea breeze often drew Myriam and me down to the shore, where we hopped from one stone to another. It was on these shores of the lake of Galilee that a little flower was born for us in this lifetime; it was soon to blossom out.

For three years we led this life, now and then interrupted by a return to our village where we never stayed for more than two months. The community was somewhat poorer than before, with fewer of us to work in the fields, but the winds of the Eternal One, we were told, were now blowing in a definite direction and it was time to speak out, to heal, and to act wherever possible. While remaining relatively discreet we were to act as leavening wherever souls were ready to listen to us to satisfy their hunger for knowledge. We did not always go to Gennesaret, which was being rebuilt little by little. Our itinerary followed a logic that was as yet incomprehensible to our minds: We went through Samaria, along the west coast, and then down to the dryness of the land of Jericho, where important Essene communities were established. The dusty and green roads of the old land of Canaan rolled by under our feet, and it was all of Nature, with its medicinal herbs and its intimate forces, which became our real home.

CHAPTER · XIII

THE CLOUD
OF PEACE

O ur sixteenth birthdays came at last, moving our hearts and awakening in us the desire to tear away the veils of childhood. Our eyes, which had been meeting in the course of even the smallest of our daily tasks, had sworn implicit oaths. We read in each other's soul and wished to be united. As was the tradition, our parents organized the ceremonies, having known for years that this day would come. We had few worldly goods, but our people's customs had always been regarded as something to value and safeguard. Joshua the potter and Ela the weaver exchanged ritual gifts: a few objects of their own making and some foodstuffs. Thus was our engagement sealed. The wedding itself was planned for a few weeks later. It was in the month of Tammuz, which was the fourth month. The vintage season had already begun and with my arms loaded with grapes I, the bridegroom, was led in a solemn procession to the house of my future wife. Our families embraced, and at last Myriam, whom I had been forbidden to see for three days, appeared on the threshold of her humble dwelling. It was just at nightfall, and as was the custom, she stood there in the dancing glow of the oil lamps.

She stepped forward, radiant, draped in the simplicity of a long red robe. Beneath her azure veil, I could see endless strings of painted clay beads peeping out from her red hair. I was spellbound. I had never imagined her thus, she who so often floated in an ochre-colored robe that was too big for her. But it was her gaze that I remember best: that of a little wild creature, with two huge eyes shining like emeralds. Our parents made us stand side by side, then four Brothers held over our heads a square of blue cloth with a white fringe. The eldest Brother in the village stepped forward and stopped in front of us. His thick ebony hair and his face were hidden beneath a veil of white linen. He said a short prayer of blessing, then our families intoned a high-pitched chant, and someone in the crowd who had followed us blew into a long horn. Then we had to walk through the whole village, hand in hand, between two lines of Brothers holding torches. We did not say a word during this time, and night closed over us in my parents' home. This is how it happened, at once simple and solemn, in keeping with a law thousands of years old. From that day on, there was no more Simon or Myriam, there was just a single being, a single force saying "we," a force moved by a will of which it could not always be aware.

So began our new life. The Brothers and our childhood friends helped us to build what was to be our little home, forming bricks of mud, their robes tucked up and tied about their waists, and from time to time picking and eating the sour little grapes that grew all around. It was a small cube of stone and clay, just like all the others in the village, with a single room, a terraced roof, and thin slits for windows. We lived there for five years, sharing our time between the fields of the Galilean countryside and our healing work on the roads of the land. We pressed the olives, sowed and reaped the flax and the barley. We prepared herbs according to ancient prescriptions and we spoke of the Nameless One, whenever a heart seemed willing to open. We and many others felt it was the right time for it.

With my twenty-first birthday came at last the long-awaited robe. It was given to me at the end of an important ceremony in which Joseph's father took part, a ceremony the details of which time has chosen to keep for itself. As foreseen, I was entrusted with a mission, which was expressed in the simple and concise words:

"Clear a path." As for Joseph himself, years had passed by without allowing us to see him return, climbing the sharp rise from the road to Joppa. He had, indeed, left the Krmel and been back to the village, but his visit had come at a time when we were off on the road somewhere about the land. His mother, whose presence alone was a joy, told us that Brothers from a foreign country had called him for a teaching she said she knew nothing about. Through ways unknown to us, she had once or twice received a small parchment scroll from him, saying his heart flew to her and to our land. Our twenty-second year was marked by an event of very special intensity, an event that stands out from the simple framework of this account.

We had got into the habit of sometimes taking the flocks out for several days, far from the village and its inhabitants. For us it was a pleasure that enabled us to be on our own and to feast our eyes on the pastel outlines of the hillsides and the stony little mountains. On this particular day, the setting sun stretched a purple and orange veil along the horizon. Before dusk, we had built a fire of dried twigs and rigged up a cloth shelter for protection from the damp. It was long before complete darkness settled in, and we were wrapped in our cloaks, looking up into the sky where the clouds were fraying away. We both noticed one cloud that was different from all the others, both in form and luminosity. It was a little egg-shaped mass that looked as if it were suspended in the sky, while all the other clouds around it were filing off across the night sky. After a moment of close scrutiny we felt a growing uneasiness as, from out of the cloud, there shot a first, then a second green flash that lit up half the sky.

Our emotion approached a peak when the woolly mass, instead of breaking up as we expected it to do, got bigger as it approached. It would have been natural to flee, as our people's memory was full of strange, incomprehensible tales that we did not really understand. To tell the truth, we did not have the time to think of fleeing. The soft breeze that had been blowing over the hillside abruptly subsided and a great, white light enveloped us like a net. In dead silence, an enormous vehicle, shining like a thousand fires, appeared before us, hanging in the air about two meters from the ground. We stood as if frozen, incapable of reacting or even thinking. Then, almost at once, without our being aware of where they came from, three beings were standing in front of us. They were clothed in long white robes somewhat like our own, but much finer, much silkier. It would be impossible to describe their faces. They were so perfectly pure and bright compared to our weatherbeaten, sun-browned faces, and from them emanated a form of love we had only met in our dreams. They had long blond hair that fell harmoniously to their shoulders, while their skin, slightly amber colored, seemed hairless. Were they in fact men? We could not have said, so fine were their features which many women might have envied. Instantly we felt an indescribable wave of warmth rising within us, flooding our entire being. Then the surroundings blurred, and we felt ourselves being seized in a beam of white light. We tried to reach out to grasp one another, but to no avail. We seemed to be lifted by a warm and numbing wind, or by an energy that was pulling us gently from the very matter of which we were composed. Finally, without knowing exactly what had happened, we found ourselves in an enclosed space wherein radiated a light of peace. The three beings were still there, facing us, illuminated by smiles of goodness. They approached, reassuring us in our own language that we had nothing to fear from them.

"Friends," said one of them, "allow us to address you thus, and to welcome you among the forces of the Father that travel the worlds. The glory of the Eternal One warms our hearts and we are happy to be able to speak to your souls. You are in one of the chariots that the solar winds drive through the universe. You are among those who people your little star, the star that shines brighter than all others in the firmament. You are with Moon-Sun. . . ."

What was said then would be out of place in this account, but the voice of the one who was speaking was clear, resolute, and acted immediately as a balm to our confused minds. Around us, we began to make out the walls of a large hexagonal room, having as its center something that resembled an enormous jewel, glowing in various colors. All around us there were a dozen strange-looking seats that looked like thrones. On a long table facing us were a multitude of varied objects surrounded by drawings, equally strange, some of them twinkling like stars in the night.

"You are with Moon-Sun," continued another of the beings,

in the same voice. "Your human fathers have always spoken of an infinity of inhabited worlds. Do you think it is just a legend? The Eternal One delegates his powers to all those who have the capacity to make the light grow around themselves. Thus, we are the angels of the Nameless One and our earth is the twinkling diamond that lights up the nights of your Brotherhood. Since the beginning of time, we have been sowing in this world—as well as in your hearts—the seed that will drive the darkness out. We have spoken to the men of the earth in many tongues, under many guises; we have given them gods according to their capacity, depending on the brightness of their souls. Do not be offended by these words, friends, for a light that is too bright tends to blind one who has always lived in the darkness of the night. The veils that dim the splendor of the force of the Father may only be lifted one by one, with infinite care. We know what we are talking about. There was a time when the men of this world lived on another Earth somewhere in the spiral; the light was too bright for them and it stifled the breath of their hearts. The power of the mind killed their love, and their world was catapulted to the confines of the universe. We cultivate and foster the growth of souls, and the providence of the Eternal One willed that we transplant them here, between light and gloom, to teach them how to distinguish between them. But wisdom also required that the gardener remain among the plants entrusted to him. And so, there is a place in this world where the Earth and the heavens wed, which your Brothers from the stars, from Moon-Sun and many others, have chosen as home. Rays have been shining from this place ever since the dawn of ages and are like the leavening and the guiding light for the great human civilizations. Nothing beautiful that has been done on this earth has been done without them. The time is now coming for another veil to be lifted and all those who can see must arise. This is why we have come knocking on the doors of your hearts. Our Love sends out sounds that your reason cannot perceive and that guide you toward definite places. This is why you are here.

"You must also know that one of us has come among you recently. It will be your task to recognize him and to prepare the path he must follow. Do not misunderstand us; we ask you to be servants rather than ambassadors. The noblest and strongest forces are always those that are hidden; do not forget this. You will soon come to understand that this era is like a crucible in which the blackest of substances and the brightest of lights are to meet. All these forces are often unaware of their real origin, which makes them better able to bear the vibrations of this world. It may be asked of you—and of others—to reveal them, when the time has come. Will you do this?"

It was not the first time we had been asked such a blunt question; however the being did not wait for a reply and told us to walk around the vast room in which we found ourselves. It looked like a palace, with its thousand jewels hung from the walls and its forces moving in beams of undulating light. We soon realized that a fourth being, exactly like the other three, had entered unnoticed. Nowhere, however, could we see a door or a wall hanging which might conceal an opening.

"Here is the energy of the Father transformed according to the will of our hearts," said one of the beings, embracing the whole room with one broad gesture. "All this may become as hard as rock or as transluscent as the glow of the flames of the soul. We have only to make life flow faster or slower. This is one of the forms of creation. You yourselves are creators through your own thoughts. It is these thoughts that in this realm, then in others, must come to transmute and finally to create matter as a stairway for the Spirit. You must learn to handle the ether with the force of your love. You need to know that every idea contains a particle of etheric life in a vibratory pattern; and you must understand just what matter is: myriad particles of life magnetized by the force of a persistent and directed idea. This is how man is formed, this is how this vehicle was made, and this is how you must learn to work. Matter, Spirit and Force are one—so be one with the Divine, and by this we mean with a state of mind that accepts the omnipresent creative substance.

"This does not imply the acceptance of a vague faith without discernment, for real faith requires the union of wisdom and the great laws in order to create without limits. Nor can it be a mental technique, which may only be effective in the tangible universe for lack of union with the networks of the inner sun. We are aware that you will undoubtedly be unable to understand all this until the day when you wake from the sleep that brought you here to this Earth. This does not matter at the present time, as the words instilled in a heart are forever engraved there. What we are asking from you today is that you learn to hold yourselves outside time. Time, too, has but the relative force of matter and it may be manipulated, and must be sublimated. Time, in itself, does not exist; it is but the reflection of a mind disconnected from its source. You will think in terms of periods and cycles, you will think in terms of beams of light, and thus, if your soul so desires, you will prepare, as your Brothers do, the path of the One who is to come."

The being's voice seemed to die away, like a lamp blown out by the wind, and we heard no more, except for one little phrase, which contained the brightest of gold: "May peace be with you."

We could not tell exactly what happened then. Without transition, we saw ourselves descending on a very dense shaft of white light, or rather, in the center of this shaft, somewhere within a translucent and radiant ray, a tunnel of light. Our feet touched down on the rocky soil, and all around us, the mountain seemed wrapped in a fleecy veil. A strange feeling, a diffuse oppression as well as an immense joy invaded our beings. High up in the sky we saw a ball of fire fading from sight, and then, looking around, we noticed that our sheep had not wandered away. The day was just dawning, and we understood that the night had passed through us to the rhythm of several crystalline phrases. Without a word, we both felt compelled to lie down on the ground, our faces to the earth, there among the rocks and the thin tufts of grass. This was our way—the way of Galileans of two thousand years ago—of giving thanks to a force we did not understand, but which had spoken to our inner beings. It was also a way of calming our minds in which stirred so many things that seemed beyond our reach.

We could not bring ourselves to go back to the village until many days had passed. And for quite a while our whole beings, so shaken by the recent event, kept longing for the return of the cloud of peace, in the warm solitude of the mountains.

CHAPTER XIV

IN THE LAND OF
THE RED EARTH

n those times a wind was blowing on our Earth. The children of
Essania, as well as the Nazarites and the Nazarenes, were aware of
this. It was a wind of renewal. We wanted it and felt it to be a
wind of peace. For others it was to signify the slashing of a sword.
Thus, the land of ancient promises was hesitating between consolation and rebellion.

In those times a wind was blowing, and the sons of Sdech
realized it was time to meet in the land of their forefathers, the land
of the red ancestors.

In the old land of Pharawon lived many of our people and they
sent messengers calling us to a council at which the path to follow
was to be decided. Two men arrived in the village in the dress and
weatherbeaten features of spice merchants. From among the most
learned members of our community, ten were chosen and given
leave to depart at once. We had the good fortune to be included
among them and in the following days we set off on the road to
Joppa, where we knew we had sympathizers who would hire us
little boats. It seemed easier to travel by water rather than to face the

blazing heat of the stony Sinai, or to cross the pass of Moses and the burning sands.

We had no trouble finding a boat that was used by traders going back and forth between the two countries. It was in fact a big fishing boat, rigged with a solid mast and a heavy patched sail. We slept in it, rocked by the waves and wrapped in our cloaks, sailing along the coast where fires were burning. We had decided against wearing our linen robes for the duration of the trip, so as not to attract attention to a sudden movement of Brothers to foreign parts. Thus it was a boatload of traders, fishermen, and ordinary travelers who disembarked in a little port of the Nile delta, lost among the sands, the aquatic plants, and a few ribbons of date palms.

A hot breeze was blowing when we went ashore and our first concern was to mingle with the cosmopolitan population that swarmed on the banks of the river. The atmosphere was gay, and in spite of the suffocating heat, people all around us were busy unloading cargo from the boats or emptying their nets. We had to make our way through a vast quantity of earthenware pots drying in the sun, and we took a real delight in seeing skeins of yarn of all colors hanging in the streets through which we walked. It seemed like a rich country, which made a sharp contrast with the relative austerity we were accustomed to. We also realized that a great many men and women were living in a state of servitude. We saw them pass by in small groups, wearing simple loincloths, their backs bent beneath loads of goods. We had met with similar sights in some ports of our own country, but never as bad as this.

For the most part, those who were compelled to do such hard work were people of color: Nubians or slaves deported after some conquest. As we walked through the narrow dirt streets of the little port, we saw that there, as everywhere else, the Roman army supervised everything. There was even a whole encampment, whose characteristic tents could be seen between the rows of dwellings that were so low that they appeared to have been crushed to the ground.

After getting our bearings with the help of a group of Greek merchants, we headed for one of the many arms of the river almost lost between the papyrus and the barley fields. There, we found several pomegranate trees, beneath which a man was sleeping. As we had been told, he was the owner of a felucca, and was ready to sell his services. Before we could reach our destination—a temple whose origins went back to the beginnings of our Brotherhood on Earth—we had to sail up the Nile, as far as the environs of Heliopolis. At the Krmel it was taught that Heliopolis was a city whose planning had been imposed by a race of beings who were other than human. These beings, as they evolved in the ethereal sphere of the sun, had undertaken the primordial initiation of our planet since time immemorial, and the great Brotherhood, from which the sons of Essania descended, had first originated in that part of the world. According to accounts spread by hearsay, Heliopolis was a beehive of spirituality, dispensing its honey without regard to frontiers. It was a short journey by sail; we can still see the frail skiff cleaving the waters of the Nile, while overhead passed flocks of ibis. Their cries echoed off the banks from which large frogs leapt in an ecstasy of splashing.

It was an unknown world that fascinated us all, a song of Nature in greens and reds, where the rich palm trees seemed in constant struggle with a rocky ground as red as live coals. At last the sun set and we went ashore where the bank offered us a vast wooden stairway. Women covered in bracelets and draped with blue and white veils were noisily washing great heaps of linen. We threaded our way among them, thus arousing peals of high-pitched laughter, the reason for which we could not understand. The vegetation, which was dense on the banks, was much sparser as we got farther from the shores of the river, and it became difficult to protect ourselves from the hot winds.

A tiny village, where everything was made from mud bricks, opened its life to us, as its men and women were returning from the fields that bordered the riverside. An intense activity seemed to prevail there. A troupe of children flocked around us as soon as we appeared, and following the advice of one of the Brothers, we let ourselves be guided by the dull and faraway beating of a tom-tom. There were several paths running through an oasis of date palms, and we chose the one that seemed most likely to take us to the drumming. It led us quite a way from the village, and the children fell behind as we went on. The path got narrower and narrower, following the meanders of a little brook, until it reached an ochre-colored hillock streaked with red by the last rays of the setting sun. There, a temple of medium size rose up, the like of which we had never seen. It looked rooted to the ground, as if it had been carved out of the hillside by some gigantic sculptor. The heavy but majestic building was half sunk into a little rocky cliff that rose at its back. Coming around to the front, we saw that the entrance was protected by a wide courtyard formed by two fortified walls and flanked by two colonnades. Half a dozen men with shaved heads, all of them dressed in white loincloths, filed around it, holding torches in their hands. They were probably priests.

After they had finished lighting blazing fires in each of the large basins placed between the columns, we decided to approach them. We had to speak Greek, and at once we understood that the knowledge of this language was undoubtedly one of the reasons why we had been chosen. At first, the priests acted courteously, but appeared to be wary. Before we could have any information, we had to prove that we were indeed members of the Brotherhood. We were asked many precise questions and requested to explain the meaning of the hieroglyphs carved into the columns. Most of them were familiar to us, as the walls of our bethsaïds were often decorated in that way. At last they told us that the high council would take place in two days, as many more Brothers were expected. Meals would be organized in the outer chambers of the temple, but we would have to sleep under the stars on mats that would be placed between the colonnades.

When we found ourselves once more alone, a wave of well-being washed over us all. Was it because of the place, or because of the prospect of encountering Brothers who had come from all the shores of the Mediterranean? At nightfall, we shared a meal of chickpea soup, all gathered around a crackling fire built against an outer wall of the courtyard. Men and women of Greek origin came to join us. The sound of their voices and something in their eyes made us trust them at once. Our conversation was warm and lively, and one of the newcomers, who had often traveled in the Red Land, undertook to tell us about the region and its sacred architecture. As someone had shown curiosity about the name of the land, he began a long explanation.

"No, Brother, the name is not due to the warm hues of its soil, nor to the fiery heat of its deserts. It stems from a very old tale that you already know. Have you forgotten the sunken continent from which our people directly descend? The men of this land had copper-colored skin, and those from other countries called them 'red men.' When the time came for their fall, they brought their civilization to the very land where we find ourselves today. The noblest of them, whole tribes together, came to find refuge here, bringing the fire of their soul and of their blood. It is in memory of these people, and of their ancestor Admah that the Brotherhood chose this name. Nevertheless, Brothers, you all know that a name always tends to present several faces. Red is the color of the ruby, and the powder of a certain ruby has proved capable of transmuting souls and bodies, minerals, plants and human beings, since the beginning of time . . . ."

While the Brother was speaking, whole sentences that had long ago echoed between the walls of the Krmel came back to my mind. They were those of one of our instructors, a man with eyes as blue as aquamarine: "Look upon this land as a palpitating ruby. Just like our Galilee, the land of the Red Earth is blessed with crucibles out of which has always flowed the most beautiful force. Here the greatest temples have been built, just as Nature grows plants. Everything there has always been pondered over and developed according to rhythms, inspired rather than imposed. . . .

"Thus, for ages, sacred grounds have been prepared through a sort of symbolic sowing of seeds. The priests there know how to scatter charcoal on the soil, as well as the numerous mineral salts, natural resins, and a thousand consecrated substances, according to the desires of the Eternal One. A temple is a creature that must evolve, a plant that needs a life force to be able to blossom out rhythmically, repeatedly. The secret of the great Brotherhood of these people is contained in their buildings, based exclusively on the knowledge of the force of death, which gives birth to every force of life. Never forget this, it is a mystery deeper than it may seem, one that has to be assimilated. Turn this and these words over and over in your minds. . . ."

At last, the night embraced us all, and our conversation died out with the crackling of the fire. Once more, we wrapped ourselves in our cloaks, as a sharp chill from over the sands fell upon us. We spent the following day talking and studying the paintings and the conception of the temple chambers to which we were allowed access. A priest wearing a wide blue and gold pectoral attested to our knowledge, checked the evening before.

The temple lived from the life of apparently immobile forms. Its foundations had been carefully prepared, its orientation scrupulously studied. This evinced a mystical sense coupled with practicality. The architects had based their work on the solar vibrations. They had used them in the different chambers of the temple in relation to the axis of the sun at a given moment of the day. In this way, each of the temple chambers was fully functional at a specific time of the day. Some of them even proved capable of condensing invisible rays.* The priest pointed out to us that the judicious orientation was not the only decisive factor. The precise shapes of the chambers and the thickness and density of the stone walls were just as important. For example, an initiation chamber that appeared to be square in fact was not. Its sides were made to curve slightly inward following "form waves" or energy fields, which establish a close link between cosmic mechanics and the psyche.

We went from room to room and from chamber to chamber with the definite sensation of being increasingly pierced by an infinite number of rays. Each of the chambers moreover, with its reliefs and its frescoes, seemed to produce its own specific light: we moved on from emerald to ruby, from ruby to amethyst. Under these waves of intense vibrations the frozen bas-reliefs and the hieratic characters appeared, to any sensitive eye, to move with a will of their own. Here was a flower which was, in fact, opening its petals, just as the transcending soul could blossom out with Nature's infinite evolution. We were in a boat, a solar vessel, which allowed us to penetrate the most intimate mechanisms of life. On the pediment of the temple Myriam and I had noticed a concise sentence which was full of meaning to one who was open to the message conveyed: "Look at your image."

*What today we would call ultraviolet and infrared rays.

At last it was time for the high council to begin. As required, we had put on our white robes, and in small groups we entered a vast chamber located under the cliff. It was rectangular in shape with a single row of pillars swelling slightly in the middle. The walls, which were of rare beauty, represented ochre-hued scenes of the life of Horus. We let our gaze roam from the splashes of gold to those of lapis lazuli. What a contrast to the sobriety of the Krmel: two ways of penetrating within the Great Sun; two ways, without a doubt complementary, of living one's inner fire. The flowers of the mind and the flowers of the heart could certainly find no closer harmony than in those responses to life. A path that was both twofold and singular was here offered to our understanding.

When we took our places, sitting on the floor, there were already hundreds of Brothers waiting, some of them wearing blue robes. An energizing silence fell over us instinctively, while in one corner of the chamber, lit by openings set high into the walls, a group of priests in rich attire were praying aloud amid a thick cloud of incense smoke. In front of us all, there were twelve seats, and upon these came to sit twelve men whose presence was extraordinary. Their shining auras fascinated me. I had never seen such a melody of white, gold, and violet. In a flash I realized we were probably in the presence of the high council of the Brotherhood. There were indeed twelve of them, which corresponded to the accounts that had reached our ears and that until now, we had been unable to verify. Myriam and I could not help looking at each other, as if to share our emotion. Then a shiver ran through the assembly; cool waves of energy were rising from the floor of the chamber and working up our spines. Our inner beings as well as the prevailing mood of the place were instantly overwhelmed. We understood what was happening: we knew that the presence of just one single being of peace in an assembly was sufficient to awaken the sacred force of each of its members. With a delicious slowness the triple serpent of our spines ascended the stairway of our states of consciousness and, within a few moments of total silence, we found ourselves in an extraordinary state of receptivity.

Then one of the twelve rose. He was a young-looking man, who held himself very straight; he was wearing a white robe of a very fine, carefully pleated fabric and his long blond hair was falling in straight locks to both shoulders. We did not see on him any of the ornaments that a high priest or dignitary might have displayed. He showed the sobriety of true nobility and his only official emblem was a crosier on which sparkled seven jewels, each one different in shape and color. I could not help staring at the long flames of blue light arising from him and flowing our way like a stream of love. At one moment, I was convinced that he was looking straight into my eyes, but I learned later that each of us had experienced the same thing.

"My Brothers," he began, placing his right hand over his heart, "before you, you find the descendants of those who kept the Tradition of the land of Atl. They are here by my side. Eleven they were, ten thousand years ago, eleven they are today, working tirelessly with me, the last missionary of the priests of Aton. If we have decided to hold this council, which is the first of its kind ever, it is because something infinitely solemn is being prepared on our Earth. The time has come at last for her to welcome the visit of the great solar flame that will modify the wheel of her past and prepare the trajectory of her future. I have already said much, and each of you will have understood that the word of the Logos is approaching us. But you may, no doubt, know this already, for hearts who have learnt to listen to silence know the vibrations of the universe, and may easily count the seasons of the Cosmos. We have insisted on your coming here for two reasons. First, to enable you to recognize each other more easily when the time has come. The eyes of the heart sometimes need the eyes of the flesh. Secondly, to warn you! For a long time, humanity has been in its involuted phase. The most brutal and the most selfish instincts have been developed, as the quest for divinity necessarily follows the exhaustion and the domination of the lower forces. Thus have our Brothers from other worlds allowed the most perfidious energies to invade our Earth. They gave them entire liberty in order to enable human beings to discover, and then to use, their own free wills. This will be fulfilled to a certain limit but not beyond it! The coming years are crucial ones; our Brothers in black know it just as well as we do and they are getting ready, right now, to strengthen their action. A certain number of them have just incarnated among us in order to sow disorder, hatred, and even worse, doubt. A certain number of them have been incarnated, I tell you this, and some are among us today, even here in this assembly!"

These words had been pronounced with greater emphasis than the others and they came as a shock to us. A deep murmur rippled through the assembly.

"Calm your spirits, Brothers! Are we so devoid of love that you do not want to allow *anyone* at our table? Calm your spirits, for I have indeed spoken of our 'black Brothers.' Just as we are, they too, are the sons of Aton and though they do not know it, they work for him at our side. Without knowing it they furbish for us the weapon with which we detect our own weaknesses; they offer us the darkness so that we may make the light shine all the brighter!

"Brothers of the black force who can hear me, I say this without irony and with neither malice nor design. You do not work for what is called evil. Absolute love shouts its existence into even the smallest atom of life, whereas hatred denies even itself and thus cannot be embodied. What is hatred? It can only be the love of what is opposite to the Father. It bears the face of love I tell you, which is simply hidden beneath a mask! It begins with pure love for itself, without which it could have no force of cohesion.

"Thus, my Brothers of the dark force who can bear my words, the particles composing your bodies are held together only by the force of love of the Great Aton, inside you and outside of you, without which they would instantly be thrown beyond the confines of the universe into a dance without end. Love is the only reason for everything and the only force of cohesion—its creation goes on forever! . . . "

There was great sound among the assembly, the sound of a heavy object crashing to the floor. Everyone started. Behind us in one corner of the vast chamber, a dozen men had hurriedly risen to their feet in a thick cloud of incense smoke and a crackling of embers. A few steps from there, threading his way with much difficulty among the Brothers who were still sitting, a man wearing a long white robe was fleeing awkwardly, bumping into those in his path. We understood that in his haste he had upset a basin in which the sacred incense was smouldering on incandescent embers. Fortunately, no one appeared to have been hurt and soon calm was restored. Not a word was said, but each of us understood within the silence of his own heart as well as in the furtive gaze of his neighbor. Truth is like any other force, it occasionally presents itself with such intensity that it is not for all ears to hear it.

A being had just been unmasked, not by another being but by himself, by his own inability to breathe a certain quality in the air.

Meanwhile, the Brother with the long blond hair had sat down, and the priests sent up a low chant in a language unknown to us, which moved us to contemplation. The syllables were stressed with extreme evenness and measured with the hammering of an enormous gong. Then the priests, imperturbable, made their way among us, sprinkling drops of lustral water to the right and left. The custom observed by the whole Brotherhood was, on such an occasion, to bow one's head and to hold both hands over one's heart. When they had finished, one of the twelve Brothers, whose dark face set him apart from the others, rose and asked each of the communities present to pray silently in its own dialect. It is difficult to describe what occurred in the ensuing moments of silence, but Myriam and I had the vivid sensation that a force was being woven in the atmosphere around us. We were creating a real network of thoughts that blended neatly into a logical pattern. In this way, we gave birth to a gigantic etheric weaving, a fabric into which the purest thought-forms we were capable of were threaded, one after another.

This was an ancient technique that had been taught at the Krmel as well as in the mystery schools of Greece. We were well aware of the power of such an etheric veil, whose each thought-form was as pure as a thread of gold, contributing to the rapid growth of an enormous egregore* of peace. Such power, springing at once from the mind and heart, could transform the very structure of matter and transmute the bodies of those creating it as well as those receiving it. It could be the cornerstone of a new world, the transforming ruby of all humanity. Hadn't old Zerah told us, when we were still at an age to be hopping up and down the stone wall

---

*An egregore is a collective thought-form that can be either positive or negative.

surrounding the village, that it was the very technique of transmutation? His clear, concise words echo today with the same truth.

"If only one-third of all the people on the Earth came voluntarily, all at the same time, to send forth similar ideas of peace and unconditional love then the structure of all matter would be forever transformed."

Thus it is that states of consciousness can affect states of matter. Such a simple truth, but such a difficult one to grasp fully, like a little key which may gently open locks that we would imagine frozen with rust.

In the midst of our living silence, amid the clouds of incense smoke that were rising, and caressing the frescoes on the walls, a wave of light came washing over us from a universe inaccessible to closed hearts.

Out of this wave a form emerged, a being was born. It was a man all clothed in light and wearing a robe whose folds looked like so many shafts of moonlight. He was tall, perfectly proportioned, with a beard and long hair like most of the rest of us. He took a few steps forward, trailing flames of azure, then stood in front of the twelve Brothers who were sitting with closed eyes. He did not stay among us long, his lips did not part, but in our souls he sowed words so clear that each of us believed them to be within himself.

"Brothers, receive our peace, the peace of the souls of this world and the peace of the One. Each nucleus contains its own nucleus and so on to infinity. To work as you have been asked to do, learn how to slow the pace of your desires! Thus, Brothers, you will leave the periphery of the circle of appearances to regain the focal point where all causes are conceived. Let your hearts remember these words and be aware also that the Brothers from the stars who have chosen to live in the womb of your world since the flowering of all life thank you for the task undertaken this day in the name of the One. I am Brother M and my spirit will accompany your steps until the final accomplishment."

The master of light brightened his features with a broad smile and then in a flash vanished from sight, leaving little cracklings of life in the air, testifying to his invisible presence. It was a long time before anyone dared move, even to blink his eyes. There are moments when even the slightest movement is enough to disturb an ocean of joy. We were not expecting any more from the day—our eyes and souls had been fulfilled.

The future was being traced with increasing precision, and it seemed as if a new energy had begun flowing through our veins. The assembly was dismissed by the sharp note of the hollow piece of wood that was struck by one of the priests.

Thus ended the first meeting of the high council of the Brothers in those times. Our souls' memories only retained scattered fragments of the days that followed, marked by a succession of prayers, meditations, and councils. Little real teaching was dispensed although we felt that something or someone was instilling in us a force that was deeper and stronger than ever.

I remember too that we all drank a radiant water; this was a water whose secret was known to a few and which served to enlighten the priests on the degree of purity of our auras. These priests were then to teach us signs of recognition to be used in the crucial day to come. Aware of the importance of such acts, we willingly opened our souls, and ten days later when we returned to the banks of the Nile, we had realized that the danger was among us. Naively we always believed that a white robe could never hide a black heart!

CHAPTER XV

AT THE FEET OF THE SILENT WATCHMAN

The day was just dawning as we reached the Nile, where a fishing boat was waiting for us amid the profusion of papyrus and aquatic flowers. This time of day was most pleasant; the bluish light of the dawning day played with infinite grace on the corollas of the lotus flowers that reached up above the surface of the water. To reach our skiff we had to wade out up to our thighs in the cool water, disturbing whole families of ducks nesting among the wadis. Our presence created an indescribable disorder that made us feel almost guilty. Only several crested cranes digging in the mud seemed not to mind our being there. Our boat was long and narrow, flanked by two floats made of reeds. It looked frail but it carried us for hours safely down the river. Myriam and I were delighted with the beauty of the surroundings. We made the most of those precious fleeting moments while the heat was still bearable. Thus we discovered one facet of the secret life of the great river, and even came upon several fellahs hiding in the reeds with nets in hand, waiting to capture the passing birds. We were filled with wonder but remained wary, not daring to think that our overloaded skiff might overturn, while bands of crocodiles were sliding silently through the water.

Then the vegetation became sparser, and following the orders of the Brother who was leading our little expedition, we regained dry land. We left the river behind, walking on thin strips of silt set with stones that divided half sunken fields, and once more we felt the heat weighing down on our shoulders. We passed through one village, then another, then a third—poor blocks of burnt earth where life was already in full swing. The inhabitants looked at us with the curiosity commonly reserved for strangers and we exchanged only a few smiles, taking care to ask permission before drinking from a well in one of the villages.

Thereafter there was nothing but sand, an apparently endless desert, lost beneath a white-hot sky. At the top of a small rocky rise, we at last sighted what we were looking for: several blurred silhouettes, blinding white and far in the distance, while the river still flowed imperturbably on our left. We were surprised to realize how little ground we had actually covered, and our feet were already burning. The silhouettes called to us once more. They were the gigantic buildings the Brotherhood had been telling us about since our earliest childhood, the pyramids of our red ancestors.

Nearby were several huts built with mud bricks, and we knew that ceremonies were held there regularly in these times when so many souls were preparing to act. The Brother who was leading us knew we were to make important contacts there so we asked for refuge, then waited for nightfall. Contrary to our expectation the huts that hugged the contours of the landscape were not occupied by men of this desert land. Their lighter skin immediately testified to that. As soon as our gazes met arms were crossed over hearts, theirs as well as our own. These Brothers said they were Greek physicians, members of the Brotherhood, and connected with what remained of the ancient Asklapios temples.* Along with an aged priest of Aton, they kept a fire burning permanently in one of the huts, both in memory of rites celebrated there long ago and to herald

---

*These doctors initiated in techniques of healing through the Spirit belonged to the renowned order of Therapists.

the great cosmic work now coming into being. This priest was a wizened old man whose eyes were full of playfulness and kindness. His first concern was to bring us to the base of the pyramids.

Standing there, we felt as if crushed to the ground by the imposing mass of the pyramids, which seemed to have been dropped there by some titan. Now and then, the sun would burn our eyes as it was reflected from the great slabs of limestone that covered the rock in places. We were overwhelmed with emotion. It was as if our hearts had once beat ardently, here on this sandy wasteland in some remote past. In spite of ourselves, we could not resist touching our lips to the ground before contemplating the masses of rock that looked like colossal stone stairways over which the millennia had glided.

A nomad and his family had set up camp at the foot of the largest of the pyramids. The priest assured us that he was a learned man who, though he was a stranger to the Brotherhood, possessed ancient wisdom. He had sworn to live isolated in this place where, he said, a great messenger from the Father would appear one day. Thus, his life would not have been lived in vain.

Our steps led us inexorably toward the Sphinx, still impressive in its majesty, in spite of the devastation caused by the desert winds. I was filled with joy. How many times, long ago, when I was still wearing the little monk's dark robe, had my inner eye focused on this idea of the man to come, the only man, in fact, who ever was? We had been taught this was the man whose transcendence of the four primary elements had brought him illumination, had rendered him impenetrable, untouched by the illusions that delude our minds. This was the image of the man who, to become so, had gone beyond humanity.

"Be aware," the Brothers at the Krmel used to say, "that there are two ways to be inhuman: The first is that of the wild beast, listening to the appetites of his scale-covered ego; the second is that of the master of light, whose numerous existences of action and reflection have enabled him to comprehend the real meaning of good and evil. He who knows indeed is the one who has understood the finality of these two concepts, and is not misled by the episodic morals of one epoch, of one body. The cosmos knows no morals, but only what love is, and this is enough, for it is all. Let us rather turn our souls to the face of the light and to that of the lack of light; this will enable us to act, in the pure sense of the term."

These words whirled in my memory while we were plodding over the intensely burning sands. Soon we were at the feet of the great being with his feline gaze. We immediately drew near between the two huge forelegs, which protected a sort of vast court-yard bordered by two high walls. At the far end, almost up against the thorax of the thought-being, rose a crude little altar flanked by two columns: that of the light, and the other, of the lack of light.*

We went no farther, preferring to wait for nightfall in order to meditate, as we all felt the need. We retired to the various mud huts, then darkness fell over the desert, deep, and soon cold. The little daub-walled village came alive in its own secret way and we caught glimpses of fleeting white shadows silhouetted against the walls. The blaze of a torch pierced the obscurity of the desert, then another, a third, a fourth, and soon the night was peopled with bright-eyed beings, all moved by the same fervor. We could hear camels snorting into the night air, the twinkling of little bells in the soft breeze, and the crunching sound of bare feet in the sands of the dunes. We all spontaneously embraced our neighbors, as if such spontaneity were the purest sign of recognition. Between the forelegs of the huge stone watchman was a family, a real family, beyond conventions and attachments of the flesh. Soon we were all within the walls of the enclosure between the arms of the great Sphinx. All the Brothers present were wearing the long white robes. But one of them stood out from the rest, for he had a big ring of lapis lazuli on his right hand. He drew us to the far end of the courtyard behind the altar. There we all held hands, standing in a circle, and a short chant was intoned in Greek. It was then that the Brother with the blue ring began to radiate an indescribable energy, something exhilarating that gripped at our hearts, something that rose to a climax as he took

---

*Another conception of the famous Jakim and Bohas, the two columns in ititiatic temples of ancient times. We can also compare them to Ida and Pingala, the Sanskrit terms for the subtle left and right channels of the spinal column.

from his robe a long metal rod and immediately traced something in the sand that neither Myriam nor I could make out.

We were standing up against the breast of the Sphinx, and our emotion was such that at one point we felt as if the sand had become like glue under our feet. Our bodies began to vibrate as never before. Only a strange sensation of cold that came from inside me reminded me of my supreme initiation at the Krmel. A square slab of stone began to take form under the sand at our feet. Its four corners and then its four sides emerged with the slowness of a body called back to life after a long sleep. Then it grew blurred and a stone stairway was revealed that plunged straight down into the sand. Whether it led under the altar or into the depths beneath the Sphinx, it is impossible for us to say today.

What we can say is that about thirty souls sank into the ground, down steps as steep as they were narrow. It seemed the atoms of our limbs were vibrating outside of time, as they carried us down to a narrow gallery dug into the yellow rock. The silence of stones prevailed in this place and for those who know how to listen, it was the most talkative silence that ever was. In these precious seconds we were beyond astonishment, and we walked on without even wondering about the source of the small white light that bathed the gallery. The ground seemed to slope gently downward for a time, then we were flooded with blinding light as we came to the entrance of a vast triangular room filled with a pure brilliance.

"We are beneath the largest of the pyramids," the Brother with the blue ring said softly. "This room is a sort of entryway leading to other chambers within the pyramid itself, and deeper into the ground. I say entryway, for to be able to come here, you must have been able to withstand a readjustment of the atoms of your bodies. My Brothers, we all vibrate here to a rhythm approaching the etheric plane, although this place is also perfectly concrete. Depending on your degree of purity, this triangle will allow you to enter other rooms of various shapes that emit other vibrations and require other levels of consciousness. One of these rooms contains most of what gave force to the first human who walked this Earth. It would be of no use to go there now. There you would see objects, energies, that your minds would not be able to grasp completely. Suffice it to say that more than two millennia must pass before a few human beings clothed in flesh may dare to understand, and then just a little. I myself, to whom it has been given to see one corner of the veil lifted, could never find the right words to describe my vision. I may simply state that, in the name of the forces that impel me to lead members of the Brotherhood here, all that is hidden here beneath the ground comes to us from the stars by way of the people of long ago. This is a sacred inheritance that contains the essence of the knowledge of our galaxy. This inheritance is sacred not so much because of what some religion has decreed, but rather because of the gift of love it represents and sums up. In fact, it offers the knowledge of the One, that is, of the nonduality of spirit and matter. Each of its creations is at once spirit and body, subtlety and density, so as to be able to function in all realms with absolute malleability. These are the creations of the children of Moon-Sun, of Hrma, and of many more who have managed to integrate their inner sun into the great central sun. Doesn't this suggest anything to any of you? I can imagine that a few among you are thinking, 'But why are we here? We are learning nothing; the Brother is speaking about vague things. . . .'

"Do not be deceived! Each of the terms I have just used is two-sided, and has been dictated to me precisely. Our presence here purifies us more than our narrow analytical minds can imagine. The vibrations of the form of the room we are in create myriad little matrices that transmute our cells by engraving images of peace in their memories. Let each of us unfold all his successive envelopes and his eyes will be opened."

As he led us through the vast chamber, the Brother added that the location of the pyramids had been chosen in accordance with lines of energy that crisscross the Earth. Their precise orientation, he said, served to avoid earthquakes in the material world, as well as to provide energy for the vehicles of the Brothers from the stars in the vital world, and finally to instill the impalpable among the palpable in the world of spirit.

In a flash I saw the chamber filled with an infinite number of singularly shaped jewels. Were these the primary forms, the arcana of all creation? Were they real objects that our impure hearts could not make hold still? The nostalgia of a lost paradise seized my heart, and I read similar feelings in the eyes of Myriam and of all the other Brothers present.

We went back up to the courtyard above by the way we had come, following a short meditation, without understanding any better than we still can today, that the particles of our bodies could unite with those of the desert sand, or those of the rocks in the Earth, since ultimately, in a very tangible way, they could be one with them.

Back on the surface, the Brother with the lapis lazuli ring disappeared into the silence of a little daub-walled shelter, while many of us felt the need to stay together. In the hollow of a dune not far from the glowing embers of a nomad's fire, fifteen white silhouettes gathered to commune.

"Listen to me Brothers!" One of us who seemed unwilling to sit down burst out. "I must tell you of something that has been tormenting me for such a long time!"

It was a man of about our age, with clear but wild eyes, to which the moon added a strange glow. He contrasted with our group by wearing a cloak made from uncombed wool, and by having incredibly long hair.

"Listen, all of you, for we are all like children, waiting to be beaten or to be rewarded with honey. Ever since I was a little boy, my fathers of Essania have split the world in two. They speak of themselves as a race of light and of all others as being blacker than jet. They expect everything from the stars, and they can only live within the walls of their villages. They want to teach through the Almighty, and they deny themselves the right to speak his name outside their own enclosures! The whole Earth needs cultivating. . . . We cannot sort out the good grass from the weeds just with a few principles and a bit of white linen. You content yourselves with a little healing here and there to calm your hearts. The time is coming, they tell us . . . but the time for what? I cry over the promises they make, over the morals they wave in my face. I must share this with you!"

"John!" A firm but gentle voice flew over the silence of the night among the dunes. We all turned our heads to see the tall silhouette of the Brother with the night-blue ring emerge from the darkness.

"John," he said again in the same tone of voice, "we need men like you; we need volcanoes on all the lands of the world. The sun calls out to you to overturn the stones in the desert. Your fire is needed, but be careful that it does not burn you as it did in time past. You refuse the dual path, and in this you see clearly, but be on your guard when you speak, lest the bitterness of your words should overwhelm you with the venom of duality itself.

"Take care not to judge, John; follow your path. Do not rebel against the fathers who perhaps have not been able to see clearly enough, or far enough. The spirit of the one who taps into the divine spirit is often inept and strays into a primitive moralism.

"As for you who are listening to me, you must realize that your morals are not of this world and they will not pass with the winds that sweep away civilizations. And you, John, do not take my words for those of a priest who wants to tell you what to do. They are the words of an old friend who has known the confusion you feel today. I know, and not because I was taught in the name of an impalpable god whose very shadow flees endlessly . . . I know because I have often fallen, and my heart has learned all by itself how to embrace the Force.

"Rebel, then, if this is your soul's desire, but do not let your rebellion be filled with rancor; let it rather add yet another step to your ascension, and to the ascension of others for whom, I can assure you, you are responsible."

John, the brother with the long hair, then burst into sobs. Before we could make a move, he was gone, striding wildly into the cold darkness that hung over the dunes.

"Let him go, my Brothers," the Brother with the ring said to us. "He is a strong being, and this is how he forges himself. His is the heart of all desert animals, which will tear themselves apart before they will let themselves be penned up. His eye is keen, let me tell you."

That night, my thoughts, as well as those of Myriam and many of the others among us, went out to John, wild-eyed John, whom we imagined huddled in the hollow of some rock or in the fold of a dune. And we thought of our own rebellions that we had been unable to vent, of the questions we had not dared to ask, of the endless waiting whose aim we managed to glimpse so rarely.

Where then was the Peace that the ageless Brothers kept promising? Where was the Logos of all our hearts? He who would shake us out of our shells? We would probably have to go on walking the dusty paths of Palestine and Judaea as well as resisting the exhortations of the Zealots. Which were we to choose? The peace of men or the Peace of the Nameless One?

All through that night the cold desert wind enveloped us in our questions, and when Moon-Sun twinkled once more in the firmament each of us felt its light go straight to his heart. It was a wink of the eye from those who know that the heat of the tropics and the bitter cold of the frozen wasteland always go side by side; a wink of the eye, too, from those who knew that the Great Work would at last be accomplished.

· BOOK TWO ·

BOOK TWO

CHAPTER 1

BAPTISMS

A soft warm wind was at our backs as we set forth from Jericho on our journey northward, doing our best to follow the faint tracks left by the caravans but so easily lost amid the sand and the rocks. A wealthy man by the name of Alphee often provided us with board and lodging in the old city. His help was precious to us in these troubled years, when the heavy footsteps of the Roman cohorts left their mark throughout the land.

Alphee was not of our blood, although there was no doubt that he was of our heart. He was one of those people who turn up from time to time in life, lending a helping hand just when and where it is most needed, though the reasons for it may be mysterious at the time.

"It is unsafe for you to stay here a day longer," he had told us. "Two of my servants have just come back from Jerusalem. They told me that, close behind them, there was a whole Roman legion sent to drive the Zealots out of the area. You know what pains some of them have taken to give the Romans the impression that you were implicated in their actions—the Eternal One alone knows why! Tomorrow there may be bloodshed. It would be safer for you to go away."

Simon had taken the lead of our little group of about fifteen men and women; and I, Myriam, could feel our host's parting words echoing and re-echoing in my heart, words that had sent us north toward the banks of the river Jordan.

"Look around when you get there," he had said. "I know a man there who speaks with great fervor. I do not know exactly what he wants to do, nor who he claims to be, but his eyes glow like burning embers. He will be of interest to you. The people say he is the Father's savior, the Messiah of the Scriptures; people from all over are flocking to him. . . ."

These were the words that had motivated us to leave. We did not fear the legions, who had nothing against the Brotherhood despite the rumors that some insisted on spreading. Above all, we wanted to find this man who had been moving about like the wind for months. Those who returned from the desert swore that he was the Lord's Anointed foretold by the prophets.

It had been a long time since we had returned to our own village, and we were travel-weary, tired of ministering to the injured and unwell following uprisings and epidemics here and there. Was this all that our mission entailed? Our meeting with the Brothers from the stars seemed infinitely far behind us, and we struggled within, so that the flow of hope that had been poured into our hearts would not evaporate under the hot sun of Judaea.

And thus had the years passed, seemingly interminably, punctuated by our daily ablutions and prayers whose basic pattern, sometimes, seemed forgotten. Joseph's father was no longer alive, and Simon's mother as well as my parents were sleeping peacefully beneath a rock not far from old Zerah's tomb.

The sun was almost at its highest when we reached the top of a hillock overlooking one arm of the Jordan. To our surprise, we discovered a great crowd of people sitting on the ground along the bank of the river. From them there rose a low murmur, something like the ritual chant of a people's soul, soft and meditative. Only a few men and women were walking into the water, up to their waists, threading their way through the tender green of aquatic plants. There a half-naked man appeared to be speaking to them, but we could not make out what he was saying.

Standing a few paces from us was a man in a long white robe. He, too, contemplated the scene; he seemed to regard it as having special importance. When he turned toward us, my heart gave a leap. I knew these eyes, this long face . . . but from where? I had no idea. He then smiled broadly at us, stepped forward, and placed his right hand on his heart. On one of his fingers I glimpsed a beautiful ring of lapis lazuli, and suddenly I understood. In my mind I saw this Brother, at the foot of a pyramid, at the foot of the Great Sphinx. His face had not aged at all; it was now as it had been long ago—impenetrable.

"Do you recognize me?" he asked simply. "I am of the line of the Manethon, and here ends the essence of my task. Come near, follow me, and you will understand better. I can assure you, you may keep the coming hours like jewels in your hearts. Remember my words, for there will be a time when what I am going to tell you and what you are going to see will burst into the open for the whole world to witness. You must know that I am one of the seven Brothers to whom the cosmic treasures of the land of the Red Earth are entrusted. The day when we met in this life was the day when my final mission took shape. Nothing is left to so-called chance— were you not aware of this?"

The Brother had spoken these words softly, with a little comforting smile, and without hesitation we followed him along the narrow path that led down to the bank of the river. More numerous than I had expected, the people milled about, their contemplation sometimes giving way to exaltation. At times, a shout would ring out, followed by acclamations, and then it would fade away, blended with the piercing whistle of a bird passing overhead. Silence would close down again, like a veil cast over the assembly.

"It is he! He is the Messiah!" someone shouted. "What are you waiting for?"

And men and women in small clusters rushed into the water, followed by the more humble who waded, their heads bowed. In the widest part of the river, the man responsible for all this excitement was standing up to his hips in the water where the surrounding growth of reeds left a clearing for human passage. His face was hidden by his long locks of hair and a thick beard. Dozens of men, women, and children were filing past him, and with both of his hands placed on their heads, he immersed them totally for an instant. He was speaking in a low voice, interrupting himself at times to shout hoarsely, "Be silent! Be silent! You don't know what you are saying! Let your hearts be silent."

A cry rose in my breast: "John! John!" We had gone forward, stepping over the people sitting and lying on the ground. Now I could see his face, and recognized the Brother whose inner revolt had once touched the depths of our souls, long ago, in the hollow of a dune. It was John, the rebellious Brother who had been searching for his own path. Was he, then, the long-awaited Savior? I turned my gaze toward Simon, who had gone very pale, as if deeply shaken and overwhelmed by all the questions in the world. Nearly ten years had passed since the night we had seen John stride into the darkness, alone and tormented. And now he had reappeared, haloed with all the fire he was trying hard to channel and which was consuming him.

"He wanted to be the firebrand of an inner revolution," murmured Manethon, "and that's what he is at last." He led us down closer to John. "From now on, here the people of this earth will be purified by water; it will be water that will burn away their impurities. Water, like the earth, is a matrix. Here is the force of Noah, Brothers, the second initiation! It is the second birth of those who have eyes to see, but it is also their first death.

"For years I have been preparing your brother John for these sublime hours. I have passed on to him the torch of Master M, who long ago purified others on the shores of a great lake. But be aware, my Brothers of Essania, that a symbol is of little importance compared with action."

The Brother with the blue ring paused for some time, and we followed him, holding our breath, living the moment to its fullest and counting the steps that lay between us and John. He resumed his explanations and we went on, drawn by the thread of his voice, to where a corner of the veil was being lifted.

"Remember, for you know, you know indeed," Manethon

said. And the master of the crypts of the Sphinx awakened old knowledge that lay hidden within our memories. He recalled to us the importance of baptism by total immersion, which allowed the etheric flame to escape from the body for a flash of an instant; a flash that was an eternity in another world, an eternity during which an entity of light left an indelible imprint on a human being. This was the driving impulse that linked the new initiate with the egregore of a new form of established peace. It was thus that John was building a gigantic thought-form, to which hundreds of people were joining their own renewed energy. Thus he was laying the first visible stone.

"Silence, silence!" he kept repeating while his voice was growing weaker; and the Brother whose eyes had been those of a wild beast, would take on the look of a sheep of Galilee. Was it he, then, we were expecting? Was this possible? Could our path have crossed his without our knowing?

"He is preparing," said our guide simply, reading our hearts. "See how his eyes shine . . . then look for eyes that shine a thousand times brighter. Such eyes alone belong to the One you are waiting for."

He stepped aside as a group of men passed by, and we stepped into the water, drawn by a will that commanded us to be silent.

When I came face to face with John, our eyes met for an instant. He smiled; he remembered. He did not say a word; I shut my eyes and felt the palms of his two strong hands on the crown of my head, and my body was plunged beneath the waters. I felt numbed by something intangible; I sensed the ripple of little waves running over my back, then nothing more, an eternity of silence. A sudden dizziness came over me and spun me up into a whirlwind of whiteness. . . . Then I was hovering over the Jordan, reduced, or perhaps enlarged, to a pair of eyes floating between two worlds. I gazed down upon the crowd, Simon, my immersed body and John, standing there glistening wet, with his eyes closed. My soul, my astral force, had escaped the envelope of my body and was at rest in a splash of light and bliss.

No doubt this lasted only an instant, but it was also a fragment of eternity, of energy, a dimension that expanded along with my heart.

"Time asserts itself in this way," Zerah had said, "a necessary illusion, a means to be made use of."

It seemed I could feel the pulsations of the crowd and my gaze lost itself in their souls, absorbing all their thoughts.

Finally there was a rift, something between a fleeting sensation of nausea and a torrent of happiness. My body once more enclosed my soul, and two strong hands gripped me and pushed me on, to make room for those who were waiting in line. I turned, and already Simon was coming up out of the water. Then it was the turn of little Joshua, born into our group, of Esther, of Zachaia, and many others who had realized that the time had come.

We drew off to rejoin Brother Manethon, and only then did we notice that John had traded his white robe for a loincloth made of coarsely woven camel hair. We were still under the shock of what had just occurred, and this detail was only one lost among a thousand others. It came up later, once we were back on the hillock, filled with the fervid sort of peace John had imparted to us along with a willingness to really do something at last.

"What does it matter to you?" asked the Brother with the lapis lazuli ring, seizing upon our remarks. "Does it bother you to see one of you dressed like a desert magician? John has renounced all structures, for the heart, in its depths, knows no structure. He has not renounced the soul of any race, but he has rejected time, which fixes that soul in a form. John is the magician who is kneading the souls of the waiting multitudes. As do all those who work with Nature's hidden forces, he is working on the human race from its base, by transmuting its etheric force. Camel hair, which is a repository of vital energies, helps him in this. It is the death of the animal that acts within humanity that he is now proclaiming. Be aware, Brothers, that he takes on others' animality, and works at transmuting it during his far-off nightly retreats. And this is the sign of a master, of an authentic initiator. As you have noticed, many of those who had come to be purified acknowledged their sins aloud before their immersion. John takes on each one's wrongdoing; he makes it his with the help of his love, which he has sharpened through special practices. And in this way he rids many beings of the burden of their past, by his willingness to wear their animal hides.

"Such is the true baptism; not an empty rite, but a concrete, direct act that transforms the past as well as the future and leaves an indelible imprint on the soul's eternal present—I mean a jewel, mounted in its astral form.

"This is the gift of a real master, as I have said... so few know how to love beyond words, so few have been able to rid their hearts of conditions and doubts. Your Brother is not living on buts or ifs. He is living on that which we all breathe, though we all too rarely recognize its taste."

That evening we fell asleep with our hearts full of joy, wrapped in our cloaks and huddled close together around a fire.

Manethon wanted us to stay there a few days longer. The reasons he gave for this were unclear. He seemed rather to hope for something that escaped us, or to have guessed that destiny was moving forward. We obeyed his wish, overjoyed at these hours of peace, far from the agitation of the villages. We were also pleased to be able to exchange points of view with other Brothers in white we had noticed, here and there among the throng.

The second evening, I was surprised to see Simon get up suddenly and rush toward an elderly looking man dressed in the white robe. They embraced at some length. This Brother, who was unknown to me, came and shared our meal, scrutinizing each of us, with eyes like shining pearls. It was thus I made the acquaintance of Moshab, who had taught Simon so much. The old man from the Krmel seemed happy to surprise us. For quite some time he made jokes about the hazards of life, but I had no doubt that his easygoing manner was hiding something essential.

"Myriam," he said at last, "there are times when the lives of human beings become interwoven in curious ways, don't you think?"

We spent four days in this way, on the banks of a little river whose name would echo to the four corners of the world. Four days, watching a procession of exalted men and women, of mystics come out from their mountain retreats, of simple families who had heard the call, of young people fleeing the riots in the cities. There, in the near-desert region of the old land of Canaan, among the pebbles and the reeds of the river, something was happening. John purified the people who flocked to him, spoke ardently of a coming Messiah, purified more people, isolated himself in a demanding silence, then began all over again. We hardly dared to go and greet him, but little did it matter. More than ever, I know now that some words are useless, and spoil everything because our spirits prove unable to breathe their gold into them. John had become a cry from the heart, a living prayer whose concentric waves reached us all.

The heat was unbearable; the sun, high in the sky, was beating relentlessly upon us, when, from out of the crowd, rose a tall white figure. It was a man, probably one of us, strongly built. We watched as he drew forward slowly, making his way through the crowd toward the bank. He looked determined yet gentle, and suddenly all seemed to make way for him.

John, who once more had begun baptizing, halted in mid-movement, as if frozen.

As for myself, I cannot say what came over me; my legs took it upon themselves to run . . . to run. . . . It was only when my feet touched the coolness of the water that I was able to stop.

The Brother, dressed in the long white robe of linen, had waded out into the water, halfway up to his thighs, and seemed to be speaking with John. Slowly he crossed his hands over his chest, right over left, in keeping with the ancient rite, and the baptist did likewise. The cries of the crowd had ceased. Some, who had been camping there for several weeks, rose and walked down to the bank of the river. Then John's voice seemed to rip through a veil, bursting into all of our hearts with a passion that we were never to hear again.

"Children, I tell you before the All-Highest, that here is the Long-Awaited, here is the Messiah. Cast off your chains and follow him. The hour has come for me to wane, my time stops here."

These words clapped like thunder and echoed off all the rocks. No doubt the hot wind carried them beyond the ancient sea of solitude, scattering them wide over the old volcanic lands, changing forever this whole region dear to the children of Essania. *(Today, when the images of these moments pass through our hearts, our souls know that two thousand years have not gone by; it was only yesterday, and the same force is still in them. . . .)*

Something like a silent cry pierced our hearts, like the cracking of a whip coming from other dimensions of our being. The light went totally white. The sun overwhelmed everything, the wind swept over all.

Then we saw John go through the ritual gesture. The white-robed figure sank quickly into the water and reemerged instantly, streaming with light, blazing with a flame that none could fail to see. In the radiance enveloping his body, there seemed to dance ephemeral white shadows. Was this just a projection of our souls' desires or was this reality? Each will find the key that best suits his needs. Our hands may only write what our hearts have felt.

The Great White Being waded slowly back toward the bank. A train of violet fire seemed to be flowing from his arms and legs. The throng gathered there, began to rush toward him, and he stopped short, halting all movement. Once again we saw him cross his arms over his heart. Finally he came out of the water in silence. A path opened before him, perhaps out of fear, but also respect. His tall figure spoke for itself; anything else, any words, would have been empty.

As he withdrew, up the hillocks, small groups of men, women, and children lay down upon the sand over which he had passed. Soon I could only glimpse his long auburn hair, which at last was lost from view among the yellow outlines of the rugged rocks. Two or three white figures walked on behind him.

A voice pierced our inner silence:

"What are you waiting for? Could you be afraid?" It was Brother Manethon. He gazed at us, almost with a disapproving look, but his eyes were those of the happiest being on Earth. We needed no more, and were surprised to find ourselves racing, jumping lightly from one rock to another, hardly paying heed to the thorn bushes that grew all around.

Soon the Great Being in the white robe was once again in sight. He was only a few steps ahead of us, walking with an even stride, now and then lifting his hands to his face.

We were panting, and our commotion made him turn round. This instant was the most beautiful of all, the most intense . . . gripping us at the very roots of our existence. Before us were two eyes of tremendous depth, which set us all alight within, existing only for each one of us and for all of us at once. It took me a long time to even notice his long locks of hair, still streaming with water, and his short beard. There seemed to be no imperfection in this face, no other marks than those that love had traced: several little wrinkles at the corners of his eyes, seeming to say, "It is all so simple." But there was something more there also, something in this face that forced me to turn inward, something that awoke confused feelings within me, scattering the pieces of a puzzle as if on purpose; and I felt once more like a little girl though I did not know why.

The Being placed both hands over his heart, smiled at us one last time, as if to say, "Soon . . . soon," then went slowly on his way.

A stone rattled down the path and we heard someone breathing behind us. It was Brother Manethon, who drew us after him. He had rolled his cloak into a ball which he held under his arm, and we understood that we had nothing more to do here. I looked at Simon and saw that he was paler than ever. Neither of us dared speak. We went on as in a dream, hardly allowing ourselves to hope that the hour had really come.

As we were walking toward Bethany, Simon suddenly stopped short, then hurried over to Manethon, gripping him firmly by the arm.

"It is he, Brother," he choked. "It is he, isn't it? It's Joseph! It's got to be, or else . . ."

"It is he, Simon," replied Manethon, "but there is no more Joseph. Joseph went to sleep forever at the Krmel; you know this, you were told. He was stripped of his name, of his limitations. He became Jesus, and now he is Christ, the Sun!"

These words broke like the second clap of thunder of the day. We all burst into great peals of laughter, in a flow of irrepressible joy. There was a breath, something almost insane, that broke our from our breasts. Yes, those eyes, those eyes! They were what I had been looking for, though I had failed to recognize them. They were indeed the eyes of the Joseph we had known, shining everywhere in the village, the eyes that made Zerah and many others murmur to each other.

Years and years had gone by since our last encounter. He had recognized us immediately, of that I was sure.

"The work of the whole Brotherhood may now take shape," declared Manethon, cutting short our effusions. "The Master needs to be alone for a while now, but afterwards if your hearts move you to act you may go to join him. For now, let us go on; I shall tell you his story, for the Brothers from the stars have entrusted me with its telling."

And we continued on our way to Bethany, along with others, listening to a story that many since have refused, and refuse still.

CHAPTER · II

THE SEVENTEEN YEARS

For some time, we continued down the river Jordan, along the steep slopes that overlooked the water. This was a land of sand and thorns and endless drought that led us over the barren hills of Judaea. We were thankful for the deep silence of these lonely wastes, and even avoided the company of the few shepherds who would have been happy to have someone to talk to. We only had ears for Manethon and his stupendous account, which we received as one would a sacred trust.

"Only a short time ago," our guide began while walking on briskly, "I was in the land of our Great Brother Thotmes, who established the solid foundations of our Brotherhood. I was staying in the city they call Alexandria along with six companions who had come a long way to reach this land. One of them came from the lands of Ashia, whose name means 'dawn'. This is where people's eyes are so small that they seem to be ever contemplating their inner beings. The name of the Brother who came from that part of the Earth was Mingts. Another one had come from the great country of Ishwar.* Still another, Gspar,† was from Babylon, and another from Greece. In short, all had come from the parts of the world where the true thought has sought refuge in recent times. Following orders that had come from the stars we held council for three times seven days, as the triple heptad transcends the human, as well as all matter, in the work of purification. The seven of us knew each other in ways unknown to common men. Our souls had spoken together countless times, freed from the envelope of flesh, in the land where soul converses with soul and each can conceive of the cyclical advance of the ages. We were aware that we were to welcome a being among us, a being who would bring us out of the heptad of a dying civilization, into the sign of eternity through rebirth. Thus is the flame always handed on; thus does the seven give way to the eight.

"We knew that this man was returning from a long journey whose itinerary we had ourselves prepared from the beginning. It was a journey that had lasted seventeen years, according to the will of the Brothers of Moon-Sun—a journey that had enabled him to submit his body and his soul to all the refinements that matter can endure. Remember this number seventeen, for its sum is equal to the octad, dear to the people of Ishtar, as may be seen in all the little eight-pointed stars you have always found in even the most humble dwellings of our people. The being of whom I am speaking followed his path as it was inscribed in the parchment of the zodiac, step by step. This was not, Brothers, to learn what he did not yet know, this would be a misleading way of putting it. His heart and his transcendental soul had known for an infinity of existences. . . . It was to gather all the vestiges of ancient wisdom that humanity has managed to preserve in different parts of the world, as did Isis with the pieces of her husband's body. He worked as the elect of a new Osiris, to receive the spiritual body of the light that had illuminated the ancient sages of Atl and of Ma. I am speaking of the knowledge deposited on Earth so that human beings might become

*India.
†Could this be the Gaspar referred to in the legend of the Three Wisemen?

fully human; I mean, the knowledge that generations of ignorant masses have buried beneath heaps of multicolored superstitions. Five times already, the colors of these deviations have changed, according to the winds that swept aside the five ages of our humanity, which are almost over; and according to the five races which have followed, one after the other, up until now.

"Your thought has penetrated my own, Brothers, so now you know that the Great Envoy of Moon-Sun whose glory I sing was among us only a short time ago. He was the Joseph of a little village whom several of you have known, the Jesus enrolled at the Krmel, then sent off to lands far away. The seven of us were privileged to recognize him in the land of the *Pharawon*. It was with a branch of acacia in his hand, resisting any analysis, that he put on the mantle of the traveler, seventeen years ago, in the company of two magi of the Brotherhood. His main goal was known as the realm of Ishwar, the crossroads of the thoughts and the races of humankind, and the precious crucible of humanity itself.

"He was no more than fourteen years old when his steps led him to a great white city known as Ie-Nagar,* which means 'the Creator's Rising Fire.' There the high priest Lamaas was teaching, Lamaas who was himself in quest of a vivifying synthesis of the highest knowledge. When he saw Brother Jesus coming toward him, he recognized in his gaze one of the great avatars of ancient times. He remembered the prestigious legislator of the people of Atl, then the wisdom of Zoroaster, which had filled his soul long ago. This was a great reunion, and Jesus, the Master of old, consented to become the pupil once more, in order to transcend what he had accomplished in times gone by. Only the true masters know that they will always remain pupils, Brothers, never forget this. No real humility will ever engender humiliation.

"Thus Jesus heard and studied, with Lamaas, the texts left by Gautama. The pupil became a Master once more, and donned the lion's mane, in order to gain access to his most secret lairs. The priests of this land, the children of Indra, wished to have him among them, and with them he learned the word of Krishna, his healing

---

*Today the city of Puri, India.

techniques, the reorganization of the atoms of life by drawing from the fluids of Nature, and finally, the transmutation of the elements. Now remember this: Indra was the vault of heaven, but he was also the night. There were jewels pulsating in his firmament, images of knowledge that could lead the world and all its beings, but there was also the darkness, that of dogma trying to absorb all, that of the castes creating division among all things.

"So Jesus left the priests and went to the people to speak of the Nameless One. This was in his twenty-first year. The Ganges and Varanasi* were the first to echo with his words of fire which, like a wind of love as well as reflection, swept aside all barriers. 'Learn how to recognize the Eternal One,' they proclaimed. 'Don't do good only from fear of evil.'

"In some places, the people wanted to rise up and shake off the brahmanic fetters. Only Lamaas and a few others understood. . . . They understood too that the Master was still learning, and that this land of Ishwar could not be his at that time.

"Jesus then went into retreat, and improved his art of handling images of sound, of fashioning the silhouettes that tightly envelop the ideas of the mind. But he had already spoken too much among the people, and when a priest tried to take his life, he understood that his path led him elsewhere. Do not think, my Brothers, that the light penetrates man in a single flash, even if it is the purest one. The being who will guide your lives, if you wish it so, has not always been as you will come to know him. He has become who he is because he knew that nothing that is authentic is given straight away. He knew that he had to become the transmuter of his own bodies before he could be the powder of the ruby for others, as had been asked of him.

"The sage understands the meaning of this wisdom: 'There is no elect.' Nothing is given by the Nameless One to one of us more than to another. Nothing serves better to predestine a being than what he has accomplished in the past and what he accepts to build today. Thus, my Brothers, there is no such thing as luck. Never say, 'That one is lucky, for the Father has chosen him to do His work.'

*Benares.

And if you use this word, 'luck', you must realize that 'luck' is not the reflection of divine grace; each of us has created his own 'luck', and we continue to do so with our own hands.

"No hierarchy in this world and in the multitude of other worlds is excluded from this law. All creatures are the architects of their own temples—past and to come. Your Brother Jesus has not always known what precise task would be his, nor exactly where he would undertake it. He had to learn to recognize his origin as well as his latent power; he had to open his heart to the ears of others until he could say, 'The others are nowhere but within myself. If I am not one in spirit with them, I will sing the Word of the Father off key.' These are truly the words of him who now deserves the title of Master. He pronounced them when he was among the seven in the royal chamber of the Great Pyramid, only a few moons ago."

Manethon interrupted his account for a moment, as we arrived on the outskirts of a little hamlet lodged in a hollow at the foot of a rocky hillock. An olive grove grew there where we halted for the night. At last, the Brother with the blue ring took up his tale once more as we sat around a crackling fire. One of us, as was the custom, threw several grains of resin onto the embers to melt, and the air was filled with fragrance.

"After leaving Lamaas, Jesus headed north, where the earth seems to converse with the heavens. It is a mountainous region, where the air is thin and where very few people go. Jesus knew whom he would find there. Many times already his soul had visited these places and had brought back clues to the understanding of his mission. He did not go there to expand his knowledge but to receive vibrations whose force was needed by his body. You must understand that places are like men; each one wants to be the bearer of messages as much as of energies. You must not cut yourself off from the places that call out to you. They are often capable of revealing our being, of transforming even our subtle nature. Believe me, these are not empty words . . . Jesus lived for several years in these highlands. There, he practiced some disciplines based on the mastery of breathing, and there his body, in ever more perfect union with the whole, began to vibrate differently, so that the mountaintops saw him as often in his etheric state as in the flesh. This part of our Earth, as you have been taught, is one of its vital centers, the heart, as we might say by way of analogy. In its ether there is a realm where beings control the events of our societies. It has many names, but we call it the White Star because of its total radiance and its purity. It is the guardian of all the traditions of the stars, it is the mother of our Brotherhood, the source of what motivates our actions. Ever since the dawn of time, ray-beings have lived, worked, and loved there, leaving to the kings of the world the illusion of governing. Each of these beings is associated with a flame of different color. This attribution is not arbitrary, but corresponds to the light, to the melodious note that emanates from each of them. They are the materialization of the quality they incarnate, with as much perfection as the Earth may bear. You will undoubtedly think I am telling you a tale, Brothers, such as those the nomads of the desert tell when the wind whips their faces and makes them seek the shelter of their tents. It is not so, I can assure you; this place is more real than the mountains over which we walk, though our eyes may be unable to see it. We are no more able to imagine it than the man blind from birth who tries to imagine the blue of the sky. There is matter, and there is matter! How ignorant is he who limits matter to what he can grasp in his two hands. The truth of this realm must only be revealed very gradually, Brothers, for human beings will continue for a long time to defile whatever their minds can neither understand nor accept.

You must remember from all this that it was there that Master Jesus fully understood the role he had been given. Then he left the continent of Ishwar and headed homeward, along with several of his former instructors, to the great despair of the people who wanted him to remain with them (but whom he would have led to armed revolt, which was the last thing he wished to do). He himself told me that his words were mainly misconstrued when he spoke of the 'land of Iesse', a land whose substance may be understood only by those hearts that go far beyond mere words.

"Thus Jesus came to know Chaldea and Babylon, rediscovering the traces of the one he had been long before, leafing through the texts of the Solar Prior,* and recapturing its essence, already tar-

---

*Which today is known as the Zend Avesta, and whose study was compulsory in all Essene schools.

nished by centuries of preaching. Still, one word was needed, one word only, to go a step further toward the progressive revelation that was organized from so far away, so very far beyond the stars, but also from so close to us, and to him.

"One more period of training was awaiting Master Jesus before he could receive the supreme consecration. Thus the priests of Orpheus, the sage Philo among them, made him welcome in Greece. An analysis was to be made of the advantages and the disadvantages of the form of polytheism founded long before by the beings of the White Star. This was yet another addition to the wealth of his knowledge. The masters of the high mountains, however, had not requested of Jesus a simple synthesis of the major lines of thought already in existence. Synthesis is just a sort of compilation that enables one to see more clearly, but it brings nothing new. In no way does it provide a way of attaining a higher level of consciousness. It satisfies the intellect and the ego, but rarely more than this.

"No, this was not the task set before the One we were all awaiting. Our Brotherhood has taught you that the different bodies of our being are superimposed, overlapping layers. You know that they develop as we grow in years, but depend essentially upon the inner work to which we submit ourselves. These bodies are like seven successive flames we must help to grow, then connect with one another. They are like an unbroken golden chain, linking you to the supreme consciousness, like a pure, unimpeded channel of love that enables the so-called lower and higher energies to come together.

"The one who comes into permanent contact with the seven vehicles, or bodies, of one's being is no longer bound to this world of matter. This one has mastered its laws and may be called an adept. But let us be clear, for as you know the ascent of a being does not stop there. Other flames of consciousness remain to be mastered before one may reach the threshold of the Father's dwelling. It was these other flames that Jesus was sent to gather from the moment of his birth, in order to perfect a body and a transcendental soul that some people already regarded as perfect, such that the honors they would have bestowed upon him might have caused stagnation in themselves.

"The highest state of sublimation was attained, as I have told you, in the heart of the Great Pyramid at the precise spot where all the energies may be focused into a single point, which links a being's seed-atom with the Spirit of that creation. Thus the Spirit of Christ penetrated that of Jesus. This could not have been accomplished elsewhere nor otherwise; so it had been planned ever since the arrival of the Melchizedech on this Earth. Still, one of them had to be capable of keeping the pledge to its very end, without slowing his pace. Indeed, make no mistake, whosoever comes into this world makes an alliance with Shatan, and to a certain extent submits to his law. Shatan is none other than the great adversary, whose other name is 'density'. By this I mean that every being who is born on this Earth dons a heavy cloak that weighs upon his progress. The incarnation of an avatar would be an unbearable suffering if his primary energy was not that of incommensurable love.

"Imagine for an instant, Brothers, that your consciousness, your reason, your will, that in a word your very soul were to be suddenly enclosed within the body of an animal. Imagine the things you could no longer do, the thoughts you could no longer express fully. So by way of analogy those of us who are humble will admit that there is as much difference between the Master and themselves as there is between themselves and the animals. Master Jesus's soul was not born of this world, this you have understood. It flew along with others, from Ishtar, long ago when the creatures of this Earth missed a turning point in their evolution.

"His soul is nevertheless a part of the same wave of life that created you and me, emanating from the Father of this universe. The truth is that some pupils are quicker than others. Some prefer to remain children rather than become adults, even to the point of refusing to open the doors of illusion they have themselves closed.

"So can be summed up the adventure, the drama in which the children of this Earth are called to act, Brothers . . . and the trouble begins when certain of these children assume powers that should be reserved for adults."

We rekindled the dying fire and as Manethon fell into a long silence, we thought he had ended his account. Then one of us blurted out a question, a naive question perhaps, but one that we were all undoubtedly turning over in our hearts.

"Brother, should we now follow Master Jesus, for you say that he is the only one on this Earth to have lit all seven inner lamps of consciousness, plus those beyond?"

"You see clearly in this," replied Manethon, "but it is not Master Jesus you will follow. This Master is now sleeping, just as Joseph one day faded from this reality. It is not only Christ you will listen to either, but the Solar Spirit of the Logos of our universe, He who, this very morning before your own eyes, invested the body of Jesus-Christ. Have you understood this? Have you really understood the importance of these moments, when we all drank from the same cup of joy?"

Manethon was quiet again for a while, and silence hung over us as we all seemed to search our innermost depths. Some eyes stared into the glowing embers, others were shut, shoulders sank into the folds of our cloaks. What was the meaning of such words? The scriptures spoke of Christ, the people's Anointed . . . and at last we had thought we understood, that this was Joseph, whom we could not even yet bring ourselves to call Jesus. And now we had to come to terms with the Logos! Manethon spoke again, stressing each syllable, as if to engrave key words into our memories forever.

"Christ is a being other than Master Jesus . . . Christ is the most advanced master of a whole other wave of life emitted by the Father before our own. He is the regent of our universe, the accomplished man, so luminous, so sublimated that if he were to come directly into dense matter, he would create cataclysms. As for the Logos, the 'atoms' of his being could pulverize our own by the rapidity of their dance.

"'Mihael' is the earthly transcription of his cosmic name. Keep this deep in your hearts for we must avoid casting jewels where they would not be recognized. This is one of the fundamental rules of our Brotherhood, do not forget it. This name, Mihael, sums up what you may know of that with which Kristos has been endued. Remember the exercises to practice the soft voice dear to those of Essania. The first syllable of his name, *mi*, is the vibratory basis of the exercises we used to acquire the soft voice of every Essene. What our hearts hear in *mi* is the second vibration of the triplicity of the

Nameless One. This is the very reflection of the breath of creation.*
This is one of the forces that unites him to us, and also one of the
forces you will have to share with others.

"Thus, as you now understand, only the perfection of Master
Jesus' vehicles could enable him to be invested by the continuing
presence of Christ and of the Logos. Since this morning, my
Brothers, three great beings are alive in a single body, the third
radiating into the first two in such a way as to give them unlimited
power, a capacity of love that will flow into us like a thousand
streams.

"From this time on it is up to you to know what you must do.
Many souls are ready to cross the threshold, but will you be among
those who will help them to understand? Life is such that if today
begins a new era of responses, the era of questions begins as well.
You can't offer freedom to those who want neither choice nor free
will."

When dawn spread its first golden light, few of us had been able
to sleep. Simon, who as usual said little, volunteered to go and fetch
water from the village well. We still had a long way to go before
reaching Bethany, and once we had finished our ritual ablutions we
set out once more, carrying a full basket of dates. From then on
every step on the path was taken for one reason only: to set eyes
once again on the One who had come.

*This refers to the triad do-mi-sol (C E G), often used in the oriental AUM as well as in
Gregorian chant.

CHAPTER · III

WHERE ARE YOUR REAL WEAPONS?

Bethany was a little, white-terraced village, half hidden in a palm grove. For us it was an oasis of cool shade where we spent several days in meditation. We did not quite know what to do, nor how to rejoin the true Master who at last had revealed himself to us. The joy of the news we had received flowed through us in deep waves, at times giving rise to such exaltation that we had some difficulty in keeping to the daily rites prescribed by the Brotherhood.

Within the silence of my innermost self, I asked, as did many others, "What good is all this, now that we are to follow the Master who will show us the way?" And a dialogue was started, my mind arguing as in reply: "What? Can the truth be swept away by a single being? Must the whole Brotherhood of Essania bow down before him?"

We stayed in Bethany for several weeks manning a bethsaïd at the edge of the village on the road to Jerusalem. As time passed we became aware of a mounting excitement among the people. We soon understood that it had spread from the banks of the river Jordan, and for the first time in one of the shops in the village we heard talk of a Messiah who had come to liberate the land of Palestine. We could not but add our accounts to those rumors, but we were careful not to insist too heavily. Our white robes always tended to inspire a certain reserve, and under no circumstances should the Master be taken for one more Nazarite or Nazarene spokesman.

Manethon left us, preferring to go back to Heliopolis where the mother group of the Brotherhood was probably waiting for a detailed account of the recent events. Following his advice, we left Bethany to move farther north into the heart of Galilee, as far as the shores of Lake Tiberias. The farther we went, the clearer our itinerary seemed to become. News of the arrival of the Master appeared to have spread throughout the land like wildfire. We passed through Gennesaret, where there had been another uprising incited by the announcement that the liberator was at hand. From there we took the road to Capernaum.

Rumors came to our ears, whispered almost stealthily: "He is over there. He has just come from the deserts of the land of the Red Earth . . . as was prophesied!" Indeed, the most ancient prophecies in the archives of the Brotherhood did announce this coming.

But what was happening? While we were waiting for the Awakener of souls sent by the All-Highest, it seemed that the whole of Palestine was ready to revolt. Was it the weapon or the Word that had been sent to us?

Capernaum opened its arms to us, with its marble houses, its majestic synagogue, and its marketplace, fragrant with all the treasures of Galilee. What a contrast to the harshness of the desert we had just left behind! The most subtle perfumes wafted through the streets, and it was with joy that we rediscovered the scarlet blossoms of the pomegranate trees standing out against the background of a deep blue sky. The city was calm and from the lake spread a cool tranquility. All the past discord might have been forgotten if it had not been for the leather-clad legionaries who were lingering in small groups here and there in the city.

Master Jesus was there, as we had thought. Perhaps it was some memory of the Joseph of his childhood that had drawn him to these shores not far from our little village of so long ago. From a sort of public square shaded by almond trees, narrow streets led into the mountain, toward Chorazin. There we found a gathering of a hundred people; the Master was among them, the center, the heart of the group. At first we could not see him. Row upon row of men and women formed a sort of rampart around him, but we were able to hear his voice. This was proof enough for us, if proof was needed, that our lives had not been lived in vain.

All we could see were multicolored backs, shoulders burnt by the sun and baskets balanced on heads. From somewhere in their midst came a voice, as palpable but as impossible to grasp as a cool wave; a gentle, friendly voice that, nevertheless, possessed a note of authority. At last the people in front of us decided to sit down and for the second time the Master appeared before our eyes.

"Now you must lay down your weapons," he was saying; "the Father has sent me to you so that you lay down your weapons. But where are your real weapons? These swords and knives I can see hanging from some of your belts? Or these thoughts that day by day ruin and waste your hearts? Tell me, children of Capernaum, is the real evil in the weapon or is it hiding within the idea of the weapon? By killing your enemies you kill yourselves with the poison of your ideas. I can assure you, freedom will only rise out of purity; only purity will lead you to the real land of Canaan for all men and women, to my Father's promised land."

An old woman rose out of the crowd. She had sharp, questioning eyes, as hard as the pebbles on the shores of the lake, and the color of its storms, as dark as the revolt of its fishermen.

"So who are you, Master," she cried, "you who speak in the name of the Highest? Is not the idea of Rome the scourge of this Earth?"

A murmur, almost of dissatisfaction had risen from the crowd. Who was this woman to dare take part in public discussions, dealing moreover with religious matters.

"I am the Word of the Father, Tisbeh," the Master answered. "It is your heart that has moved you to speak, and it is to your heart that I will reply. I ask you, what is evil if it is not the absence of love? Can you see the color of the eyes of the men you meet at dusk? In the same way the soul darkened by hatred is unable to discern the Father's plan. What do you know of your enemy if you have not seen the human being in him? What do you know of the forces that have led him to you? I can assure you, the one who sees the enemy in another contemplates his own image deformed by a mirror. He feeds on his own rancor and condemns himself to live among the shadows.

"There is in this world only one weapon that deserves to be honored, the only weapon furbished for you by your Father: Love. So love one another as I love you! Does the sun send its rays to one of you more than to another?"

The Master was silent, and for a long while nothing happened. Nothing happened? How could we dare say for sure? There are moments when words are superfluous, seconds during which one may search one's soul and find out more than in a thousand years. These were no doubt such moments, when one met another's gaze and understood the essence. But how long would we retain our understanding? We had to grasp this ultimate feeling and not let it go. Some in the crowd stood and approached the Master, who himself had got up. I did not hear their words, but between two women pushing on in front of me, I saw the tall white form of the Master as he placed his two hands on the forehead of a very dark little man wearing a plain gray tunic.

Simon, the others, and I wanted to go forward and tell him that we were there, ready to listen to him, to speak with him, to follow him. However, two or three men, apparently disappointed, left the crowd, insensitive to the presence which moved us so.

"Myriam," Zerah had once said to me, one day when we were alone in the mountains, not far from the village, "if you gave some gold to your donkey, what do you think it could do with it? Even if that gold was to be brought to it by a king in a silver manger the animal would still prefer a handful of fodder left over from last winter. Thus it is with people as well; as it is said, to each his own. The path of evolution is a long one, and the perception of what is authentic is acquired only with difficulty. To those who can only see divinity among the trees, speak of a god who turned into a tree. Learn to accept differences, for you cannot force spiritual gold on people."

At last we were able to approach. He stood there before us

with all the simplicity of long ago, and still so different. His bearing was the same, his eyes were still full of the same kindness, with something more, something like lightning that carried us away, so far. . . . He was still wearing the Brotherhood rosary composed of one hundred and eight beads, but the little black bag that had hung at his chest was gone. Our gazes met.

"That is good," he said simply, "that is good."

He came forward and embraced us, openly showing that he recognized us, that he remembered. No words could capture these moments. Then he took two steps back and added, warmly, "I ask you to wait a while longer . . . a very short while, in truth. Your hour is approaching."

We were overcome with emotion. One of us started to kneel, but the crowd was gaining on us and we were absorbed by the flood of people. I saw Simon hoist himself onto an old millstone, and he held out his hand for me to climb up beside him. Our equilibrium was more than precarious, but we could see, and that was all that mattered. The crowd had grown out of all proportion, and looking back on that scene it was as if all Capernaum had gathered there, suddenly, some perhaps without even knowing why, others because they had just begun to understand. They were those who, for ages, had been willing to mold their beings, to be ready for the day when they would stand before a presence, the Presence. From the top of our millstone, we could see men and women who were striving to understand and others who thought they already understood, all together forming a motley crowd.

The Master drew off at last into a shaded narrow alleyway, followed by two Brothers we did not know and the dark little man he had blessed. Overwhelmed with an intense emotion, the gathering slowly began to disperse and we walked down toward the shores of the lake. There we saw fishermen who, unaware of what was happening, were emptying their nets and filling little baskets with their still flapping fish.

We had to rest and to wait for what we called the "signs of fate" that would help us to understand where we would be needed.

That night we slept out under the stars. The following morning we learned that the Master had left the village, and was walking along the lakeshore, visiting the isolated dwellings and the little fishing villages. We stayed where we were and waited calmly until a few days later, when we were aroused by a shout from the road to Beth Saïda. Three men were running on the road lined with big fig trees. We stood up and saw, coming toward them down from the mountains, a small group of people who were walking at a fairly good pace. We quickly recognized the Master among them because of his height, and also because of something else, something we could not name, that told us: "It is he." Were we expected to jump up and run to him as the three men were doing? We were not sure. He would probably tell us to wait once more, and after all, what could we suggest to him that he had not already decided to do? Even so, we timidly walked forward to meet him. He greeted us and in so doing he closed the inner distance between us.

"Jacob, Myriam, Simon, Saul, and Esther, come closer and recognize these men as your own. From now on, they will be by my side, for my Father needs them."

The four men he introduced were of varying heights, but all had steadfast gazes. Their hands were calloused, their tunics patched, and they did not look like the scribes who most often surrounded priests and doctors. We did not learn their names immediately but this did not matter, since he had already accepted them among us. Seeing that they were not wearing the robes of white linen, our eyes must have reflected our surprise, for the Master added, "Do not look so astonished. A hard worker is not to be recognized by the quality of his loincloth but by the breadth of his shoulders. Listen to my words, for the children of the sun may be recruited from all the lands of the Earth; no two of them wear the same cloak, though all speak the same language. What I have to say to you is not only for the ears of the Brothers of Essania. Now the age of unlimited sharing begins, and no doubt many will be shocked. The Father calls out for men who pray, men who heal, but also for men who act like leaven, those who are to be found in the very heart of the people."

Then the Master was silent and his gaze seemed to lose itself over the lake, beyond the gray mountains that rose on the far shore.

"We must go," he said gently. "We have so much to do." And he glanced our way, giving us to understand that we were accepted.

We had almost forgotten the three men who had been running up the road a few moments before and who had drawn back, perhaps intimidated by the gathering of the long linen robes. Before they could speak, the Master put a hand on the shoulder of one of them and asked, "Where are you leading me?"

"To my son, Rabbi, if you will," he replied. "I have been looking for you for two days. There are fishermen and merchants saying that you are the Messiah spoken of by the ancient prophets. They say that you can do anything . . . anything!"

The man, about forty years old, was beginning to tremble and found it hard to go on.

"My son has been unable to walk for two years now . . . I thought you might be able to ask the Eternal One. . . . "

The Master gazed at the man steadily, then smiled at him, and replied simply, "The most important thing, you see, is that you have already asked the Eternal One."

The man was visibly at a loss for what to think and all he could do was to point the way to his home with embarrased gestures. Our little group took the path back to Capernaum, from which we had not gone far. The Master led the way, preceded at times by those who had come to request his help, but who felt uneasy about it. As for us, we chose to hold back a few paces, leaving the Master with the four men he had introduced to us. Now and then he gazed back at us with an amused look full of tenderness. What more could we wish for? It seemed that ages passed in this way, time crumbled into eternity, and everything else could wait because he was with us. No words have ever been able to convey such emotion; they can only make a parody of it, deforming it by projecting nothing but its shadow, open to ridicule. Yet the emotion of these moments is not the only thing preserved by my soul; there is something else, something even more subtle based on a sort of tangible knowing, which cannot be communicated.

Morning was drawing to its end when we reached the first poor dwellings of Capernaum, white and ochre blocks that soon gave way to the wealthy homes of the town. A small group of children in rags ran to meet us and then, as if aware of our destination, led us on through the maze of streets. We walked past Sadducean houses with their impressive marble pillars. The whole place was bathed in a pale bluish light and we let ourselves be guided to a narrow lane situated behind the synagogue. The three men halted before a rather large house and climbed up a ladder that gave access to a terrace above. The Master went up at once, and we decided to follow him. It was a large terrace bordered by great basins filled with soil, where clusters of white and violet flowers grew. From there we had a beautiful view of the Sea of Galilee, blue with patches of sparkling white. Other ladders led upward to other terraces and to inner rooms, but we did not climb any farther. Following the three men, the Master stepped over to one corner of the terrace where a rope bed had been stretched beneath the shelter of two high daub walls. There lay a young man of about twenty, propped up on his elbows.

"He has been lying like that for two years now," said one of the men, approaching. "He had a high fever and since then, he has been unable to walk or even get up."

The young man smiled at us and made a gesture of welcome, obviously unaware of the identity of this tall man in white who had already taken his hand. When the Master knelt at his side, however, the look on his face changed, showing both puzzlement and surprise. Who were these Nazarites who had crossed his threshold in such a way?

We watched as the Master raised his left hand to his heart and with his right pressed the hand he had already taken. He shut his eyes, and the paralyzed young man stretched out abruptly as if shaken by a spasm and leaving his whole body trembling. We were ready to intone one of our chants to assist the Master, as was the practice among the members of the Brotherhood, but he had already released the man's wrist and his eyes were once more open. The young man raised himself to his elbows again and two tears were forming in the corners of his eyes. He pretended to be surprised at this, with a small twist of a smile and a raise of his eyebrows, but the extreme pallor that had come over his face showed how much he had been shaken.

The Master then rose and declared imperatively, "Come!"

His voice echoed on the nearby terraces where we noticed then that groups of men and women had gathered. Still seized by long spasms the paralyzed man lowered his two feet to the floor and with great effort raised himself on his legs. A complete silence seemed to fall over the whole town. It was a living silence that swallowed even the strident cries of the flocks of birds soaring over the surface of the lake.

The young man stepped forward with one foot then the other, jerkily, and began walking all over the terrace with the wide eyes of a child discovering how to walk. From the nearby rooftop terraces came a resounding explosion of joy and we could hear the news spreading through the streets below. The young man and his father remained mute, as we all did. We had witnessed this event perhaps from too close up to be able to grasp all its implications.

At last one of the three men who had escorted us managed to utter a sound: "Rabbi! Rabbi!"

"Remember this" said the Master, "It takes only one man to make a request of my father and he will be answered; it takes only three men to ask in my name, with a single impulse and their wish will be fulfilled. This I can assure you."

He smiled and then embraced the three men who had called for him. Then without further delay, he walked toward the ladder. I felt as if my mind was suddenly drained. I could not manage to think, to formulate even a single coherent idea. We all followed the Master and in no time we were once again in the street, engulfed by a shouting motley crowd.

What had happened? Simon and I had, of course, seen such wonders; our long years of healing work in villages all over the land had enabled us to witness more than one sudden cure of this sort, most often carried out by an aged brother who would lose himself in endless prayers, his hands on the patient's forehead. Of course, we knew that the spirit was all-powerful; we had been given evidence of this, countless times, on all the paths and hillsides of Galilee and Judaea . . . but such ease . . . such apparent lack of technique . . . such promptness in emitting the wave of the purest love! This was what overcame me . . . and then there was his gaze that penetrated us all the way down to our very core!

It was not easy to thread our way through the growing throng.

How had the news spread so quickly? Had it been some sort of inner call felt by the multitudes—a whisper of intuition saying, "You must be there!" Our white robes had the effect of associating us with the wonder that had just occurred and Simon and I felt somewhat embarrassed. We had done nothing and deserved no attention whatsoever. We had to summon up all the reserve the Brothers had taught us, to bring back with a few warm syllables the sort of calm around us that our hearts were longing for. This was a technique considered to be one of the secrets of the Brotherhood, and was in no case to be used frequently nor divulged. Sounds may bear silence just as they may bear noise, and may engender peace as well as war. There are some which act as quick as lightning upon the soul of a crowd. It is all a matter of breath, of rhythm, and of focusing the will on a specific spot. This knowledge was a double-edged sword, as we knew. It might enable one to manipulate masses of people and was to be used only with extreme parsimony, since it left so little room for the play of free will. Calm settled quickly over the crowd and in a moment people were whispering to each other softly, commenting on what they had just seen.

Only then did we realize that the Master was no longer among us. The four men he had introduced us to were still there, but he himself had apparently vanished into thin air. We did our best to do the same, having no other desire than to find him. Only later that evening did we come upon him a little outside of the town on the shore of the lake, where he had found shelter beneath an overturned skiff. As we approached we saw there was an animal with him, a goat, and he seemed to be murmuring to it. After a brief exchange of greetings Simon was the first to mention what our hearts could hardly contain.

"Master," he said, "this miracle—"

"What miracle, Simon?" he replied softly, leaving us at a loss for words. "Have you so quickly forgotten the teachings of the Krmel? What the Father has sent through me today should not make you forget the laws of Nature that are for all of us always the same.

"The real miracle, the only miracle, is the life we breathe. The sad thing is that all the beings on this earth cannot perceive it. They go through life without grasping all the little ferments that are just waiting to become forces of healing. Miracles are for those whose hearts are blind, my Brothers; do not pretend you have forgotten this! All the force of the worlds is at your fingertips. You may sometimes see it sparkling within your hearts when you meditate, or when you pray. Give your willpower, your hands, to your heart and you will direct this force as and wherever it is needed. You will not be able to command this force with your minds, as it rebels against order. I tell you truly, to control any wave of life you must be its eternal lover; you must become the wave itself, without a glance behind you, or around you.

"Use this cool wave as you will, my Brothers, it has been put in the great surrounding cosmic reservoir by the Father to suit your purpose. Thus, you may be sure that you are within the Force. It is your consciousness of being yourself, one little being isolated from all the others, and your far too analytical thinking, that prevent you from taking hold of the Force, in one flash, and from breathing it into matter that calls out for it.

"Do not forget my words, you seekers! Techniques are the disciplines of the body and the mind, and they can change the course of things, and of beings—but how long will it take? So practice them up to a point—in the hope of awakening the technique of the heart. The heart is simply all-powerful, and forever so. We may stifle it or we may listen to it. Often we think we are listening to it, though we are hardly letting it breathe beneath the weight of reason and the excuses of the mind. You are aware that I am not speaking of the heart that beats inside us, in time with the seasons. I am speaking of the inner sun which links us to the chain of transcendental worlds. You are in the universe of being, Brothers, be now in the universe of becoming. Abolish all barriers, for they subject you for a while to techniques and to time itself. Learn simply to ask, without worrying about the answer, for the answer is always the same: Yes. The force of my Father is unconditionally yours, as it is anyone's. Do you not even hear within yourselves the echo of his eternal will, of his presence?"

We kept silent, hardly daring to breathe, the better to absorb the flood of light that poured from the Master into our hearts. Each of his words was a world to explore, a resonant blue star weaving a pattern of peace. We were all sitting on the boulders that lined the shore with the wind from the lake blowing in our hair. At last the sun set and we felt it better to leave the Master there alone.

In the following days we saw little of him in the streets of Capernaum though from time to time we met one of the four men who accompanied him. This one had the sturdy look of a fisherman, with the guileless smile of one who is loyal, and who gives himself wholly with a single glance. He said his name was Andrew, and told us that the Master was spending his time in the countryside around the lake. We finally decided to remain for a time in Capernaum. With the agreement of the council of Brothers in Jerusalem, from whom we had heard, we took it upon ourselves to open a little bethsaïd near the edge of town, on the road to Magdala. This gave us something to do and afforded us time to wait for a sign from the Master. We heard his name pronounced often in conversations overheard in the harbor or on the steps of the synagogue. Many spoke of him as the Great White Rabbi or the Nazarite, which always upset us a bit. We found that many stories concerning him had spread, few of which were true. There was talk of his prodigious healing in the little nearby villages. Once a rabbi violently interrupted such a conversation, urging the people not to trust those accounts. What disturbed us most, however, were the outbursts of the Zealots exacerbated by the rumors. They were determined to find a Messiah who would brandish the sword.

Finally one morning we recognized the Master sitting beneath a doorway near the little square. There was already a big throng around him, listening to him talk about the only Earth in which they could have hope. At his side were about a dozen men, two of whom must have belonged to our people.

At the same time that peace was being urged upon those who were listening, a small group of Roman soldiers suddenly broke upon the square and dispersed the crowd with a great outburst of shouting. The Master did not say a word and we watched as he walked over to the side of the centurion's mount and placed his hand on the horse's forehead.

All at once we felt irrationally joyful. Perhaps we understood that a message that disturbs is a message that is beginning to be heard.

CHAPTER · IV

FOOD AND
TABERNACLES

A t times the Master stayed in our bethsaïd, but he delighted in making clear to the people of Capernaum that his heart belonged to the Brothers in white no more than to the rest of Palestine. For that reason he used to accept any invitation, no matter who offered it. At first we could feel that curiosity as much as respect was the underlying motive of those who invited the "Great Rabbi in White." The Sadducees and the Pharisees alone resolutely maintained their habitual reserve. When heated arguments were heard among the colonnades in the synagogue, we sensed that they were concerned about the Master's sudden appearance in the region. What was he after? they wondered. What was the goal of this Nazarite who failed to observe the reserve typical of other Nazarites, who healed the people and who dared claim he was the son of the Eternal One? The Master's presence was disturbing, his self-assurance embarrassing.

As the weeks passed, his tall figure in the markets and the ports of the little lakeshore villages became a familiar sight. It was known that at certain times of the day he would most likely be in such and such a place, and so he was. The priests became involved in the discussions he inspired among the people who thronged about him. As a rule, he used to base his talks on some everyday occurrence, something that had just happened "by chance" to people he met on his way. I am now convinced that he somehow called forth these chance happenings. He had a way of knowing who or what would cross his path, and how he could make use of it in spreading the Word.

We weren't able to follow him everywhere he went, as the bethsaïd, which became busier and busier, took up much of our time. Nevertheless, whenever possible we discreetly accompanied him through the streets of Capernaum on his daily walk that had become a sort of ritual.

I remember one of these occasions. The little market under the arcades was just coming to life that morning. The merchants in their ample, earth-colored robes were still unpacking their wares, and fishermen wearing short tunics were just laying out their silvery catch on the great stone slabs of the marketplace. Camels and donkeys were constantly in the way, no matter where they were tethered. The Master stopped in front of one of the stalls where several men were arguing over the parts of a butchered sheep.

"My Father would be pleased if you could argue so vehemently about the way to put his Word into practice," he said, with an air of amused exasperation, much to the delight of the early shoppers in the market, who burst into laughter. A little circle who enjoyed a good joke formed quickly around the "rabbi."

I noticed a Sadducee among the crowd, dressed in a rich, shimmering robe, his fingers laden with heavy rings, who seemed not at all unhappy to have the chance to benefit from an exchange, that in other circumstances might have cost him his reputation. Others joined in the fun, but the Master, with his strong yet gentle voice, cut this short.

"My words are in no way intended to make fun of you, my Brothers; I appreciate the ardor with which you seek your nourishment. My Father likes to see you take care of the body he gave you to harbor your soul."

These words caused the onlookers to pause, and a hush fell

upon the crowd. It was more customary for the priests, the doctors, and members of ascetic groups to preach the virtue of fasting.

"Look, my Brothers, at this big, wonderful house you have built for the Eternal One," he said, pointing to one corner of the synagogue. "Look at these colonnades under which you listen to the discourses on the law. You can see them from here, look how sturdy they are. Think of the love and the force that you or your fathers put into carving the foundation stones. Truly, I can assure you that your body is just like this house that rises toward the heavens. It has all the value and promise of a cornerstone. Thus must one work on the base that enables one to rise toward the kingdom.

"But what would you think of a builder whose art consisted in piling all sorts of stones one on the other, without distinction as to how or what sort? What would you think of a builder who had no regard for the grain of the stone, who knew nothing of squares and chisels that give to the work the craftsmanship it deserves? You would think him mad. Truly I say to you, my Brothers, behave in such a way that the Father who lives within you will have no reason to complain about his temple. I do not preach to you about the dimensions nor the quality of the stones you make your own; I am speaking about the heart that makes it possible for you to grasp their meaning and their purpose. I am speaking also for the heart that helps you to understand their origin. Thus, you will not kill in order to satisfy the demands of your body, without first making sure of the constructive finality of such an act. You are fond of animal flesh but be careful that the animal doesn't leave too big a trace in your own flesh, as it may impart upon you its primary vitality.*

"It is the force that your souls still impose upon this Earth that causes you to crave such food. Let those who may, remember the words from the ancient scripture: I offer you all the grasses bearing seed on the surface of the whole Earth, and all the trees bearing fruit and giving seed; this will be your food.'"†

"Do you mean, Rabbi," someone asked, "that we must abstain from all meat?"

---

*Certainly an allusion to the etheric body of the animal present in meat, but which is reduced in the flesh of animals that have been bled.
†Gen. 1:29.

"I mean," he replied, "that a ready heart finds the path all by itself, and can keep to it without effort. If your body craves animal flesh, give it animal flesh, but be aware that with it, as with all things, you absorb a parcel of the Father, a grain of his Life that has germinated with love and that is given to you with love."

These words, which reflected the opinion of the Brotherhood, caused a sensation among the throng. Several of those present even reacted in scorn or mockery and walked away. Questions were flung from all directions but the man who must have been a Sadducee, raised his voice above the others.

"How can you say, Rabbi, that the Eternal One dwells within all things? If this were true, how could I dare to eat anything?"

Some smiled at this, and the Master said nothing in reply but made his way through the people over to a little stall where hunks of meat were piled high. He took one and handed it around, offering it to whoever wanted it. All were silent, not knowing what he meant by this. Then, in the palm of his outstretched hand tiny blue and white flames flickered into life, crackling and licking the edges of the morsel of meat. It was as if there were a burning gas or some secret energy that flared up, then dispersed in little puffs of life.

The people stepped back a pace.

"He is a magician!" someone cried, "we must report him to the Sanhedrin!"

"Where do you see magic, my Brothers? You wanted an answer and your Father himself spoke to you. Do you think he is so far away that he cannot hear you? So I can assure you, and may these words remain forever in your hearts: Every day you partake of my Father who gives himself willingly; you take his life. So you must be the purest tabernacles for this life that you take. Learn to transform your appetite for material things into love for the Eternal One, who sleeps within the objects of your desire. In this way you will come to know the Divine, which shines in all things. Here begins the true path."

At this point, what sounded like a scuffle broke out in the crowd and we heard John, Andrew, James, and others calling to each other. A group formed around the Master as if to protect him, but he was quick to free himself from their circle.

Two women and three men were trying vainly to elbow their way through the crowd of people gathered in the little square. I saw the Master's tall white form slowly move toward them, place a hand on each of their foreheads, then slip between two market stands and vanish into a little alleyway. We made no effort to follow him, for we were beginning to understand his recurrent need for solitude. Then timidly we attempted to explain to those who lingered on what we thought the "rabbi" had meant.

Andrew, John, and the eight others who were with them, tried to do likewise, and perhaps their poor, patched robes made this easier for them, in a sense, lending them a sort of honest credibility. In the eyes of many we represented a philosophy, and this made things more difficult for us. We dared not mingle with Andrew and his companions. The Master seemed to have chosen them, and perhaps tested them individually. As for us, we wondered if our goal would ever become clear.

"Patience forges the soul," we told each other, hoping at the same time that it wouldn't also blunt its edge. All this waiting was gnawing at the self within each of us, as we were well aware, but for some it came close to tarnishing the joy that we felt flooding the streets of Capernaum.

The following morning we went up into the mountains. We needed some herbs for our decoctions. Before the onset of the scorching summer months, we had to gather the herbs at dawn, at the precise moment when the force rising from the Earth forms pearls of shining dewdrops in the hollows of the flowercups. One of the Brotherhood's customs was to roll naked in the morning dew. This was said to have the effect of recharging the vital body, of giving it a youthfulness that many potions tried in vain to restore. Ancient tradition had it that a little of the Earth Mother and Cosmic Father were to be found in every drop of dew, something like the wedding of a single force now differentiated, a union of two apparently contrary principles. This union could engender a sort of liquid gold, if only we could catch the moment when the sun darts its first rays over the Earth.

That morning four of us—two women of the Brotherhood, Simon, and I—were making our way up the side of the mountain when we met a slender man with very dark hair. He called out to us, and we recognized him as one of Andrew's companions. He was heading our way, walking surprisingly fast, and his red, calf-length robe whipped around his legs in the cool morning breeze. Was it us he wanted to see? How could he possibly know we were there? It turned out that he was indeed looking for us, certain he would find us there.

"The Master is up there if you wish to see him," he said, pointing to the rounded top of the mountain, dotted with huge gray rocks. We set off at once, cutting straight through the thornbushes, thistles, and myrtle and frightening away stray ewes startled by our sudden approach.

We found the Master sitting with his back up against what remained of an old tree trunk, talking there with two of those we had come to regard as his close disciples. We saluted him after the fashion of the Brotherhood and he returned our greeting. We did not know whether we should take part in the discussion or not; it was obviously dealing with what had been said in town the day before.

"Teach the people to work on the base of their beings," he was saying, in a voice that was like a chant. "You would like them to have wings to fly, while in reality they have yet to find their feet. If they do not recognize the Earth as the Mother who feeds them, who nurses them, you may expect that they will spend their whole lives desperately seeking my Father.

"One of your tasks, you whose hearts aspire to open the hearts of others, is to teach the people of the Earth to purify themselves from the base up. By this, I mean to help them become aware of the divinity inherent in even the smallest of things and to live accordingly. It may seem to you that you can succeed in this easily, but make no mistake, for it is easy to persuade people. The one who speaks from the heart uses the full weight of his words. Your task is not to persuade people but to make them understand, and truly the two terms stand worlds apart. One who is persuaded is only the plaything of his intellect and words make him fluctuate according to the fancies of philosophies; one who understands is one who knows, for he has plunged into his own essence. 'So,' you will say in the name of my Father, 'look deep within your inner being, you who seek without realizing that you have already found; you who are already men and who possess all things within you.' But be careful, my Brothers, to teach only what your souls are now able to live. If your cup of love is only half full, very few indeed will be able to drink from it. In the name of all that enables us to live these moments, I ask you to reform your bodies so that you may transcend those of the multitudes. Learn to eat the eternal essence in all the food of the Earth. Let every meal be a celebration. The primordial art of true humanity consists in taming one's food, making it vibrate in rhythm with one's own body.

"These are not just words that I am offering you, but the description of a concrete yet infinitely subtle phenomenon. To tame your food is to tame your thoughts, which represent the only force that may either poison or purify your food. If you were able to see where and how your celestial creation took place, you would not dare anymore to give your body even one-fourth of what you are accustomed to feeding it. You must vivify matter as you eat it. You must understand too that as you eat matter, you serve the great plan of creation, for you have the gift of sublimating what you absorb. It is not the work of your bodies that should strike you as being essential in this, but that of the spirit you summon that issues its orders to your etheric flame. I tell you, Brothers, your love is capable of ordering your etheric being to alter the vital particles of anything you eat. It may cause these particles to be transmuted in view of other incarnations in realms of their own. Thus you see how great is the responsibility of human beings on this Earth. They are the sphere of exchanges, the field where the transmutation of forces takes place."

"Master," interrupted the man who had guided us, "what about wine? There are many merchants of Greek origin who come to this region, and who hold this drink to be sacred, although we can all see that it clouds one's reasoning."

"Have you not answered your own question, Jude? A man without reason is like a ship without a rudder. Even so, what is said by the Greeks is not altogether unfounded. What is true in Greece is also true in the land of the Red Earth; this country remains a privileged heir to the knowledge of the land of Atl, even if thousands of years ago it revolted against its rule.

"The preparation of fermented drinks was introduced to humanity toward the end of the domination by the continent of Atl. My Father's Elohim saw that the great majority of human beings had fallen into excessive materiality. The feats they accomplished by means of their rites were no longer in harmony with the omnipresence of the Great Force. They dominated by virtue of their willpower, while they were no longer aware of the realms it affected. Little by little they lost touch with their higher states of consciousness. Inspired by the stars, a high priest of the One, whose name was Mayan, taught the people to make a drink from fermented grain. This drink enabled one, through certain rites and in certain proportions, to experience the multiplicity of bodies that one can inhabit. This was not the wine we know today, which men themselves dicovered by analogy much later. This drink, my Brothers, had the capacity to offer redemption through the door it opened at one particular moment in history.* I can assure you that it did offer redemption, for its preparation and consumption were governed by rites that were respected in a state of mind similar to the one I have taught you.

"Now that you know these things, tell me if the use of wine seems advisable to you today, now that humanity is once more aware of the higher dimension of its being—even if this awareness is as yet very vague?"

"Then we must abstain from wine, Master?"

"I did not say that, Jude. To a certain extent you must conform to the times you live in. If you want to be heard, do not be too different from others. The difference that is willfully displayed is often the sign of unshakable pride. If you wish the divinity within you to be heard, do not turn your back on the humanity that serves as its support. If you do not respect this rule you will be feared more than loved. What you will say and do then be at once scattered to the winds.

"Thus, Jude, my Father has given me all the force that is promised to Man, but also all the attributes of a human being. I shall

---

*One can recognize in the drink the ancients' use of barley beer, mead, ambrosia, and soma.

drink the wine that is offered me. My willpower alone will limit the quantity. I am the reconciler, my Brothers, not the prophet of ascetics in the mountains!"

With these words, the Master rose and began to walk along the crest of the hilltop.

"What does it matter if they no longer know how to prepare wine? All you have to do is know how to drink it, while remembering my words. What is good for one era may be evil for another. Only when you have realized the Divine within you, will you fuse these two notions in your being, unifying them with the play of your love.

"What are you waiting for before you sublimate the dual tendencies in a single point of your being? The image of choice, in the form of the cross, has always been born from the encounter between the Earth and the Cosmos. Learn how to place yourself in its center; it is there that my Father's solar fire resides, and it is there that the quintessence will blossom within you."

We followed a mule path toward a place where tall cedar trees grew. The sun had not yet managed to pierce the morning mist, and as we walked we looked down on the lake, surrounded by an almost blinding, bluish light.

Walking in silence, Simon and I realized clearly that the Master's teaching offered two different aspects. One of them was addressed to the people of Palestine as a whole, the other to a smaller group of men and women among whom we were fortunate to be counted. For a time we thought this was in order to create a school reserved for an elite, but it was not so. The Master wished to speak to people according to their capacity to understand, and perhaps the ten who were following him more closely at this time had the benefit of a third form of teaching?

These apparent differences mattered little to us. We had learned to see them as yet another illusion, a trick of the mind, which is forever trying to take over everything in order to create divisions. The Master's words that we drank in were like a stairway leading us always upward, always further. On which step were we then standing? In the end, we did not even care since the stairway was one. We were walking beside a sun, and this was All to us.

CHAPTER · V

THE TREE WITH SEVEN ROOTS

W e came upon them time after time, in every town from Magdala to Tiberias. Among the crowds, curious faces attracted our attention. Sometimes it would be a rich landowner, sometimes a fisherman there with his whole family, or a vagabond who happened to be traveling that way, or even a merchant who looked embarrassed to linger on, unable to leave. Three months had passed since we had arrived on the shores of the Sea of Galilee, and we found ourselves in the midst of a group, as yet informal, which had formed around the person of the Master. None of us knew any of the others, or at least so it seemed, yet everything led us to believe that old souls were reuniting, wearing the masks of earthly roles and karmas. Though we could not find the words to express this, we were inwardly convinced that it was true. These souls met and met again, became entwined, though our only common language was that of silence. In the meantime, he to whom we dedicated our every breath went on, going here and there throughout the region with surprising speed, lingering in the squares and marketplaces of every village, along every shore. It was as if he wished to appreciate the different atmospheres, and to leave a tangible trace of his passing. The healings and discourses were now countless. Groups of men and women arrived from Samaria and Judaea, and set up camps. The military and religious authorities turned a deaf ear to him, for the words of "the Nazarene" tended toward a general appeasement, and seemed to reflect just the opposite of any desire for power. In the eyes of many, he must have seemed to be just another prophet.

Very few Brothers of Essania showed themselves at our sides. We knew this had to be so, for most of them had been given orders not to frequent the Master too openly. These decisions came from the high council of Jerusalem, which had received the word from Heliopolis. It became clear that the Envoy had to remain pure from any preexisting doctrine, even if the body of Jesus linked him to the Brotherhood forever. As for us, we used discretion in our choice of a time and place to approach him and did not hesitate to leave our white robes for the tunic of a fisherman, or of any other man or woman from among the people. That was how we were dressed when we gathered around him a few times on the shores of the lake on the way to Magdala, some distance from any dwellings. Once more Jude acted as our guide. As we walked along the path, he seemed to be highly excited. Like others we had met, he was expecting something to happen soon. He said it was urgent for the whole of Palestine to rise up and for all, faced with the increasing number of spectacular healings, to become aware of the obvious. We must join forces with the Zealots, he argued, and combine force and faith. We listened in silence, somewhat troubled by the reactions of a man we had supposed far above such ideas. We wondered why he had been chosen when his heart was filled more with revolt than with peace. We had hardly arrived before the Master when he seemed to have guessed our secret questioning. About fifteen men were already at his side, sitting on the stones along the shore, and then still others arrived, perhaps five, among whom we recognized some faces we had seen before in one place or another.

"Who do you think were the envoys of other times sent by the Highest?" asked the tall white form, his back to the sea. "They were not so much philosophers as men of combat. I see surprise written on your faces, my Brothers—but do you really know what a man of combat is? He is a man who knows no rest, one of those workers—goldsmith of the soul—who is not afraid of even the hardest work. What remains of words, if they are only the promises of deeds? What remains of words if they are betrayed by deeds? Let your discourse be at the same time an act. Understand what I am saying: a word may be fully charged with love and go forth to encounter humanity. I am speaking of a tangible world that penetrates another one. When the word becomes an act, the goal is met, for it transmutes.

"This is therefore the only energy you should work with, the only one that contains any real power, for it is the only energy that creates. The celestial sword can have no other form than that of the point of your heart. When you know this law, the battle is won even before it begins; it takes the form of a gift. Love, I can assure you, knows nothing of the force of division it faces, since the victory is forever expressed in the world to which love alone has access. . . ."

The Master observed a few moments of silence, and in our breasts echoed the wash of the waves over the bluish stones on the beach.

His tall silhouette stood out so brightly against the dark mass of water behind him that we almost had to lower our eyes. This was not a sign of submission . . . one does not lower oneself before real love, but rather becomes one with it. It was an awareness of how far we had yet to go. We felt at once gigantic and minuscule; something was boiling within us, a decoction of pride and humility. A royal path was opening before us, but we had to walk it with the simplicity due to a mule path.

Once more the deep voice made us look up.

"For days and days I have been speaking to you of my Father, of love, and of the heart of all humanity. I am aware that some of you, as you listen to what I say, see images, reflections of invisible worlds which are perhaps tiresome for you and this question comes to mind: What can be done to link the mental images created by each of you out of words back to their source, and not to leave them like empty shells that people try to fill with philosophical concepts. I tell you that you must begin by restoring the flow that unites you to Nature. So many forms of life are bursting with joy all around you, above you, and below you, and you have forgotten them.

"Remember this: A human being is just one more variety of tree on this Earth. The Cosmos has endowed him with seven roots and seven branches. Now and then his consciousness suspects the existence of one or two of them, and a few buds open, but in what disorder! His seven roots are the terrestrial forces that nourish him. Unlike the roots of the plant kingdom, they are visible, and their names are Mother-Root, Earth-Root, Life, Joy, Sun, Water, and Air. They are the channels for our nourishment, but they are also a whole people of beings who instill in us the saps of the Great Matrix.

"His seven branches grow and have consciousness in the transcendental ether. Their names are Cosmic Father, Eternal Fluid, Creative Force, Peace, Power, Love, and Wisdom.

"Thus you are like a tree that is still seeking a harmonious way to develop, one in which there are two tendencies that the trunk, because of its coarse bark is apparently unable to bring together . . . and for now, so that the earthly and cosmic saps may flood through you, here are the rules by which you will live."

We all turned to look at one another, and the Master paused. Until this moment he had always spoken of a total, immediate love that would fill our beings as soon as we had acquired perfect consciousness of it. It was simply a matter of loving and not of adopting new disciplines.

"What do you want to love?" he queried as if he had read our thoughts. "The total love to which you aspire will never be vague and uncontrolled. It follows the lines of force whose ramifications spread across the whole universe. For now, you must learn to recognize these channels, to tame them so they may become an extension of your bodies.

"This is not a discipline I want to impose upon you, my Brothers, it is rather the key to a purification I suggest to you, so that in full trust you will feel yourselves the allies of my Father. For this reason, for three moons, you must practice two daily meditations and eat nothing that has perished in fire, in water, or by frost, nothing prepared at a temperature higher than that of the human body.

"There is nothing arbitrary about this. Any heat above the temperature of human blood destroys the primary impalpable qualities of creative life."

Those instructions initiated the second stage of our growing awareness. We had to change our way of life in order to experience the inner light in a tangible way. As it had been made clear, the Master did not wish us to become ascetics, but to change our habits. At the same time, this was a reinstatement of an ancient code by then long forgotten, but that he knew to be of value.

Twice a day we practiced guided meditations in the courtyard of the bethsaïd, beneath the shade of several date palms. Often we felt a tall white presence at our side. We knew that he was there, even if he was also far away, in some fishing boat or under a tent high up the mountain where he was speaking of his Father. Then we felt happy to carry out the advice he had given us. Friday had always been the day that was sacred to the Brotherhood—the day consecrated to Moon-Sun*—and on that day we had been told to begin the purification of the various flames of our beings. As soon as the sun rose we were to enter into communion with the many forces of Nature, carrying the rites taught by the Brotherhood even further.

Above all else, the Master wanted us to refine the etheric nature of our bodies through the focusing of our willpower. He taught us that in most cases, human desires propagated a wavelike phenomenon that disturbed the beings living within the element earth. We understood that humans could be severed from their roots by parasitic thought forms that permeate the very matter supporting them. These were the themes for meditation given us by the Christ Jesus, and we pondered them day after day for nearly three months.

Friday mornings were devoted to breathing exercises, in which our minds concentrated on the absorption of subtle energies. On Friday evenings, we meditated on the Cosmic Father and on the union with his creative flow. Saturday mornings were dedicated to the Mother-Root. We sought an intimate comprehension of the

*The French word for Friday, *vendredi*, is etymologically linked to Venus. In English, Friday was dedicated to the goddess Frigg, the Anglo-Saxon counterpart of Venus.

unity of our own physical bodies, as well as of the nurturing vocation of tangible Nature. We meditated essentially on the basis of nourishment and on the phenomenon of absorption. Saturday evenings we spent examining the meaning of the eternity of existence, and in a state of conscious receptivity, we worked to develop our capacity to look into the future.

Sunday was devoted to the Spirit of the Earth and to all the powers of generation, both those of Nature and those inherent to human beings. We became sensitive to the basic energy called kundalini and for our personal regeneration, tried to channel it by guiding its fire through each of our endocrine glands.

Sunday evenings our meditation focused on the concept of creativity and on the importance of the arts for the full expansion of our consciousness. We had to send forth the purest flow of love we were capable of.

At sunrise on Monday, we gave thanks for life and reflected on the harmony between the parallel realms of the microcosm and the macrocosm. This reflection, which was implicitly a form of prayer, was concluded by a long communion with a mature tree that we hugged in our arms. This might be seen as only a symbol, but to us it was much more than that.

On Monday evening we gave ourselves to an inner invocation of the Spirit of Peace, which is not just an idea, nor a symbol either, but a living entity whose help can be sought.

Tuesday mornings were devoted to the notion of joy through the contemplation of Nature's wonders. We consciously experienced one of the faces of serenity that enabled us, in the evening, to charge ourselves with all the energies from the planets. We mentally directed their rays to the corresponding organs of our bodies.

Early the following morning we did the same with the sun, whose action on the skin and also on the chakras we tried to perceive consciously. This was the exercise that was the most effective in developing our healing capacities. We ended the evening with a meditation on another form of love: Compassion.

The theme for Thursday mornings was the circulation of water in the universe, with its eternal cycles of renewal that was to offer us a new perception of the circulation of the blood within our own bodies, as well as a clearer understanding of its fundamental laws. We saw our bodies as worlds crisscrossed by regenerating rivers. We learned how to control the quality of our blood through careful analysis of the soul. All this led on Thursday evening to the exploration of wisdom. The Master expected us to let our minds merge into the cosmic ocean.

These practices went on for nearly three moons. We were not in any case to "force" our meditations, for that would have rendered them meaningless. This way of life, which was similar to the ideals Zerah had tried to teach us, transformed us all with astonishing effectiveness. During this time, we were not to remain isolated from the outside world. As soon as we had finished our exercises we resumed our everyday tasks. We treated the ill who came to us from all over the countryside, and we mingled with the crowds who came more and more often to listen to "the rabbi" opposite the synagogue or in the shade of the archways. As we were nearing the end of our attunement with the Spirit of the Earth, something happened that was full of meaning for us.

It was not uncommon that after a time of sustained meditation, the perception of our physical bodies would escape us altogether. We knew that we lived in a sort of shell, and that very easily this shell could vanish below us, leaving our soul free to float in a universe of indescribable beauty. Simon and I had experienced this a number of times, he at the Krmel and I in the company of Zerah. The Brotherhood officially recognized the multiplicity of the realms open to both the transcendental soul and the soul still dominated by the self. We sensed this as being something wholly natural, and rejoiced at being able to experience what many philosophers spent their time trying to prove theoretically. The truth, we used to tell ourselves at these times, is that nothing is to be proved and everything is to be lived. It was not thus the simple fact of leaving our bodies behind, leaning against a little brick wall, that engraved this morning of the month of Tishri* in my mind.

My body of light floated for a while over the shore of the lake

*Mid-September.

amid the leafy branches of the olive trees, as the Galilean pastels gave
way to a rainbow of crystalline splashes of light. I wanted nothing
more than to let myself be gently rocked by this mysterious astral
plane that, without any obvious aim, guides souls who are still close
to the Earth. But suddenly there was a blinding flash and the waters,
the fields, and the olive groves vanished. Above me there was a
gigantic cone of light that called out to me, and then engulfed me.
This took place in only an instant, just the time it took for a heart
to open itself to a wave of love. I found myself in an immense room
with countless columns, more transparent than crystal: I could feel
everything vibrating, which made me think I was in a living palace,
in a place unknown to our fleshly body, but where the soul feels the
caress of Divinity. In the middle of this wonderful place of light
stood the Master, his arms ritually crossed over his breast.

"You see, Myriam," he said without even parting his lips, "this
place is the concrete manifestation of all our wishes for peace. It is
a place of forces, one of those places where thought and love are
greatly multiplied. From now on, when you sleep, you and all
others who have heard my Father's call will gather here. I shall be
among you, and together we shall prepare the way. It is up to all
people living on the Earth to build such sanctuaries where every
night they may work for humanity. But they must want to, Myriam,
for only love and willpower are needed in order to create worlds and
palaces of peace. It is really so easy to build!

"From now on my plans for peace will be elaborated here, as
well as on Earth. You will not always be conscious of it, but my goal
will be revealed to you here. My goal is not to help beings but to
help beings to help themselves . . . only this will enable them to
escape from their cocoons!"

Then the Master broke into a sublime smile and his gaze was
filled with tenderness. I remember feeling an irresistible desire to
walk toward him, to weep from joy . . . or from some stronger
emotion that does not exist in our hearts. There was a white flash,
and once again all this vanished, as the heaviness of my body had
called me back. It was there or rather I was there, below me, waiting
with the rigidity of one dead, leaning against the wall of the
bethsaïd, splashed with light. Simon and two Brothers were still

sunk in meditation. Quickly I felt the warm contact of the bricks, the touch of the sun on my feet. And where are you, little particles of earth, of water and fire, having borne my weight all the while? Where have the feet of men taken you? No doubt you still remember this moment when my soul took wing. . . .

CHAPTER VI

ON THE ROAD TO JERICHO

"It was John who traced this path for us and gathered us here. Almost all of us listened to him for weeks as he preached, up to his waist in the water at the ford."

The man who spoke had an aquiline nose and his eyes testified to the great distance he had already traveled. His name was James, and he was one of the small group the Master had chosen. Like most of his companions, he was wearing a rudimentary sword at his side, over a knee-length tunic made of coarse cloth. It was early afternoon and we were making our way up to the top of a mountain where we often met the Master. The first weeks of winter had cast their mantle of coolness over Palestine, and a weak sun escorted us in our ascent among the brushwood.

"This is how it happened," continued James. "For too long, Andrew, all the others, and I, had felt that something had to change. We felt smothered here, at the mercy of the Zealots' least move, of the Roman legions, and even of the uncertain yield of the fishing. That's why we were drawn to John. There was nothing but talk of him here and the stories people told about him were so different from what we had experienced all our lives. No, Myriam, what the people in town who point and stare at me keep whispering is untrue. I was never close to the Eternal One before I was drawn to the banks of the Jordan. It was just that I had had enough of this life, of this uncontrolled anxiety that was gnawing at my heart and that I could not explain. And just about the same thing is true for all the others too, except for Simon and Levi.* When we met John, we were all totally dazzled; and as for myself, I do believe I would have stayed there with him if he hadn't directed us to a man in the midst of the crowd there, a man dressed in white, who seemed to be praying, his head in his hands, in the shade of a large rock. The rest you can imagine! We didn't dare to go to him right away, however, and we returned to Capernaum certain that he would go there. But believe me, everything that happened was not of our own doing. It was as if someone had placed us first here and then there, and had put feelings in our hearts that seem foolish to me today.

"I can't say if I am free to do as I wish, Myriam. I still don't know whether the Master and John are magicians who have stolen my soul. I don't know where I am heading but only one thing is certain: I can't turn back! It was the Master himself who came to me as I was unloading my boat. I did not realize he had just arrived in town, but he seemed to know all about me and my family."

"Does that really surprise you?" interrupted Simon, breaking into our conversation. With an embarrassed smile James admitted that it did not, then confided that the Master had told him he had met him long ago, close by Elijah. I could tell that this frightened him a little but that he was more proud than afraid.

When we reached the top of the mountain, an icy wind was whipping our faces. We found the Master in a rocky hollow. We had not seen him for three weeks, and although he looked considerably thinner, his body and his bearing had become even more luminous. During the years we spent with him we noticed this wasting away a number of times. It always occurred after periods of time when he would disappear completely, not even seeing his closest disciples. It was only much later that we discovered the

*Simon Peter and Matthew.

reason for his prolonged absences. Two high initiates of the Brotherhood had been given the task of watching over him by the council of Heliopolis. We were told that the body of Jesus, permanently invested by two spiritual forces of unimaginable intensity, was constantly submitted to radiations of such a nature as would totally overwhelm any other human organism. It was for this reason that he required long periods of isolation, rest, and fasting, during which time the envoys from Heliopolis watched over his physical body, while the Logos withdrew somewhat.

"We must leave this region," said the Master, rising as we approached him, his eyes shining like flames of kindness. His force, of this we had no doubt, came from a land where human beings had not yet managed to set foot. We came to an abrupt halt, our eyes on this tall white figure whose hair was blowing in the wind.

"My father would have his words heard elsewhere than on these shores. Is there anyone among you who will follow me as far as Jericho?" he asked.

He did not appear to expect a reply, and sat down again in the shelter of the rock. We all rushed forward, assuring him of our aid, however humble it might be.

Our departure took place at dawn of the following day, while Capernaum was still asleep. There were more than twenty of us who met at the outskirts of the village on the road to Tiberias. Several oil lamps were still burning on the scattered terraces as we set out, wrapped in our cloaks. As the sun rose higher and we passed through small towns our group grew to include several beggars, three ex-Zealots, and two Brothers, one of whom had been a companion of Simon at the Krmel.

The Master did more teaching with his actions than with his words. One look, one hand placed upon a shoulder, one name said aloud, were enough to work wonders; souls were opened wide as if they had known him forever. Two blind men were healed on the first day of our journey in two neighboring villages. Hoarse voices had called out, "Rabbi! Rabbi!" and he had simply put a bit of his saliva on the sealed eyelids. . . . That was all; it was so easy!

"Your saliva is yourself," replied the Master to those who pressed around him full of wonder, "your hair is yourself, the sweat of your brow and the dust on your skin is yourself. Let love now be yourself, and my Father will work in you, will work through you."

And he set out once more, soberly throwing his cloak back over his shoulders, knowing that the questions he left in suspense would ripen in time, depending on the awakening of each soul. We stayed in Beth Shean for two days. The Master's reputation had preceded him and the people vied with one another for the honor of his presence beneath their roofs. The second evening there, overburdened with questions and requests, he rose and left an assembly without even pronouncing a single word. After this incident, we perceived some sadness in his eyes.

"What sort of show are they expecting from me?" he asked when we had rejoined him in the darkness of a street. "There is not one person in this town who sees my Father in me. They want me to work wonders, but they do not care about the Force behind them. I can tell you, Brothers, in everything there must be a limit. The one who fills people's eyes with miracles misses his mark for though he intends to reveal the Father, it is only he they are looking at. He wishes to open hearts, but only manifests egoism. Why do you think they fight amongst themselves to see who will offer me lodging? There is probably not one of them who wishes for anything else than a healing achieved or a prophecy told within his home. Let them search in the desert: that is where they will find the magicians they are looking for. Their hearts hunger for something, can they not realize this? Where are the wishes formulated by the heart rather than by the lips? These will be fulfilled, I tell you. My Father's succor is not for sale to the highest bidder, but belongs to whoever knows how to seek it out where it is waiting for him. You may be sure that the one who does not want to be a spring will always go thirsty."

Several beggars wrapped in rags had lit a crackling wood fire that filled the little street with its fragrance. In the light of the flames, we searched one another's eyes and understood that the abundance of wonders that had adorned the Master's path would now decrease. The means was not to be mistaken for the end.

The following morning, a throng of peasants, craftsmen, and

shepherds were waiting for the Master before the door of the house where he had spent the night. Some of these people greeted him with hostility in their voices.

"How can you claim to be the son of the Eternal One, you who will not even listen to our requests? Do we live too far from Capernaum, with its beautiful synagogues? Of course, the accounts of your wonders would be forgotten in the solitude of our valleys. We know what you can do; is it through pride that you hesitate like this, Rabbi? If what they say about you is true, there is not a man in the land who would not swear to obey you."

Half crushed by the packed crowd, we could only catch a glimpse of the tall white figure of the Master as he threaded his way through the mass of people to approach the one who had taken him to task. Then his words rang out with the purity of crystal and a silence fell over the crowd.

"I do not wish to be obeyed, my Brother; neither my Father nor I wish this. Obedience has just a single ally, and that is fear. The Eternal One speaks of love, and he only wishes for one thing: that you recognize him within yourself; the rest is nothing but the consequence of this recognition. You want miracles? Work them first in your heart; learn to cherish love for love's sake. Learn to stop feeling different from others. It is that difference that complicates everything. I can tell you, you who listen to me, that only the sensation of total unity with the Father and all his creation will set you free. If you count mentally up to two, already you fall into duality, into the endless cycle of desire and satisfaction. If some of you refuse these words, you are certainly seeking a Master, and I am not a Master. I am the One who has come to break the chains."

A heavy silence hung over the crowd. We saw the tall white figure go back into the house then reappear shortly after, his cloak over his shoulders. We knew it was time to leave. A thin winter rain began to fall. One last time we heard the Master address the crowd.

"When you are really cold, you will know that I am near."

How many understood these words? The people stood there as if frozen, their eyes wide, marveling more at the presence before them than at his words. As we were leaving town a hirsute shepherd, huddling beneath a rough sack to protect himself from the rain, cried out to us.

"Stay off the path that leads to the road following the Jordan," he said. "The Romans were through here a few days ago and they captured about ten of our Zealot brothers. They put them up on crosses on a little hill about a kilometer out of town that way, and it is forbidden to go near!"

We took the advised detour, but in the distance, standing out against the blue-gray background of a hill, the sinister assemblage of crudely hewn tree trunks and gallows was visible all the same, with its sad burden already prey to the birds. We passed with clenched teeth, horrified by such barbarism.

What had happened here? We had always heard that the Romans allowed the families of the executed to reclaim the bodies. Perhaps in this case they had wanted to deal more severely than usual in order to set an example. We never found out.

Soon our road led through the hills; the grass grew thinner, the soil was redder, and the rather naked mountainside offered a view, here and there, of cave dwellings. At last a ray of sunlight pierced the clouds, bringing warmth to our hearts, numbed and pained by our experience in Beth Shean.

Beth Shean! That meant "the dwelling of the serpent god." Which serpent did the name refer to? Was it the great adversary spoken of in Genesis? The Master gave us the answer to this enigma, an answer that led us toward further horizons than we might have guessed.

"There are two serpent forces in the universe," he said. "They are hardly related to each other, and their antagonism gives rise to terrible confusion. My Brothers of Essania are familiar with the first of these two, the triple tongue of fire that sleeps within, coiled at the base of every human spine. This is the Mother Force, which awaits the Cosmic Prince, and when it springs up to meet him, it unfolds the multiple flowers of consciousness. This is to a certain extent the transcendental soul of the Earth that rises up within us.

"The second serpent power, on the other hand, is of a totally opposite nature. It is a power of destabilization, a rampant, crawling energy, even if it does come from the stars—from certain stars. You must know, my Brothers, that not everything that comes from the heavens is an example of great purity. There are sparkling worlds in our universe where the inhabitants work for my Father; and there are others that look luminous, but where the inhabitants work for their own satisfaction out of pride and lack of love, because they have not understood yet.

"These are the realms of the serpent race. The ancients of this Earth named them thus because of the duplicity of their words. They know how to dominate but not how to tame. Theirs are the powers of the mind rather than the invincible capacities of the heart.

"I tell you, they are far from Ishtar, and unfortunately, close to mankind in their deceit. You must know that since the dawn of time, they have visited our world on clouds of illusory light, the unknowing agents of the force of darkness. They will continue to come for a long time yet."

"Are they the 'Shatan' of our scriptures, Master?" someone asked.

"Shatan is not a being, nor even a spirit. He is the hidden energy of the cosmos, the force of differentiation, the dark breath that the Nameless One has released for you, so that you may learn to choose. Shatan is also the collective thought-form* of men who experiment with destruction before becoming builders. He is less a force to fight against than one to go beyond. Now, my Brothers, you will find that the serpent of Beth Shean is indeed a god, issued from the terrestrial flow of love. This you will learn soon."

It took us several days' walking to reach the ford of the Jordan, where the Master knew that John was still ministering to the forces that were coming alive in Israel. We followed the banks of the river at times, climbed down wild little gorges, and spent the night in palm groves. Simon and I were fond of the rugged, wild landscape, with its orange rock and all its little stones that surely had so much to tell. They seemed to murmur the tales of the patriarchs of long ago. Never was the approach to the desert more invigorating for me than in those days. We had established a sort of complicity with the proud poverty of the soil.

The nights got colder, and the days hotter; the world seemed to overflow with white sunlight. One morning we found ourselves face to face with John at the top of a hillock. At our feet, the Jordan

*The egregore.

was flowing by, and about a hundred people thronged the banks, waiting for the moment that would confirm their awakening.

John was still glowing with the same inner fire, but I could feel a tenderness in him whose flow had not been visible before. He, too, was advancing on his path, there was no doubt about this. Though he had limited himself to his small patch of rocky land bordering the river, his was the most beautiful path.

We left him alone with the Master all morning long. Someone, however, discovered the two of them in a secluded hollow of the terrain, and they immediately found themselves overwhelmed by the throng's eagerness. They blessed the crowd together, and both spoke to the people at great length. Were we then aware of how precious these moments were? I do not remember, but we were at that time living in the present moment and did not yet know that it would never be renewed.

That afternoon, while the Master went on speaking to the people and we were waiting for him to leave, John came to us, with a shapeless bundle of brown woolen cloth in his hand.

"Here," he said, handing it to one of the Master's close disciples, whose name was also John.

"This was Elijah's; now it is your burden, until the Christ shows you where it is to be laid down."

The disciple gaped at him, realizing only after a moment that it was a cloak made of camel hair.

"I will take care of it," he said simply, holding it tight against his chest.

And the eyes of the two Johns shone with equal brilliance, like little sapphires, communicating far beyond words. From that time on, John the disciple from Capernaum was not the same. He became at once more serious and more radiant. We never learned what became of the cloak of Elijah and the Precursor. It was most likely hidden somewhere and will probably come to light, or perhaps has already come to light, on a day of great hope.

Jericho welcomed the Master in triumph. His presence aroused such enthusiasm among the people that a detachment of soldiers, not all of whom were Romans this time, was sent to intervene, as had happened in Capernaum. That night we felt it would be better to

seek lodging outside the town. Our group was unusually vocal in
Jericho. So many men and women had come to acclaim the Master
that we could hardly doubt the power of his message. Even more
than before, wherever he went he diffused a wave of love that spread
among the people. In Jericho this took on the proportions of a tidal
wave. . . But how can one speak in appropriate terms of a being of
peace who often had only to appear for the impossible to occur?
There were still, of course, those who looked on in mocking
disbelief, but most people were drawn to listen and to ask questions.
Something was stirring in the depths of their hearts, some little seed
that from one existence to another, would preserve the imprint of
these moments when the soul of humanity was shedding its outer
layers.

After Jericho we set out toward the north of the country by
way of Samaria. The Master did not want to push as far as Jerusalem;
on the contrary, his wish was quite deliberately to avoid it. Through
a few remarks he passed incidentally, we gathered that he feared the
political consequences of his presence in the capital of Judaea. He
wanted to be associated neither with an era nor with a people, but
he knew that others did not see things in the same way. The people
of Palestine, oppressed and longing for a renewed spirit, wanted
nothing better than to claim him as theirs. The Zealots were ever-
present, even in the most remote places where we stopped. One
may now consider the possibility that an organized network of
people was watching every move made by the "Great Rabbi" and
his ever-growing group of disciples. Was not the Master the ideal
leader for an uprising against the oppressor? Faced with the unquestionable authority he showed in every matter and wherever he
went, even his closest companions came to wonder about this.
Three of these companions had, after all, recently fought among the
ranks of the Zealots. Simon and I recalled Manethon mentioning
the troubles that the one who was then simply called Jesus had
caused because of his words near Varanasi. Was the temporal necessarily bound to hinder the progress of the spiritual? Above all, the
Master took great pains to avoid even the slightest political confron-
tation, and this was his heaviest burden.

"I am the prince of a realm that is not of this Earth," he said repeatedly. "Would you chain down the bird who wants to fly away after coming to announce the arrival of spring? Listen to its song, for it brings the message your heart longs to hear. It is attuned to the march of the worlds and will teach you the secret law of its epochs."

Our progress was slow, taking us weeks to travel through the heart of the mild Palestinian winter. One day toward the end of that season, as we were camped in the region of Samaria, we saw a Brother in white coming up the road on a recalcitrant little donkey.

"I must tell you about John," he cried out, overcome by emotion. "The soldiers arrested him three days ago!"

This news threw us into dismay and I must admit that a wind of fear blew over our group. Thus John had fallen into the trap that the Master dreaded: attacking the people in power, their methods, and their dissolute morals.

As the Brother was relating the details of his story, the Master drew away to be alone. A deep sadness in his eyes was there for all to see, and made us all feel closer to him. We could not have followed an impassive sage who, in his quest for absolute values would shut his heart to joy as well as to pain. The one we loved was human in all respects. The Logos and Christ were living among us, but they did not overwhelm the tenderness of Jesus.

One of the places where we had decided to stop on this journey, was the little village of our childhood.* We arrived one evening, exhausted from a long march through the hills. From a kilometer away it seemed I could recognize all of the atmosphere that was dear to my heart. There are fragrances that our sense of smell is incapable of perceiving, but that in an impulse of love, our deeper sensibilities manage to perceive somewhere in the realm of the invisible. Once within the village walls I could make out the familiar glow of several fires, and I knew it was the time of the evening when the communal meal that was shared at nightfall was being prepared. An old woman came forward to greet us. It was Sarah, and I felt sorry to see her hobbling so, almost doubled over, she who so long ago had charmed me with the legends of our

---

*Not Nazareth, whose name was given only centuries later, due to the repeated confusion between Nazarites and Essenes.

people. She had never married, but as was the custom of Essania, she had adopted a son who now worked with Simon's father making pottery.

The Master had especially insisted on stopping here because he wanted to take his mother and two of his brothers with us to Gennesaret or Capernaum.

Once the joy of our reunion with the faces and the streets of our childhood had subsided, we became more and more aware that something had changed. At first this was a vague impression, but it was confirmed by several comments we heard that led us to understand that the presence here of men and women who did not belong to the Brotherhood was disturbing. Some did not seem to understand what was happening. As far as they were concerned, the Master was still Joseph. Hardly did they recognize him as a high initiate, perhaps of the rank of a priest of Helios in Jerusalem. Just as a body is often unaware of its inner sun, our village refused to recognize the one it had sheltered as a child. The Master did not seem concerned, chatting like an old friend with everyone, astonishing some with the warmth of his presence, but also offending others by his words thought to be too liberal. The rumor spread that he had taught the throngs of Samaria truths that up until that time had been exclusively communicated from Initiates of the Brotherhood to their disciples. These concerned some details about reincarnation and about the close links existing between what people call good and evil. The elders of the village, who so far had limited their comments to disgruntled murmurings, reacted with an unconditional refusal when the Master suggested sharing the communal meal with Andrew, Jude, and the others. If only Zerah had been there! Would he perhaps have seen in the eyes of these sometimes rough men the flame of initiates of another time? They were twelve who had drunk the water of forgetfulness from the fountain of Lethe, twelve who had traded their wisdom of the past for the plain garb of fishermen—but this is too often forgotten.

The letter of the law seemed to have supplanted its spirit, and for the first time, those who to me had once symbolized tolerance and clear-sightedness appeared bound by the same chains of ignorance that restrained so many others among the common people.

As we were leaving the village my face must have reflected sadness or bitterness, for an old man who had long ago worked at the looms with my father put his hand on my arm.

"Why such a hard look, Myriam?" he asked. "The Brotherhood had been entrusted with the coming of a Messiah as its essential goal. This has almost been achieved; it may now recede into the background. Those you seek, those who knew and who still do know how to see clearly, are no longer here within these walls. Like you and Simon and the others they have heard the call and they have taken to the roads. The members of the deeper Brotherhood are scattered all over the Earth, and have in many cases left their white robes behind, in order to work more discreetly.

"Do not be sad; what is happening had to happen. The life of the Master is a symbol, don't you understand? He has all the power of a hieroglyph! Do you think he failed to realize when he arrived here in what manner he would be received, with what mistrust he would be regarded? The Master is not a man, Myriam, he sees further with the eyes of Man, and I mean with the eyes of the authentic Man. He knows that certain things he does hasten the rotting of the ancient world. Look into his eyes. What do you see?"

"I have seen love there, old Jacob," I replied. "I have seen love, and now, thanks to you, I see joy as well."

The Master walked down the steep path and we all followed him, pushing forward the several donkeys that had been given to us. The old Brother had seen true; there was no sadness, no rancor in the Master's eyes. And when several of our company pressed him with questions about the attitudes of some of the Brothers, he only smiled in silence. As planned, his mother was coming with us. She seemed not to have changed with the passing of the years, as if she had refused the process of aging.

We headed straight for Capernaum, cutting through the olive groves. On the way, as we were leaving Tiberias by the trail that bordered the shores of the lake, we were suddenly accosted be a group of armed men.

"Are you the Nazarene?" asked one of them, approaching the Master. "We want to have a word with you."

None of us took part in the discussion, which took place at a certain distance and continued for a long time. On seeing the abrupt gestures of the strangers we were filled with apprehension. Nothing came of it, and the little band of men dispersed into the hills as rapidly as they had arrived. They were Zealots, this we had understood at a glance. They had probably counted heavily on this meeting, for Tiberias, which was one of the symbols of Roman domination in Palestine, housed a number of cohorts that were continually patrolling. When the Zealots were taken, they were usually summarily executed like plain highwaymen.

It was pitch-dark when the glow of a fire or two and myriad tiny oil lamps signaled our arrival on the edges of Capernaum. We entered the town by walking along the shore of the lake, preferring the musical lapping of the waves to the noisy company of the travelers who lingered along the road. The air was strangely sweet, laden with the smell of fish and of the smoke from cooking fires. This place had become a sort of home to us. After months of wending our way over the roads of the whole country, this came to us as a very clear feeling. Something we found nowhere else vibrated in this place: the prolonged presence of the Master had already breathed Life into it.

As we made our way in silence toward the stable of the bethsaïd, a stocky figure loomed up out of the darkness, barring our way.

"Rabbi! Rabbi!" we heard him say, "I am here ! I knew I would find you here!"

In the glow of an earthen lamp we recognized the face of the man from Beth Shean, the man whose words had seemed so harsh. His eyes were like two big gray pearls, and we could see that he wanted only one thing: to learn.

CHAPTER · VII

THE ONE HUNDRED
AND TWENTY

The semidarkness was thick, relieved only slightly by the little oil lamps placed here and there sending up thin ribbons of blackish smoke. There were many of us crowded together in this underground room that one of the Master's disciples had put at our disposal. It was late in the afternoon, and we were sitting on the rock floor, waiting. Andrew had sent out a call for us to come, taking great care to be discreet, as it had been made clear that the assembly was to remain rigorously secret. It seems to me that we were all ignorant of the reason for such secrecy. We simply knew that the Master was going to come, and that was enough to draw us there.

Eyes met in the half-light, souls penetrated each other, and little gestures, barely sketched out, were exchanged. We all knew one another without ever having dared to start a conversation in the streets of Capernaum or on the roads of Palestine; we shared a sort of intimate complicity, and we simply enjoyed being together.

Simon and I were huddled against one of the damp walls, speaking in whispers with a man in his fifties who sat in front of us.

"My name is Nicodemus," he whispered. "I have been listening to the Master for only a few months now, so I was surprised when one of his disciples invited me to this meeting. I do not know what is happening; everything and everyone looks different. Only two months ago I had to hide from my own people the fact that I went to listen to the Master and now that he seems to have nothing more to fear, we are asked to observe absolute discretion."

This man was speaking with deep emotion, looking for words, and searching our eyes with his own. I felt him to be one who had spent a long time looking, and who had loved without restraint. The heat was so intense that he removed the veil that covered his head, revealing thick silvery hair that hung in tight curls and two large sparkling eyes. There was a glow in his eyes that night, a real glow that may be seen in those who have looked upon the truth.

"I was with the Master yesterday," he went on, half shutting his eyes as if to look inward. "I had heard that he was returning from the land of the Gadarenes, on the other side of the lake. Like so many others, I went to wait for his boat to land on the little beach. When he stepped out of the boat and onto the shore there was an indescribable turmoil, and I found myself pushed quite a distance from the Master. Everywhere people were yelling and shouting so loudly that I began to fear that the Romans would intervene. From the reaction of the crowd I gathered that some miracle must have occurred.* The Master seemed unconcerned with all this confusion, as if he were a thousand miles from us all. He looked right through us, threading his way through the throng so easily that I had the impression he projected an incredible force around himself. In a moment he was drawn to one side by Jairus of the synagogue, who led him to his home. All along the way, the poor man was unable to contain his sobbing, for his daughter had just died. I know Jairus well, so I was lucky enough to be able to enter his home along with the Master.

"There were mourners all around the little body making an awful din, crying and stamping their feet on the floor. When the

---

*No doubt this is a reference to the healing of the woman mentioned in the Gospels (Mark 5:25–34).

Master saw this, he ordered them to be silent and to leave the room.

"'Get out of this house!' he said with authority. 'There is nothing like despair to foster death. Your thoughts of sadness are poisoning the air in this room. I can assure you, souls feed on an air whose existence you do not suspect. Open that window wide and rejoice in your hearts! Jairus, your daughter is only sleeping, as she does every night. Can you not see her smiling at me?

"'What you call death is just someone flying away. Has my Father ever forbidden a bird to perch on a branch of one of his trees? Sometimes it happens that the branch lacks a bit of the sap necessary to support the bird's weight.'"

"Then we saw him step over to the little body, kneel beside it, and without touching it, he blew between the girl's two eyebrows and whispered a few words. . . .

"I believe I have never seen anyone so radiant as he was at that moment. Until now, my eyes have never had the chance to see something that I could not hold in my hands. At that moment, the Master looked like a white flame. At first I thought it was some force he had called to him, but now I know that the force came from within him, that he breathed it out; he gave a part of himself. Perhaps he gave himself entirely.

"A being such as he does not give away only a part of himself, does he?" Nicodemus asked, looking at me.

His eyes were blue-gray, like the color of the water in the lake, and as deep too. I don't believe I replied, the answer seemed so obvious to me. No, the Master never gave partly of himself; we had his whole being within each of us, in the promise of a future that we could draw toward the present, toward the eternal present he spoke of, but that we could never quite grasp.

Tears in his eyes, Nicodemus made a gesture as if to wipe the sweat from his forehead, then went on.

"Then the Master took a few steps back and Jairus's daughter began blinking her eyes rapidly. I heard a clamor behind me that someone tried to stifle, and I felt myself pushed forward by the unruly crowd. The Master stepped forward again, took the little one by the hand as if to pull her out of a long dream, and then she stood up! Do you hear me? She stood up!

"At that moment I found myself propelled to the center of the room; Jairus's family and friends were beside themselves with joy. They did not know what to do but kiss the Master's feet, as well as those of the little girl, who stood there, rubbing her cheeks.

"I will remember this sight forever! This tall figure, all of white fire, holding the child's hand, just where a thin ray of light was falling in through the doorway. And I tell you the Master did not want any of their foot kissing, and wasted no time in taking the child outside, repeating softly that death was only for those who were blind in their hearts.

"'Death is the forgetting of my Father's word,' he said. Then he asked for some bread, adding: 'Give her something to eat, and thus you will complete the awakening of her sanguine soul.'*

"Later, as we returned together, I decided to ask him why he did not do such acts more often. I knew that, countless times, he had been begged to intervene in similar circumstances.

"'The flight of the soul out of the body is not a punishment for the one who experiences it,' he replied. 'The hour of death has very often been decided by the deceased themselves, in other times, in other worlds. The reasons and the moment of death, believe me, are only the consequence of a multitude of past actions. Calling a soul back to life on Earth, Nicodemus, means intervening in the being's destiny well beyond what we know of its existence. A soul that flies to the realm that is its own only follows its path faithfully, all for the greater accomplishment of the goal. You must understand that. This is not injustice, but the application of very subtle laws.

"'The heart of this little girl, as well as that of others to come, has long been attuned to the heart of my Father. Calling her back to life did not mean intervening in the unfolding of her evolution, but revealing one aspect of the omnipresence of the Nameless One. Jairus's daughter, I assure you, placed herself upon my path so that what had to be accomplished came to pass.

"'So you see, Nicodemus, and all of you who are listening to my words, whoever rekindles the life of the flesh must be sure to

*Or vital soul, another Essene name for the etheric body.

do so with good reason, that is, without transgressing the laws that govern a being's evolution. Giving life is easy, my Brothers, but knowing why we give life, and whether or not it is just—there lies the difficulty.

"'If people knew how to spread a little love, the answers to these questions would come readily to their own lips . . . but they allow only a semblance of love to blossom, clothed in ulterior motives.

"'You will heal in my name, this I tell you. You will do this with a single impulse of your heart, not for the glory of it, nor out of pride in your own power, but rather to correct mistakes. Bodies and souls who suffer are, in all cases, human offenses against the deeper nature of the worlds.

"'Look within yourselves; in his perfection my Father never makes mistakes. He will point to the path that your illusory personality tries to hide. Be no longer who you think you are, my Brothers, for however sweet your dream may be, it is bound to fall short of the truth. Become your Essence, and then both the Knowledge and the Force of the worlds will radiate in your mind and in your hands.'"

Nicodemus ended his account of the Master's words with his eyes to the ground, as if he were bent under their weight. I felt he was looking for the right words, that he wanted to supplement what he had told us with one more detail, with something the Master had said and that he had forgotten, but nothing more came. Simon and I knew this feeling all too well, a fear of having left out what was most important, of having blunted a message so pure that it lost something in the telling. . . a fear of defiling something perfect, of letting it fade. . . .

At last Nicodemus looked up, and with a smile reached out to take our hands in his own, a way of communicating what could not be said, of opening the ears of the heart.

Then a murmur swept through those assembled in the underground room, and once more we sought each other's eyes. Simon glanced up to the top of the narrow stone stairway, and following his gaze, I saw a tall white figure slowly coming down among us. Silence fell over us at once, punctuated from time to time by some dry coughing owing to the acrid smell of the oil lamps. It was too dark to distinguish the Master's features with precision, but this mattered little, as the atmosphere of the room was already forgotten.

The warm voice that resounded against the walls of rock and earth was the link that united us all, making our assembly a single, unshakable edifice.

"This is the first time I have asked you to meet together," he said, "but you have all known each other since time immemorial."

Such were the first words that we received from the Master that evening; such was also the reminder of the common will that had always inspired us, whether we were weavers, merchants, tailors, shepherds, Brothers affiliated with some group, or wore still some other mask. Nothing of that mattered at all.

"Perhaps you have counted. There are one hundred and twenty of you here. I have been teaching you long enough now for you to know that this number is not due to chance. It corresponds to a place within the cosmic geography of the Nameless One, to one-third of his force of creation that whirls endlessly through the eternal cycle.* It is now your task to create a material center, like the pit of a fruit, and to grow methodically. You have expressed the desire to cultivate the 'Awakener of souls' within you. The time has come, my Brothers, to get organized, to meet, to come to know each other, and to deploy yourselves according to the harmonies inscribed in the stars. In this I do not ask you to conform to the numbers, nor to the architecture that rules the universe, but that you respect them, that you love them, and that you make them yours, so that they may help you in your work.

"My Father does not need those who are slaves to his celestial mathematics; he only wants those who are the lovers of his laws. I can assure you, these laws are not laws at all, in the human sense of the term; nothing arbitrary went into their formulation, for they are harmony above all else, and this is true throughout all eternity.

"Within the space of two years, your goal will be to become

*This is a reference to the sacred geometry practiced among the Essenes. One hundred twenty is one-third of the 360 degrees in a circle. This number is associated with one of the forces of the cosmic trinity.

three hundred and sixty, the pulp of the fruit. You will grow in such a way as to respect this proportion until the fruit is whole, ready to be planted, ready to let the energy of generation develop within it. The tree will grow from there. It will be a tree of human beings, ready for all the passing birds to alight upon its branches. . . . These are the twelve flames who will nourish the seeds, and this is my mother, who has always worked at my side."

The Master then stepped into the seated assembly, and folded his arms around the small group of his close disciples; then he put his hands on the shoulders of a woman in a long white veil, a woman who sat very straight. She had been so discreet that we had often forgotten her. She was the mother of Joseph—not of Christ, not of the Logos—and it was probably because of this that we had been unaware of the importance of her hidden work. Too often we had forgotten that she had been the dove of Essania, the high vestal of our people's initiates; that she herself had been initiated into the most ancient rites of the Red Land, as the living symbol of the Primordial Mother. She was the physical support of the one who would one day be known as the Mother of All Peoples.

"What is the reason for my presence among you, my Brothers?" he continued, standing in our midst. "You have probably asked yourselves this question time and time again. I have no set answer for you, for when a thousand beings listen to the words the Father brings to my lips, there are a thousand solutions to the enigma. The true reply to the quest of souls will forever be an individual one. I am here for each one of you, for what you have been and what your Earth can no longer be responsible for, for what you signify today and for what you will become. The universal cycles have chosen the time and place. The vital body of your world is now overladen with the weight of past human failures to understand. This weight slows down its growing march through the aeons, bogs it down in the karmic remains of the earths of old. The cloaks of complacency and of lack of love are crying out to be rent asunder, in order to let the Breath that is to come blow through. This is the role that my Father has given me, making me a breaker of chains.

"You will see me as a sword—a sword that represents a crossroads, the spearhead of the Nameless One combined with the weakness of a man's body. Because of this, you will love me, but also because of this, you will fail to understand me. . . .

"So learn to open your eyes. There are one hundred and eight beads that I have always worn around my neck.* May you who recognize me identify yourselves with these beads by penetrating my heart, by searching beyond the words it shapes.

"In order that you may serve my Father, I shall ask that you begin by grasping the double meaning of my words. I will not speak in fine phrases, but in images, so that all may read without having to learn to read. I shall be a teller of tales, so that the flower of love may bloom rather than the intellect. Tales are like clay that each of you may shape according to the secrets of your soul; or like a well where irreconcilable thirsts may be quenched. Do not expect trenchant truths from me, my Brothers, nor dogmas, but a song that follows the waves on the sea as well as the rising and falling of flames.

"At each full moon we shall assemble here and I shall teach you of the worlds that are awaiting you. This will take place as it has tonight, in the darkest secrecy, for germination occurs only under the Earth, sheltered from the raging of winds and the shining of the light. I shall give you a sign, and you will know it as your own when the times turn a more troubled face."

As he said this, the Master stepped over to the smoothest of the walls, and with a thin twig he quickly drew a grid formed with four vertical lines and four horizontal lines.

"This is one of the designs of my Father's stone," he added. "Matter is unified, but it creates its own network of subtle energies in order to work."

I had forgotten the suffocating heat of this cellar, located in the heart of Capernaum, in a little street that passed not far from the synagogue. I glanced at Simon, who had just covered himself with the cloak he had brought as a precaution—a ritual Essene act that had become an unconscious gesture, a way of enclosing something

---

*This refers to the rosary composed of 108 beads generally worn by the Essene initiates. One hundred and eight corresponds to 120 minus the 12 disciples. Note the 108 years making up the Rosicrucian cycles and the 108 beads forming the Hindu and Tibetan rosaries.

sacred, the better to nourish it with his contemplation. To Simon too, this damp heat meant nothing at all.

For a short moment, the Master stopped speaking and glanced around the room at us, one after the other, from face to face, throwing up a bridge of light between himself and each of us. There was nothing theatrical in this, nor in anything else he ever did. He acted—and always urged us to act—spontaneously, putting his whole being into even a brief glance of his eyes. He knew instinctively, naturally, which was the right word, the right detail that would flood a soul with peace, enabling it to span the ages. Every one of his gestures thus became a lesson in itself, a hieroglyph to be traced and treasured. His long auburn hair, his fine beard, his long fingers, and even the folds of his robe were parts of a story that told of his being, of his force, and of the long chain of love that linked him to the Great Source, beyond any concept. Two thousand years are nothing. The form of the One who had come to console will remain forever in the hearts of those who beheld him.

More than before, the Master appeared to be the reformer of the human soul, a living force come to bring peace to human minds, but also to disturb them in their comfort. His goal seemed clear: through our coordinated action he wanted to create a network, invisible at first, but capable of spreading the basis of a new way of being, or rather of bringing to light the basis that each of us possesses but rejects.

"People are blinded by pride," he told us, "and they certainly have every reason to be proud of themselves as they are standing at a crossroads that enables them to act limitlessly. But this is not the pride that they flaunt. In the limitations of matter they have projected their own dreams and now pride themselves on dominating them."

Never before had he spoken to us of a new religion, nor even of a new philosophy to be advocated. This seemed to be far from his mind, and perhaps it was just the opposite of what was in his mind. He kept repeating that the truth bore no face at all, that people should seek truth within themselves through their own work; we were all, he said, the atoms of a single body, whether we were aware of it or not—the body of his Father.

So it was that when we had the opportunity to speak with the people, following his passage through some small town or village, we had no precepts, in the usual sense of the word, to dictate to the masses who were more and more impressed. There was only a spirit of love to be breathed, and this is what we attempted to share with them once the Master had moved on again.

Our task was to help the people rediscover a forgotten sensitivity, and to teach the principles of the universe to those who were most prepared.

It was at this time that we really began to become acquainted with the little clan of the one hundred and eight. Some of the names have come down through the ages, such as Martha, Simon of Cyrene, and Joseph of Arimathea. These men and women did not all live around Tiberias, Capernaum, or Magdala. At each full moon they came discreetly from Samaria, Jerusalem, or Bethany, taking advantage of passing camel trains under the pretext of some business to conclude in Capernaum. They came from different social classes of the Palestinian population. Not all were Essenes—far from it. Their knowledge of the hidden truths varied a great deal, but all managed to find the right words to convey the message.

It was in the dark of the night that we took leave of the Master, at the end of our first secret assembly. In order to avoid suspicion we filed out into the alleyway one by one, at a signal from one of us who kept watch in a doorway. To let others know about our meeting would have provoked those in power, and we would have certainly run the risk of mass arrest. The shadow of the Zealots was still hanging over us.

On our return, we found ourselves back again within the warm walls of the bethsaïd, which reminded us that life as usual would have to be resumed: caring for the ill, feeding passing vagabonds dressed in rags, talking to the people at the entrance to the synagogue, and following the Master on his long walks along the shores of the lake or over the mountain paths.

But it could no longer continue as before. A new page had been turned, and as we were lying on our mats, watching the last oil lamp flicker out, we knew that at last our mission had begun.

CHAPTER · VIII

BENEATH THE
SUN OF
MAGDALA

t was during the year after the first assembly of the one hundred and twenty that most of the wonders immortalized in the scriptures took place. Simon and I were fortunate enough to witness several of them. These events that are known as miracles were, however, far more numerous than is described in the remaining texts. They were not the result of some boundless energy spent without regard for measure, but the fruit of a force that knew where to direct itself, and when.

"The giving of material gifts without discernment is possible only in an adult world," the Master often said. This was in keeping with the Essene rule that advised us, through a harsh metaphor, not to cast our pearls before swine. By this we understood that the human race was as yet a race of children, and satisfying their desires too quickly could not be of any lasting help to them.

The Master was not content with simply healing bodies and souls; what became known as the miracle of the loaves testifies to this. He gave birth to matter as easily as a shepherd plays music on his flute. It was after one of these miracles that always aroused such enthusiasm from the people that we joined him beneath a porch in

Magdala. We found ourselves in a little square, flooded by the white light of the noonday sun. The village was calm at that time of day, crushed beneath the weight of the summer heat. The deserted streets were full of the fragrance of spices and barley cakes that floated out from the coolness of the houses. And yet, under the pomegranate and fig trees growing in the fish market there were about a hundred men and women who had gathered around the Master. They were sitting wherever they could, squinting their eyes the better to see him as he was leaning back against a large earthenware jar, a long, white linen veil over his head. They were fishermen and peasants, listening with great respect to his words, only rarely asking a question, perhaps for fear of breaking the spell he cast over them. They formed a mosaic of ochres, whites, and reds, of ragged beards and dark skin dripping with sweat. All the humble people of Israel were represented there, trying to understand what many refused to accept. They were still in shock from what had happened earlier in the morning: a dozen heavy bunches of grapes had suddenly appeared in the Master's cupped hands as he was walking along the shore of the lake, deep in conversation with these simple folks. "These grapes were all around me," he was now explaining. "I only had to see them, and to pick them out of the air, after asking my Father for them.

"You will do the same, I can assure you. There are many others waiting in the air we breathe all around us. My Brothers, this is not a metaphor I'm using now. I speak clearly to you of what is already there; it is only your mind that refuses to believe. In this universe that your hearts are beginning to apprehend, everything has always existed. You only have to give form to what you desire, and to help it through the doors of this Earth with your love and your willpower. Ask simply with the calm conviction of one who knows that his wish has already been granted. My Father's soul and the soul of this world only know the language of simplicity. Why then complicate things with the conditions you impose upon yourselves? Your own human thoughts create your own limitations."

"You say this, Rabbi, you say you act only through your Father's power. I am filled with wonder at what I saw this morning, but the merchants who travel throughout the country often speak about magicians they have met. Two of them who live in the region

of Samaria are said to be able to create things just the way you do.*
Who am I to believe?"

The young man who had asked the question was wearing a
short peasant tunic, one corner of which was hitched up to his belt.
We had seen him stand up in the middle of the assembly, and his
deep voice betrayed his emotion.

"There are two ways of doing the things we are talking about,"
replied the Master. "One of these corresponds to what we call the
white willpower, and this is what we mentioned earlier. The other
belongs to the realm of black desire. Most people see no difference
between the two, for the eyes of the flesh see only the results. By
'black desire' I mean the techniques of those who do not create, but
who use their power to steal something that already exists. This is
the secret method of those who make matter move through space.
These magicians project the rays of their soul to the object of their
desire, cause it to undergo a transformation, and then bring it to
themselves.† Must theft be called a miracle, and their usurped
authority a gift of the Lord?

The one who creates, does so out of love; the one who
appropriates what is already created does so out of desire. Desire will
destroy you if you are not wary; it forces you to take without giving
in exchange. The laws of the Nameless One are the opposite of
those you have established on this Earth, my Brothers. The one who
accumulates and distributes nothing can only become inexorably
poorer and poorer. Instead of drinking from an inexhaustible well,
his body of light becomes rooted to the Earth life after life, age after
age. If your eyes had learned to see, rather than to look, they would
weep at the sight of those who come and go about their sepulchers,
searching for their wealth among the worms caught in the muck of
their powers and their illusory possessions. How long will it take
them to see the ray of light that has come to help them out of their
pits? I do not intend to give you power, but understanding. To
understand is to love. That is how everything is accomplished. Your
Earth, my Brothers, has been created in the image of all those in the
universe. You must see it as a being with countless vestments, each

*One of these may be Simon Magus, mentioned in the Acts of the Apostles.
†This is teleportation of objects by dematerialization and rematerialization.

of them more subtle the farther it is from the skin. The vestments of the Earth are like vessels that are more abundant as they are less visible. Visible Nature, which nourishes you and whose resources are wrongly thought to be infinite, figures among the first of these vestments; while invisible Nature exists beyond, toward the sun. It is there and nowhere else that you must go to gather the things that your heart really longs for. Gather them there, where they really are, in the spirit and the soul of your Earth."*

Then a woman rose out of the crowd and spoke. She was wearing a long blue robe, and her self-assurance showed she was used to the harsh haggling of the camel drivers.

"Rabbi," she said, "I have faith in what you say but your explanations are still mysterious. They do not really explain how you obtain what your heart desires."

The Master smiled, and lowered his voice as if to be closer to the woman who questioned him.

"My heart desires nothing . . . it *is*. Hearts that desire only exist. Don't you understand that you cannot desire what you already have? What I have, woman, I do not own, for it has ever been a part of my being.

"The same is true for you—and for you, my Brothers. Stop thinking of yourselves as one-armed and blind, for you are *one* with what *is*. The extensions of your life are these stones, these plants, these animals that you dream of dominating, though in fact they are another self, another 'you' that you should discover and treat with love.

"These words may seem obscure, I know, but I cannot say this more simply without giving you the answer that you must find yourselves, individually. To you, woman, I can repeat that there is no method by which we can create what you have seen. We must simply not deny ourselves the possibility, not even in the most secret, the innermost part of our being. My Brothers, you do not

---

*Shortly after, the Master went more deeply into this for the 120, making a clear distinction between "naturing Nature" and "natured Nature." He made a special effort to demonstrate the analogy between the spirit, the soul, and the body of the earth, and the world of ideas (the "principial" world), agents (the active astral forces), and phenomena (material effects to be transcended).

know how to love! Why is this? When you have found the true answer to this question, by ceasing to elude it, then you will have come more than half the way you must travel."

Suddenly we heard the sound of hurried footsteps coming from a nearby street. We all turned our heads to see a group of armed men burst upon the little square bathed in sunlight. They were not wearing the uniform of the legion, but plain short tunics. I felt Simon getting tense by my side: we had recognized the Zealots. In a flash, ten of them came to within a few paces of the Master. Two of his close disciples were already on their feet, and in their hands were the swords they always wore at their belts.

"Leave off," he said, calmly and firmly, "these men won't do us any harm."

There was a confused noise in the crowd and several people fled, no doubt fearing the worst. I felt apprehensive myself and stayed where I was, sitting beside Simon and the others, to conceal my emotion. It was not the first time I had seen two close disciples react in such a way. It displeased me all the more since I knew the Master did not approve. Those two men, one of them named Simon, were quick-tempered and nothing could be done to alter their behavior. Their attitude remained unchanged during the years we were fortunate enough to follow the Master; they neither gave up their habit of carrying swords nor overcame the turbulent ways of the Zealots they had once been.

The Master explained to them time and again that the sword could only attract other swords, but he did not forbid them to bear arms. His first care was to respect individualities and differences; and so his disciples were all unlike one another, most of them very close to the common people.

The one who seemed to be the leader of the Zealot troop came still closer to the Master. His tunic, which must have once been orange, was torn in many places and crisscrossed with leather trappings. From his belt hung two cutlasses and a worn sword. His hair was long, the color of ebony, and his flaring nostrils revealed him to be a man prompt to take action and avid for adventure. I could see his profile, and in the way he looked boldly at the Master he reminded me of an eagle.

"Rabbi," he said, trying to catch his breath, "my men have

contacted you many times and today, at great risk, I have come to speak with you myself. My name is Barabbas. That should say something to you. You know that I am the leader of the rebellion against Rome in a good part of the country."

There were muffled sounds from behind; I turned my head in time to see a number of men and women hastily leaving the scene, obviously fearing to be involved in what looked like trouble.

"Rabbi," the Zealot leader continued, "I call these inhabitants of Magdala to witness. I want to say in front of them that the people of Palestine need you! They want to make you their symbol against the Roman legions, they want you for their king. I have men all over the land, men of the soil, those who work, who pray, and who await the Messiah of the Lord. They are talking about you in every valley, in every vineyard, and they see only one hope left: all Israel is crying out to you.

"Walk unarmed before our fighters, and our whole Earth will regain its freedom. Then all will listen to the word of your Father; they will listen to your appeal and you will explain your faith to them."

These words, uttered in a loud, raw voice triggered an outburst among the crowd, which counted no more than fifty people at this point. They rose at once to their feet and exploded into applause at the declarations of the Zealot leader. I even saw a few of our group smile and step closer to the Master, swept away by the wave of enthusiasm.

Simon and I, along with several other members of the Brotherhood, did not know what to do. For all those gathered there this was a blaze of joy. The leader, Barabbas, proud of the impact of his words, stepped onto a big stone and raised his hands to call for silence. He wanted to go on but no one paid attention to him. It seemed, however, that people were now coming from all sides to join in the tumult. It was as if ears had been listening behind the walls of stone and dried brick surrounding the little square. They had heard a call to revolt. . . . And what if Barabbas was right? What if he had been sent so the Master could spread the word at the head of the whole nation?

These questions flashed through me like lightning. Had John

not proclaimed him the Messiah? And was not the place of a Messiah at the head of a nation? The enthusiasm had almost won me over, but within me something snapped, and I felt a growing resistance to this oncoming feeling; something from the ancient teachings of the Essene sages saying: No, no, the real Messiah, the one we were waiting for, could not accept this offer. He was to transform the human race, not to insinuate himself into its old established inner workings. At the very most he could wish to be the grain of sand likely to halt the mechanistic cycle of illusion. Old Zerah had said, "The light must not be imprisoned in an institution; it is not to be seated on a throne, for it is like a breath of life that flows on and on and is endlessly renewed."

I had always treasured these words within my innermost self, and now they surged into my consciousness all by themselves. How many years had passed, Zerah, since your last "farewell"! Nearly twenty perhaps, and you were still there, still there with the right answer!

Simon had not moved, and when his eyes met mine, I could see that he, too, disapproved of what was happening. Suddenly all was quiet again. The Master, one hand spread wide before him, stepped through the crowd. His tall white form was impressive. His eyes were half shut, and a deep feeling of sadness appeared to mark his features.

"You are like young saplings with giant roots," he said, his voice full of love. "Is your attachment to this Earth so strong that you cannot take a step forward? I tell you, my Brothers, the one who will make of me a king among men turns his back on my Father and refuses to look at himself. I am already king of all eternity as each one of you is, but my realm is not of this Earth."

"Do not play with words, Rabbi, the Lord will have nothing to do with a people who does not shake off the yoke of slavery!"

Thus spoke Barrabas, who had just risen to claim his turn to address the crowd; but he had no time to continue, as a heavy clashing of metal made us all jump to our feet. Suddenly, from the corner of a street that gave onto the square, a Roman detachment burst upon the scene, their metal helmets flashing bright spots of sunlight on the ochre of the walls and the dark green of the pomegranate trees. A wave of panic swept the crowd and people began screaming and running in all directions, trampling their neighbors in a mad effort to escape. There was a clanking of metal, orders were shouted over the harsh cries of the crowd, and we watched the band of Zealots rush into a narrow street, their weapons in their hands, with three mounted Roman officers at their heels.

Terror seized the center of Magdala. Cries seemed to come even from within the surrounding dwellings, as if the army had dispatched soldiers with orders to search all the houses.

Those of the one hundred and twenty who were there had the presence of mind to assemble quickly around the Master, forming a nucleus that was immediately encircled by a row of menacing spears. My throat was knotted, and I grabbed Simon's hand as he pressed me close to him. Could it all end there and then?—it was too absurd!

We turned to look at the Master, who had not said a word. Suddenly something happened, still engraved upon my memory with incredible sharpness. I had the sensation that our group was enveloped in a bluish halo, in a veil of cool silence. My head was clear but the noise around us died out, giving way to a strong feeling of tranquility. It seemed as if the Master had enfolded us all in his arms, and indeed, this was probably true in a way. A pure spirit can weave veils of peace, true shields, tangible thoughts of love that make the verb *to love* more than just a word.

Thus it was without fear that we then saw an officer clad in leather approach us. His gaze was like ice and with a quick signal of his hand, he indicated we were to be arrested. The Master then smiled at each of us in turn, which further anchored and strengthened our tranquility. The Romans at last marched us away through the streets of Magdala and we were able to witness the consequences of their intervention. Beneath an arcade two men lay in the dust, blood still flowing from deep wounds in their sides. I clenched my teeth. We came to the edge of the town where several strongly fortified houses served as the high command of the garrison. Behind them we could see a vast camp, protected by short walls of dried mud as yet unfinished. I glanced furtively beyond the camp toward the lake, sparkling in the distance beyond a row of date palms. We were quickly separated from the Master; it was obvious they knew who he was.

An officer in a long purple cloak made us enter a courtyard where we sat on the ground, guarded by a dozen armed men in the shade of an acacia. One of these men seemed to me to look friendly, despite his heavy leather and metal armor. After a moment, he smiled tentatively at us. We returned his smile, and a simple sort of dialogue was established, in silence, but nevertheless rich in meaning.

Perhaps at that time the Master already counted a number of disciples among the Romans who sometimes lingered to listen to him. Were they moved to admiration, to curiosity, or were they merely watching him? We never knew. Perhaps it was all three at once.

The afternoon passed peacefully, and we felt no apprehension whatsoever, neither for the Master nor for ourselves. He was no doubt being questioned about the reasons for his presence in Magdala, and about his ties with the Zealot leader.

Only our contact with Barabbas could get us into any real trouble, surely a long prison sentence. But this was of little importance; it seemed now that we could go through any ordeal and not be affected by it. Something we could not explain had suddenly conferred a sort of invulnerability upon us. Miraculously any attack against us had only the force of childish insults, bearing no real weight.

"What you must awaken is that part of me which is asleep within you."

Was that it? Perhaps the words of Christ had begun to have the effect of the balm we had so long hoped for. Perhaps they were drawing us out of a long lethargy.

Late in the afternoon the Master reappeared, his white veil still harmoniously draped over his head. He was escorted by two legionaries with spears in their hands, looking like mere puppets.

"Come," he said warmly, "we must now find somewhere to sleep."

We suppressed our joy, in an effort to maintain an attitude of dignity until we were alone. Soon after, the heavy wooden doors of the Roman garrison headquarters in Magdala creaked shut behind us. Several soldiers escorted us another hundred yards, then they left us. The setting sun reddened the horizon, and the soft breeze that blew in from the lake was just enough to freshen the air a little. We decided to walk toward the lake. A few palm trees growing in the midst of pleasant greenery there might provide us with shelter for the night. John and Andrew built a fire, and we gathered around the Master to hold a council about what to do next. It was now obvious that the Zealots were bent on exploiting his authority in an effort to gain credibility for future actions.

"We must be very vigilant," said one of us, so quietly that we had to strain our ears to hear him. "In the crowd this morning I heard a man and a woman speaking of a rabbi named Jesus who, according to them, was marching with the Zealots in the region of Bethany. That is all I could grasp of what they were saying, but this means that people are probably beginning to spread false rumors."

Aghast at this news, we lapsed into silence, meeting one another's gazes over the crackling fire.

"There is nothing surprising about that," said the Master, pausing for a long time to let us reflect on our companion's words. "I once observed a young man named Joseph. . . ."

We waited for him to go on, but he broke off, as if to search further within himself. I met Simon's gaze instinctively and together we came to a gradual realization. This took us back into the past, when we were adolescents in the burnt-out streets of Gennesaret. But it was a vague recollection, and still we did not understand.

When nothing remained of the fire but glowing embers, we decided to intone a chant in memory of the two victims of the morning's violence. We knew that the vibrations of the voice united with those of the soul gave birth to beings suffused with love in the realms where bodies of light live. These were chants of joy rather than bitterness or sorrow. Finally, as our humble ceremony came to an end, two members of the Brotherhood moved off from the group. Their task was to escort the deceased to their home of light, far beyond the traps of the etheric ocean.

CHAPTER · IX

THE WAY OF
TRANSMUTATION

I n the months that followed the events in Magdala, the Master, as
well as many of his disciples, were again solicited a number of
times by Barabbas and his followers, whose requests met with the
same categorical refusal. Such eagerness on the part of the Zealots
began to trouble us, the more so as their leader ran increasingly
greater risks to meet the Master whom they still called the Great
White Rabbi. The people, however, gradually stopped calling him
by this name. His growing popularity made him a more familiar
figure, and in many places, he was known as Jesus the Nazarite.*

The Romans seemed not to want to intervene any more; they
were even strangely absent. Much later we learned that a certain
number of men and women of Israel were working for them,
reporting to highly placed officers whatever the Master did or said,
although we did not know this at the time.

We had been in Capernaum for two years when the Master
told us one day that he would leave us for longer than usual.

---

*Due to a confusion with the religious sect mentioned at the beginning of this work and
which was unquestionably better known than the Essene Brotherhood.

"I need some time to be alone," he said, "to compare the path I have taken with the one that still lies ahead of me. A father does not make of his son a device to carry out his plans. Therefore, in giving me a man's body, my celestial Father gave me a man's freedom as well. This is a sign of love that you must understand. The two hands of the human creature, the choice open to him in the making of his life here on Earth are the first fruits of his oncoming grandeur, more than you can imagine. Strip these ideas of the words which cover them. I show you a pathway for humanity. Looking at the times that are to come, I fear one thing: that which is not understood gives rise to terror, fanaticism, or a withering devotion. So I tell you, do not make a god of me."

We were left somewhat perplexed. Why had he said this? John came forward with an answer to our question several days later while the three of us were off the coast of Capernaum in a little boat. A fragrant breeze was blowing, like a caress to our faces. We were alone, and we let the boat drift where it would as we contemplated the shoreline with its trees in blossom and its tender green hills. It was a time for sharing secrets, for opening up our hearts in all confidence.

"We often forget that the Master is a man," said John. "He has said this himself. Of course, there are the two incommensurable forces that speak and act through him, but his resistance is still that of any human body. We must not make an idol of him in imitation of those of ancient times. This is not his wish. He will never be someone who is stuck in some hieratic form, free from questioning, hunger, or fatigue. Within him lies all the force of the Cosmos, but also all the weakness of a man. This is his greatness, Myriam. He is not, all of a piece, the son of the Eternal One, but the revealing sign of an authentic human path.

"I know the Zealots' proposals hurt him at times, in that they offer him a choice that only someone who is forever bound by the chains of his destiny could make without hesitation or temptation. As he has said, we must decide whether we prefer to have an idol or a being such as himself who understands our suffering because he has accepted the whole range of human experience as a consequence of his birth.

"I spoke of the Zealots, but have you never noticed the women who are always trying to get his attention? No doubt they love him—how could it be otherwise? You can't blame them, but do they know what the forces are that use them as they try to attract his attention? Oh, I am not thinking of the devil, you know too well that the only demon that exists is the malice stagnant within the hearts of human beings. No, I mean the energy of dispersion inherent in the matter of our universe. The Master works at gathering and concentrating that which is authentic, whereas what we see as being exterior to him works at the undoing of his action by any means available.

"The weakness of matter holds no real sway over him, but its presence enables him to sharpen his own freedom. So you see, Myriam, now we can better understand what he meant when he said we must render to Rome the things that are Rome's. We do not serve two opposing forces. We must try to understand what makes us think they oppose each other. We must accept them both, and bring them together to be able to grow."

"Do you think the Master would yield so much as an inch to Barabbas?" asked Simon.

"He will not, although he knows his words must be based on the matter in this world."

John was smiling, these days he was all smiles. He asked Simon for the oars and we made our way back to a little wooden pier where fishermen, dangling their feet in the water, were mending their nets.

During the week that followed one of the one hundred and eight died. Upon his return from the mountains, the Master replaced him by a woman from Magdala who, for some time, had been following him. She was tall and thin, and her name was Myriam, or Mary. She was a little older than we were, and her eyes reflected unfathomable sadness. She must once have had a fiery temperament and reminded us of a sleeping volcano, of a force that because it is contained, may one day explode with all the more violence. In the streets of Capernaum it was said that she had led a dissolute life. Her personality and her sometimes quick and often disconcerting reactions tended for several weeks to throw discredit on the Master's entourage. To our knowledge, however, none of the one hundred and twenty ever mentioned this.

Soon a day came when the Master requested our company for a journey of several weeks over the mountains of Galilee. It was the beginning of spring. I can still see how we ran to the bethsaïd, where we had been working shifts with three other Brothers, to pick up our woolen cloaks and our cloth bags. There were twenty of us who had been chosen for that trip aimed at visiting a number of isolated villages.

We gathered beneath a porch on the edge of Capernaum, then set out towards the highlands by way of the shepherds' paths that climbed the moutain. Simon and I enjoyed picking our way among the hawthorn bushes and the rue, as it reminded us of our childhood escapades in the hills around our village.

The blue fringe of the lake was lost to view behind us, and we progressed along a humpbacked ridge amid gray rocks and the almond trees in full blossom.

As we headed toward the north of the country, the landscape became greener and high, snowcapped mountain peaks towered above the cedar forests. The air was still cool and we set a brisk pace, occasionally questioning the Master. His isolation during the past weeks seemed to have reinforced his self-confidence. He was more adamant than ever about the impossibility of establishing what he referred to as his true kingdom among the beings of this Earth, at least as he saw it at that time. He took care to explain this clearly, and this was to be of great help for us later.

"These mountains, these plants, your bodies, everything that is alive or seems to be asleep—in this world and in a multitude of other worlds—is like a bowstring that is plucked at regular intervals by a willing finger. You have no doubt noticed this: when a string is plucked, it vibrates in such a way as to become invisible for an instant. Our bodies function in the same way: they vibrate continually, at the touch of forces unknown to our senses. They vibrate so slowly, however, that their movement is beyond our understanding. That is what makes them dense and palpable. Imagine now what would happen if you acted upon them, if you plucked the bowstring with the most powerful energy there is, the energy of love. Their vibrations would make them invisible to any ordinary human eye.

"Thus it is with my kingdom and its inhabitants. The atoms of which they are composed vibrate so quickly that our eyes cannot see them, nor can our hands grasp them. Know then, my Brothers, that what is called the 'real world' wears a number of faces that defy the reasoning and logic elaborated by certain human beings.

"I may now tell you clearly, my Brothers, that my task is not to establish my kingdom on this Earth, but to bring this Earth closer to my kingdom.

"I will activate the life of your world by inducing subtle vibrations within your hearts. Never, perhaps, have I expressed myself as concretely as I do now. My words are not a form of poetry so much as they are an expression of a geometry of the heart and soul.

"The universes as well as the heavens you contemplate every evening, evolve according to the same rules. They bathe in an ocean of life, where an invisible finger makes them vibrate periodically following ever-accelerating rhythms. The multitudes of heavenly bodies progress in this way, cyclically transmuted, propelled from one reality to the next, inexorably fleeing the limitations of density. The Eternal One, my Brothers, is a musician who sounds notes at ever-higher pitches. The key born of his breath, goes up one note every two thousand years, and at the end of the sixth of these keys, the worlds enter a new vibratory stage. I tell you truly, I am the master craftsman of the sixth key, a catalyst whose task it is to make the doors of the heart vibrate in a new way by the end of the next two millenia.

"The rock must become a gem; the grass, trees; animals must awaken to their humanity and humans emerge as initiates, the equals of the Brothers from the stars.

"In the angel must blossom the archangel, the planet bloom as a sun, and the sun expand into a central cosmic fire. This will first take place in our universe as an etherization of matter and consciousness, subsequent to an internal and external purification of each form of existence.

"It is all a question of the level of consciousness, my Brothers. Everything else is but an application of this principle."

These explanations made us feel giddy. We were not used to such technical language on the part of the Master. Nevertheless, we felt the urgent need for such precise knowledge, which strengthened our understanding of the harmonics of the universe. Those of us who were children of Essania were accustomed to hearing the world spoken of in terms of vibrations, and had little trouble following the Master, but this was not true of the others, more sensitive to familiar images, even if they contained double meanings, than to this form of mathematics.

We felt the need to make a halt on a sloping hillside. In the valley below, the bleating of sheep acted as a reminder that we were not alone in the world, and that one day we would have to share these newly revealed truths with others.

"You will not explain these things to the people," said the Master, as if he had felt our anxiety. "Never turn more than one page of the revelation at a time. For everything there is a season, for every person there is a book. You must be able to speak of the harvest to those who work in the fields and the vineyards, of fishing to those whose universe is a boat and the waters it floats upon. Knowing is not enough, you must know how to be silent, not to hide anything, but to go to the essential, avoiding horizons which are apt to arouse fear in people. The art I ask you to practice may be expressed in three words: love, progression, and discernment."

With this the Master paused for quite a while, and stepped several paces away from the rest of us who sat waiting in the grass.

"Lie down on the ground," he said, coming back calmly. We did as he asked without question, overcome by such an unexpected request.

"It would be well for you to look upon the dance of the worlds," he said, as he, too, lay down in our midst, "so that you will know something of the celestial finger that plucks the bowstring of the universe, and makes it vibrate. You have nothing to fear from this experience. It will make you weep with joy rather than from fear. I am going to operate within you a separation between consciousness and flesh, that you may soar free of all apparent ties and follow me."

The Master then asked us not to move at all and to be absolutely silent. We lay there, our eyes closed, listening to the singing of the birds. A long time passed. I felt my energy draining downward, soaking into the ground beneath me, organ by organ. Then I was one with the Earth. I was sure that I had sunk into the Earth, physically as well as mentally. I could no longer feel any connection with my limbs. The circulation of my blood had most certainly slowed down to the point where any effort to move would have been in vain—but then I had no desire to try. I felt a deep serenity in my body and soul, an absolute ataraxy. The mask of my personality and the shell of my physical body were forgotten. It was a state I knew well, whose mastery was taught by the Brotherhood. It represented neither an escape from awareness nor a dulling of consciousness. Quite the contrary, it was the prerequisite to an awakening to the real world, the key needed to open the door to true perception.

"Open your aura."

The Master's three simple words slipped almost imperceptibly into our beings, as if whispered to each of our cells. Then I had the impression that someone touched me in the hollow of my belly, and I felt myself slowly slide out of my body and into a translucent cone of light, up through the crown of my head. This happened so distinctly, with my breath feeling easy and deep . . . I could see my body below me, seemingly asleep in a sort of semirigidity, a smile on its lips. I soon realized that the same thing had happened to my companions, and that their physical envelopes lay abandoned in the grass. We were hovering lightly on the air, our luminous bodies straining to maintain stability, in loose formation about a source of dazzling light that was the Master. His willpower had enabled us all to leave our bodies altogether.

Nature had clothed herself in myriad iridescent splashes of light, a display of hues I had never seen before. The grass below, the flowers, whole valleys were united in one vast and splendid rainbow, sparkling with life. This was the real world, the truth of life on our planet that humankind kept denying. Our thoughts mingled and we spoke from heart to heart, exchanging subtle impressions and images words could never convey. This was surely an approach to boundless love, a fusion with the vital and cosmic forces that nurture all life.

Simon reached out to me and we moved together, like two

veils of silk, with the wind whispering through us. We whirled and plunged down toward a tuft of grass, making ourselves so small that we could follow the meanders of the unfolding shoots. We condensed and expanded our light bodies according to our will and love, watching all the energy of the world pulsating in the calyx of a flower or in a splinter of stone. We knew then that barriers are unknown to the soul, and that life is a single force that our minds relentlessly try to differentiate, an eternal sharing that escapes the understanding of the small self. As human-shaped flames, we gathered around the Master, clothed in light.

"Come," he said, addressing each of us. "Soar with me beyond these mountains, beyond the clouds."

He smiled and it was like a ray of sunshine leading us ever upward, our sleeping bodies and the copses of Galilee fading into the distance below us. It seemed that our astral bodies had woven cocoons of white light around us as we rose into the air at dizzying speed. But then, was it really air? really speed? The soul does not categorize, nor does it differentiate between places, based on notions of distance. The soul evolves in a realm of tangible thought that laughs at our world of logic.

Now we were no more than a milky sphere hovering around the Master, surrounded by the blackness of the firmament, which somehow was suffused with a secret light. I could see the throbbing of myriad stars, the versicolored fires of planets that seemed to have been drawn into a whirlwind. This was beyond the comprehension of my Galilean intelligence, versed though I was in the abstractions of the Brotherhood. Through my mind flashed thoughts of the Brothers of the stars, of the mists on which they traveled through the different worlds. Then followed a flurry of incomprehensible images. Once more I felt our pace accelerating, and the structure of our bodies seemed transformed.

Away to one side I saw a gaseous-looking form flecked with tiny blue, yellow, and red stains. It looked like an enormous cloud that was stretched and torn in places, pierced by blinding little flashes of light. I recognized our galaxy and its suns.

"Here is the sum of your worlds," said the Master, his soft voice coming from within each of us. "It is a body where suns, moons, and earths like your own are born, live, and die, where planetary systems interlace and revolve around a great force of a subtle nature, the fire of all the transcended suns, the fire of my Father. In the cosmic immensity, there are an infinite number of bodies like this one. The Nameless One has harmoniously submitted each of them to cycles within cycles and so on, eternally. These bodies are interlocked, as are their cycles. This is the truth I share with you today, for you to learn and reflect upon. Whoever knows the cycles of his own body knows those of all the bodies in the cosmic ocean. The same principles are infinitely reproduced in variations the human mind cannot penetrate, though arbitrary chance plays no part there.

"Look at all the physical worlds into which you are born as a function of your karma and according to what you need in order to evolve. The Nameless One's finger is slowly approaching these worlds, and in the form of a fantastic cloud of energies he will penetrate them. You cannot feel it yet, but within two thousand years all of your planets and stars will be transformed by his intervention. He will make them vibrate at a higher pitch, which will cause their etherization.

"You can realize now the importance of preparing the beings of your world for such a transformation, which is a necessary step on the path to happiness. Never forget this, my Brothers, never forget to see the grand scale of things, for all is grand. Little means nothing, except within the prison of narrow minds. Let your love be grand then, for it is the only inexhaustible force that envelops all. Now you must understand that the worlds shining before you and of which you can only perceive the coarsest, outermost shells, are the organs of my Father's body.

"The perfect Human Being is no other than my Father, and you are his children, as you are the particles of his body. He calls you to Him so that you may grow incommensurably in consciousness, so that you, too, may become perfect men, creators of worlds.

"I am His son because I am his heart, the sun, the part of his body that shows you the path. From now on, you must become aware of each of the cells of your bodies. Identify yourselves with them, and may they identify themselves with you. In truth there is no difference between them and you. In this knowledge, and especially in this love, let the seven fundamental suns of your body blaze with all their fire. Let them be the seven seals and the seven churches of your alliance with your own flesh. This is the royal path of transmutation!"

With these words, our exploration of the cosmic ocean came to an end. We felt ourselves plunging at dizzying speed into a bottomless well. All around us, multicolored ribbons of light were infinitely unfolded, penetrating us at times with a tingling, ringing music. This did not last very long, but we focused on every detail as would a musician suddenly discovering a new melody.

Our bodies awaited us like silent sleepers, and we reentered them with some difficulty. It seemed that our blood had almost frozen in our veins, and our stiffened muscles were in need of vigorous massage. The Master then embraced us as if to welcome us into a new and radically different reality. Afterwards, we set off once more, on the path that led down into the valley.

News of the Master's arrival had preceded him, and even after all we had experienced this day, we marveled at this little detail.

CHAPTER X

AND THEY WERE BUILDING HIM A THRONE OF STONE

T he months and the seasons went by. The Master continued his teaching throughout the land, from time to time making brief trips into Jerusalem. The priests of the high temple there always awaited him eagerly, hoping to provoke him before the people in the merchants' courtyard. Though the twelve were with him nearly everywhere he went, our nucleus of one hundred and eight followers was momentarily split into two groups; it was our task to spread the message throughout the whole of Palestine and to calm the public tension aroused by the Zealots' disturbances.

The Master rarely spent the night in Jerusalem, preferring to stay at a little house in Bethany—Martha's house—which thus became a meeting place. Nevertheless, he went more and more frequently into Jerusalem, where he made a habit of speaking in the temple courtyard every Friday. Soon, crowds of people would gather there, awaiting his arrival. Whenever possible, we mingled with the teeming throng of merchants, craftsmen, shepherds, and pilgrims, our ears open to the various reactions voiced by those who were listening to the Master. Our aim was to avoid any form of uprising that might result in the sort of thing which had happened in Magdala. We feared an excess of enthusiasm from the people as much as the possibility of an acute reaction triggered by the priests. From what we heard here and there in the streets and in the court of the temple, it became progressively clearer that the Pharisees and the Sadducees were split into two groups with diverging opinions. Some were categorically opposed to the "Nazarite," whereas others were more lenient or even sympathetic.

Simon related the words of a priest he had overheard talking to the owner of a little shop:

"What do we have to fear from him save that he disturbs our tranquility? Is this not what prophets have always done? Few people loved them while they lived, refusing them even the title that was rightfully theirs. For many, only death establishes a man as someone; prophets always belong to the past. Living ones are always regarded as troublemakers!"

This priest had perhaps not grasped the full meaning of the Master's words, but we could not deny that he spoke with some common sense.

Nevertheless, it was during this period that we feared the worst. The critical situation reached a climax on the day when the Master was greeted by an eager crowd, carrying palm branches. Many people looked but did not see, listened but did not hear.

In our frequent discussions outside the walls of the city, we attempted to make sense of the situation. We did not know what to think of the enthusiastic reactions of the people of Jerusalem, or rather, we suspected the truth, without daring to acknowledge it. The Roman army remained silent, but we felt it to be ever present. Barabbas was to be seen no more—we had learned of his arrest—but his men were scattered among the crowds, perhaps watching for the most favorable moment to urge the people to rise up. Their actions seemed frighteningly clear to us, as they spread their robes on the ground for the Master to walk upon. They were building for the "Nazarite Rabbi" the throne of stone he did not want. They were, in the words of the Master himself, "crowning the only king their hearts could conceive of."

The confusion and the exaltation that reigned among the people reached a new pitch when rumors of a small Zealot band led by Jesus continued to spread. James, Simon Peter and several of the one hundred and twenty who were present at the time were sent by the Master to discover the origin of these rumors. They returned with news that filled us with indignation. The Zealots had resolved to take advantage of the resemblance between one of their men and the Master. Thus, there were many who affirmed in good faith that they had seen the Great White Rabbi leading attacks against the Romans. The Zealots apparently felt they could force the Master's hand by presenting an image of him that corresponded to the wishes of the majority. They reasoned that he would at last give in and answer the people's call.

It was an obvious trap, whose indisputable force caused us great harm. Walls of incomprehension were being raised before us, just at a moment when an ever-growing number of men and women had begun to look within themselves. Simon and I were moved to discouragement and rebellion. From long ago came a vision—quite explicit now—of eyes like live embers, those of Joseph the Zealot in the streets of Gennesaret. It was certainly he who was the instrument of the dark forces that the masters of the Brotherhood had told us of, during our stay in the land of the Red Earth. There was no longer any doubt of it. We found it hard to suppress a wave of hatred rising within us. This was a new feeling, a terrifying feeling. The Master must have felt its presence among us, no doubt, for he cut through the heavy silence with a few simple words at once full of both reproach and love.

"Hatred feeds on hatred. I tell you, my Brothers, do not strengthen the energies of those who do not yet know how to see."

We gathered around him, as if we all felt the need to find peace, to mentally weave what had been our force until then: the web of white light—our shield, our bridge from one heart to another.

"I would recommend, however, neither weakness nor passivity," he added. "A being must rebel against all forms of lies and errors. But when one chooses to act, let it be from healthy anger. Anger, I can assure you, may be a manifestation of love as much as of hatred. If it is to be constructive it must be controlled, in no way resembling an overflow of animal-like impulses. Only then does it become a directed action, an instrument of equity rather than a satisfaction of instincts or immediate desires."

Through a curious conjunction of events, it was in the days that followed this declaration that the Master vehemently criticized the temple merchants. The news of his angry outburst spread like wildfire through the streets of Jerusalem, silencing the complaints of those who feared that his words revealed a much too tender heart. Though we did not witness this scene personally, we saw in it an illustration of the double aspect of Moon-Sun, our Venus: rebellious and renovating in the morning, peaceful at night.

As he did not want to cause any trouble for Martha, the Master entrusted Philip, one of the twelve, with the task of finding a place within the walls of Jerusalem for the secret meetings of the one hundred and twenty. We met frequently then, as we shared a vague feeling that we had no time to lose in organizing our work.

Unexpectedly, the place that was chosen was located in a busy Jerusalem street. This turned out to be a judicious choice, as a few more people added to the hustle and bustle of the noisy, motley crowd could hardly draw attention to us. It was what we called a high room, located over a dwelling place. Narrow little windows cut into the walls looked out onto a few of the shops below, and allowed thin rays of light to enter the room. The atmosphere there was soft, all in halftones. There was a permanent chiaroscuro effect as the orange rays of light played with the darkness, creating an intimacy that uplifted our hearts. It was a tiny universe surrounded by four walls of sunbaked bricks, a perfect place for the transmutation of awakening souls. We felt safe there, sheltered from the turbulence and the incomprehension that reigned outside.

Our tranquility was, however, as illusory as it was short lived. It was under this roof that we heard the news that destroyed the hopes we had nourished. The Master had arrived as usual, late one afternoon, in his long white linen robe, with a veil over his head. His tall form had appeared at the top of the little wooden stairway, before coming to sit facing us. In the streets below a lively commotion still prevailed; we could hear the cries of the donkey drivers as they unloaded their baskets before the merchants' stands. The noise was hardly filtered by the drapes of coarse cloth we had hung here and there, and we feared we would hear nothing of what the Master had to say. Yet his voice, although discreetly hushed, reached our ears as if it traveled on paths unknown to the laws of our physical world.

"Soon," he said, "I will have to leave you."

We sat there, as if frozen. His first words of the day were pronounced with a voice that was calm but underscored with gravity.

"Whatever happens," he went on, "will be good, for it will be my Father's will, as well as my own. You will receive my counsel in good time, so that the stream of love may become a river. Understand what the Eternal One expects of you. What I have to say to you today leaves no room for interpretation, as all is perfectly clear.

"Soon you will be called to go across the mountains and beyond the seas. You will understand the purpose of your own acts, but above all, you must acknowledge the deeper meaning and the very goal for which you strive. I do not ask you to speak of Jesus. My own physical personality is of little importance. Your world may forget my name, it is of little consequence. What is important is to lay the foundations of an immense Brotherhood based on mutual giving and union with all the forces of creation. It is essential that you console men and women through your acts and through the repetition of the words that my Father has placed in my mouth. Remember this well. It is not the person of Jesus who has addressed you for the past three years, but a truth without age, expressed through him. You will tell people that you have known the meeting point of the forces of renewal and that these forces are theirs. I have called you here to prevent you from establishing dogmas in my name or in the name of my Father. Dogma is human, and we are not human. Teach our works and our harmony, but not a law.

"Here then is my first wish: Do not create one more religion, thinking you serve the Eternal One. His desire is that the people of your Earth go beyond that notion of religion, that they transcend it in order to rediscover the original unity. Teach their hearts and their minds how to break down the barriers that divide them, but do not raise up one more wall to surround them through the commentaries of my words, which, thus, would become dead letter. Will you be able to accept this? I fear that the mirrors of time will distort the truth, my Brothers. I fear that the human race on earth, for the time being, is only to walk on one leg.

"Link their hearts to their true source, but do not invent yet another model image for them. Above all, do not shape for them the contours of a new god, rather awaken their memories apart from any moral values.

"The gods will always wear masks of warlords copied from those of the humans as they are whisked into the dance of the cosmic cycles. Teach the multitudes to melt into my heart, for it is thus that they will melt into my Father. Their privilege will become that of Man, which is to perceive all the beings in the creation, to become one with all at once; to be part of their countless lives and deaths, the plan and consequence of which they will be able to order in a single impulse of love.

"Sages and prophets have thought it necessary to create methods and techniques in order to achieve the supreme union. These you may regard as the rungs of a ladder but not as the ladder itself. Above all, you must take care not to let yourselves be caught in the web of illusions woven by the satisfactions of your own minds. This is to be dreaded even more than a lack of love, for it is a lack of love itself that is disguised as wisdom.

"I tell you my Brothers, be of those who may be recognized by the light flowing from their hearts. The sun of the mind, only able to speak to its kind, hasn't any positive energy to offer. It destroys itself.

"Let it be understood that my life is the life of those who go barefoot, those who are without artifice, who have rediscovered their roots. It is a shorter distance from the soles of the feet to the heart than Earthly logic would allow you to believe."

Darkness was invading the room and several of the Brothers busied themselves with lighting big earthenware oil lamps. Their shadows danced over the walls, mingling with the long ribbons of incense smoke that curled into the air. Two men then left the room, down the narrow stairway, and reappeared shortly with a basket of barley cakes.

This was to be the last meal taken by the one hundred and

twenty gathered around the Master. We passed the flat, round little breadcakes amongst us, and ate them with a spread made from cereals. A few olives and some bitter wine completed our repast. I remember we tried to make it a happy meal in spite of the misgivings aroused in us by the Master's opening words. We did not know exactly what he had meant, but in our hearts we felt the weight of those who realize they are becoming orphans. Throughout the meal and after the following short ritual prayer, the Master made his way among our little group, joking with us and comforting those who told him they no longer understood. It was a moving experience, though no one could quite explain what was happening.

Meanwhile, about ten of us took turns to watch the front of the house and the street below in order to remain on alert for any sign of danger. We used a secret code that changed every week. The Master knew he was being closely watched, and seemed for the first time to fear a direct attack by the Sanhedrin or the Roman command. Before he left us that evening, he spoke at length of his journeys in the lands of the East and of the many sacred texts he had studied there. During this account, interrupted by questions, he spoke frequently of himself in the third person as if he were referring to a being other than himself, and whose reactions he was analyzing. It was Christ addressing us, which better allowed us to appreciate the superhuman force that had incarnated in the body of the little Joseph of our childhood. It almost made me dizzy to think of this, and memories of times gone by were awakened in me.

I saw once more the travelers, rich or miserable, who regularly had come to visit Joseph in the secret of his earth-colored home. No doubt they had already known. Who were they all, these pilgrims of the soul whose very names have been lost to time? That evening I paid special attention to a few sentences the Master spoke about a vast land located far to the North, beyond the sea. A number of divinities were to be found there, with names that sounded strange to our ears: Aesus, Hukadern, Karito Winda.* Of these he spoke

---

*This refers to a Celtic trinity: Hukadern represents the Logos, son of God, the physical and spiritual sun; Karito Winda (or Koridwen), the black virgin, the true Egyptian Isis, was Hukadern's mystical spouse and symbolized the primary matter of nature. Aesus (Teutates) is the Cosmic Father. His name suggests the root As or Ase of the words Essene and Iesse, one of Jesus' ancestors on his mother's side.

briefly, lingering rather over a stag god whose symbolic life was not dissimilar to the legends of our people. This stag, whose name was Cernunnos, was the keystone of the whole mythology. The Master described it as being the regent of the energies of fecundity, as one of the forces of Nature, dying and being cyclically reborn. The people of the North prepared a sacred drink from fermented mashed grain.* This drink represented Nature's blood, the energy able to give visions and to hasten reintegration into the initial divine source. The god Cernunnos was spoken of as the initiator, the solar stag whose antlers were like roots, reminding us of our link to the celestial forces. We were asked to see him as the supreme sacrificial being: while the grain was being mashed during the ritual the stag was tortured to death, in order to be born again at the spring equinox in the young germinating seeds.

This was a universal image we were to contemplate. Such a reference to beliefs foreign to our people was a reminder advising us not to turn away from the wisdom of diverse teachings and the fraternal bonds that united them.

"My path," said the Master, "is not opposed to those of ancient times. The message you are called upon to spread is the end result of a thousand others and is addressed to all the species of the Earth. The history of humanity, my Brothers, is that of a rough stone fallen from the Heavens, fallen from so high that it became planted in the Earth and believed it was one with her. It is the history of that stone to which the solar winds give a cubic form and which they will transform into a jewel of one hundred and forty-four thousand facets when its time has come to regain the heavenly gardens.†

"Try to understand this, and to retain its essence. The whole mystery of the human race is to be found there."

With these words, the Master rose and drew the long veil of white linen over his face. He crossed his arms on his breast, and we

---

*Barley beer.

†This is apparently a reference to the two extreme chakras and to the levels of consciousness linked to them. The four represents the earth, as well as the stable base; the cube represents the energy of transmutation; while the number 144,000 (the number of the elect in Revelation 7:4) is the number of the petals of the crown chakra, the lotus of Christ consciousness, which includes those of the other chakras.

did the same in deep silence. The eyes of our souls then became aware of vivid blue flames all around him and sparks of gold that gathered and rose in spirals to the rough-hewn beams of the ceiling. This perception lasted a long, long time, so long it seemed that a flood of love, unknown to us until now, caught at our throats and swelled our hearts.

Outside, night had fallen. As we walked down the winding streets that led beyond the walls and toward the bethsaïd, we caught a glimpse of a single twinkling light in the sky. It was Moon-Sun. As in the past, it was calling out to us and spreading its thousand hands of white peace, hands that made of each heart a crucible.

CHAPTER · XI

THE NIGHT OF GETHSEMANE

I t was pitch-dark and we had just entered Jerusalem through a gate the Roman militia failed to watch as closely as the others. At such a late hour, it was not easy to gain entry through the ramparts of the city. There were only three of us—Simon, Zachariah (who was also a member of the Brotherhood), and myself, and we gave as an excuse for our late arrival the long and hazardous nature of our journey. We were out of breath, having run most of the way, and the last steps, up a steep and rocky path that wound among the fragrant shrubs, had been the worst of all. And to all that was added the fear of being recognized as companions of the Master. Simon's and Zachariah's long hair in itself was enough to betray our identity, and after what we had just witnessed we could indeed fear the worst.

For some time now we had already taken care not to wear our white robes anymore, for they had become too recognizable; but we had the feeling that there was something else in us that was likely to give us away . . . as if a way of looking at someone or a way of speaking were enough to signal that we were among the partisans of the Master. Partisans! Indeed, it had gone that far; more than ever before, the whole city was split into two factions. There were those who declared themselves in favor of the "Nazarite" and those who were doubtful about his political neutrality. Fortunately, Passover was approaching, and Jerusalem was packed with people from far and wide. With a little luck, we might be able to blend in with the flood of pilgrims. Whatever the danger, we had to reach the home of Massalia, a young man we trusted implicitly, who had offered to help us countless times when we were in the temple courtyard. His home, in a dark street beneath the city walls, had often served as a meeting place for some of us. We felt that he alone, at such an hour, might be able to advise us as to where the Master would be sleeping that night. Getting there was no easy matter. At all costs we had to avoid the armed soldiers that were patrolling along the streets. Luckily, they were not given to being silent. The clanking of their weapons echoed in rhythmic cadence off the walls and the paved streets, and warned us whether they were near at hand.

The lower part of Massalia's house sheltered a warehouse of jugs and jars filled with grain and wine. The door was easily opened, and we slipped in, gasping for breath. We must have been lacking in discretion, for from the room above we heard the sound of quick muffled footsteps. We thought it a good idea to announce ourselves out loud before something unpleasant might happen to us. It was pitch-black in there, and we had to grope carefully among the earthenware vessels. At last we heard the voice of Massalia, and the darkness was pierced by a small flame that appeared in one corner of the ceiling. There we could make out a ladder, then a half-clad form that descended it, an oil lamp in hand.

"What's the matter?" Massalia asked in a worried voice, raising his lamp high to see us better. His eyes were haggard, and his hair was tangled. We hardly heard his question, trying so hard to hold back ours.

"Where is the Master?" Simon asked immediately. "We absolutely have to see him at once. Something very important has just happened near Bethany. We did not even think we could make it all the way here!"

"You had better come upstairs," replied Massalia. "I know where the Master is, but it is impossible to reach him at this time of the night. I saw James at nightfall and he told me he was leaving for Gethsemane. You know that for some time they have been going there almost every evening to pray. He also told me that the Master hardly spoke, and that he seemed worried. However, as I said, you cannot reach him now; the soldiers will not let you out of the city until daylight. There has been a strange unrest since the morning."

Massalia's words seemed full of wisdom, and momentarily calmed, we followed him up the ladder that led to the upper room. His wife and daughter were there. We found them sitting on a mat on the floor, wrapped in a blanket of coarse wool. We sat beside them and in a hushed voice Simon undertook to relate briefly the events we had witnessed.

"We were on our way back from Martha's, and we were in a hurry to reach the Bethsaïd at the outskirts of the city before dark. We had even been given donkeys by someone at Martha's house in order to speed our return, but to no avail, as we had to abandon them at the first house we came upon, for fear of drawing attention to our presence. On foot it is easier to slip unseen among the rocks and the gullies. But this is what happened: We had hardly left Bethany when we came upon some shepherd huts half buried in the earth, close by the high road. We could see fires already burning there. As we approached, we heard screaming and shouting that seemed to be coming from every stone on the mountain. As we drew even closer to the huts, we saw that a great number of men were fighting amid a cloud of dust. Some of them were on horseback, and were striking wherever they could. We saw at once they were Romans. As for the others, they responded to the onslaught with incredible determination. A few of them were wearing dark headbands, which indentified them as Zealots.

"We did not know what to do, Massalia; could we interfere? It was a real slaughter. About thirty men were dragging themselves painfully on the ground, and on either side, about fifty more were still fighting. Suddenly we saw two centurions on their mounts, a little way off, coldly observing the massacre. We thought it best to run to them, and beg them to stop the fight. We hurried their way, our arms raised to make it clear that we were unarmed—but this was a real mistake. They received us with the flat of their swords, not even giving us a chance to speak. Then they knocked us to the ground, with the rumps of their horses. By the time we got to our feet again, they were galloping toward their troops. The struggle was over in no time. We understood that the legionaries had made quick work of the rebels, as they soon gathered to chase the last ones fleeing among the nearby rocks. We heard a few more earsplitting cries, and then all was silent. They rode away in formation after picking up their own casualties. Their leader gazed at us suspiciously from afar, then he, too, turned around and left. Bruised and in pain, we rushed to the side of the Zealot victims. It was obvious there could be no survivors, as moments before we had watched with horror the Romans killing those who were merely wounded.''

A heavy silence fell over us all. I could tell that Simon had no desire to continue his account. As for myself, I was unhappy, and I still thought we had to see the Master as soon as possible. Zachariah picked up where Simon had left off. What he had to say seemed even more important, but Massalia, troubled, had stood up abruptly and was now pacing back and forth over the dusty floor of the room. We saw his silhouette fade into the darkness, then reappear, and each time he seemed more nervous than before.

"The sight of the bodies was horrible," said Zachariah.

"Among the victims we recognized the two shepherds who had been camped there, and who must have been caught in the middle of the fight. But most unbelievable, Massalia, was to find, covered with wounds, the Zealot leader who had been passing himself off as the Master in the past months. I do not know if his death should come as a relief to us or if it is a sign of the danger facing the Master. This may be the sign of a major offensive on the part of Rome.

"We hardly had time to recite the ritual prayers amidst this butchery, when we heard people galloping our way. We thought it safer to hide in the biggest of the shepherds' huts and from there we watched as a number of Roman soldiers loaded the body of the Zealot leader onto a wagon. It all happened quickly, then they left, abandoning the other bodies.

"There was nothing else we could do but come here, as fast as possible, and that was not easy, Massalia. Night fell, which slowed our pace down, and we dared not take the high road. It was a good thing too, for twice, from afar, we saw Roman detachments passing there in great haste."

Massalia fastened his robe and took his cloak.

"You were right," Massalia agreed. "The Master must be warned. All this seems too serious not to."

Without a word, we followed him down the ladder, and slipped noiselessly into the street. I was exhausted from the long walk earlier, and I was surprised to feel a new burst of energy rising from some inner reserve. Waiting there would have been still more of a strain. We did not go far, however. Beneath a little archway near the stables we came abruptly face-to-face with another furtive figure hugging the walls. My heart rose in my throat, and we could hardly keep from crying out . . . it was John! Our eyes met, searching . . . then he rushed toward us, overwhelmed by an intense emotion.

"The Master! The Master!" he stammered, in a choked voice. "They have just taken him away!"

John could say no more, but burst into tears, and I feared he was about to smash his head against the walls. For the three of us time stood still for a second, for an hour, I cannot say. Our minds became dull, frozen, and it was as if all life had suddenly withdrawn from our bodies. Then Simon was at last able to whisper a few words:

"We cannot stay here, all we can do is return to Massalia's!" John said nothing and burst into tears once more but we saw that his eyes had taken on a new expression. There was a blue flame in them, a flame that pierced the darkness, a flame of murdered hope but one that wanted to live . . . to live! . . .

As we made our way in the shadows under the walls, we could smell the dying scent of incense, and for the first time this fragrance pained me; so bitter it seemed, so heady that it wearied the heart. I made an effort to reason myself into calmness, however, to examine the facts logically. Had we not already been arrested in Magdala? Nothing had come of it, and the Master had taken great care to prove his political neutrality. But what if it was the Sanhedrin?

Massalia's door was once more closed behind us, and we hastened to the upper room, where we would be more at ease to ponder our next move.

"It was the Iscariot," murmured John, as he let himself fall onto the mats. "It was he who betrayed the Master's presence in Gethsemane. We all saw him, he did not even try to hide, arriving shortly after the soldiers. I should have known something was wrong. I had never seen the Master as he was this evening. After the long prayer that we always said together in the garden, he drew away from us, and refused to say any more, although he usually commented on some words.

"Simon and I tried to approach him several times. It was getting quite cool and we found it increasingly difficult to sit there motionless, but he said nothing we could understand, other than he wished to be left alone because he was speaking with his Father."

John ran his fingers through his hair, then over his face. He seemed to hesitate, to search for his words, then he took a deep breath, forcibly, and went on.

"It is too stupid! Why didn't I suspect? . . . I had never seen the Master like that. It was pitch-dark, but I think I saw tears in his eyes. It had happened before, but never like that, no. . . . When the soldiers fell on us, they put chains on his wrists immediately! They would never have dared that in Magdala! Those of us who were armed did what they could to try to defend him, but it was of no avail. The altercation was very sharp. I think that two of the Romans were wounded, but it was as if the Master gave himself up. It was he who intervened to stop the fight. By then the chains on his wrists were gone, which made the Romans step back in awe: they thought it was magic! That was when the Iscariot arrived. He pretended not to understand what was happening, and he mumbled something to the Master. Then the fight began again and we all ended up running away, scattering among the olive trees. We all ran, do you hear? We all turned and ran! Even I! That's the worst part. . . . My Brothers, I think we have understood nothing of what has happened here in Jerusalem, right from the beginning!

"I don't know where the others are, I thought I would find some of them if I came here. Perhaps they have gathered at the bethsaïd?"

"Does anyone else know about this?" I whispered.

"Nicodemus and Joseph,"* he said. "They were sitting not far from us among the olive trees. I met them as I came down toward the valley. They said they were going to the palace of Pilate, as they have friends there who might be able to do something. Perhaps Pilate himself, in fact."

John paused, seemed to reflect for a moment, then placed his two hands over his heart.

"Listen," he said, "and promise me you will not repeat what I am going to tell you. The reputation and perhaps the life of a whole family depend on your silence.

"This afternoon, as I was alone with the Master, we were accosted by a man who led us to a rich home. The Master recognized him as one of his secret followers in the palace. We accompanied him with complete trust. In the back room of the house, Pilate himself awaited us. I thought it was a trap, but it was not, and I even found him to be very courteous. I assure you, he is not as opposed to our cause as they say! The exchange was very brief; he simply asked the Master to observe great caution, as, he said, he himself was not informed of all that was happening. I was struck by the trembling of his lips, as if he were very unsure of himself."

John straightened up again, then rose suddenly, and we did the same. Words were useless. His anxiety was now our own, in the darkest moment of the night when everything seemed to waver. One of us came up with the idea that we should rejoin the others, and without further delay we drew our cloaks around us and went down the little ladder. As we did so, there came a heavy sound of footsteps, a cadenced, metallic clanking: it was the Romans.

We waited silently amid the disorder of the grain jars, until the din faded away into the night. We had to cross more than half the city, avoiding the patrols, and manage to get through the gates, in order to reach the Bethsaïd. On the way, during the brief moments

---

*Joseph of Arimathea.

when we paused to catch our breath, an idea germinated in our minds and little by little took form. The best way to make it past the guards was for one of us to pretend to be ill on approaching the main gates, thus giving the others the excuse to carry him to the Bethsaïd outside the walls to be cared for by the Brothers. Our destination would then be known, but still it seemed to be the best strategy. We were fortunate enough to find a makeshift stretcher in a little shed that belonged to one of our people in the city. The men decided I was the one to play the role of the patient. I settled into the precarious construction of wood and branches and tried to moan as genuinely as possible. The legionaries suspected nothing, but simply lifted my cloak to get a look at my face.

That is how we got outside the walls of the city. Not a word was exchanged, but I felt my bearers hasten their pace, stumbling now and then on stones in the path. Lifting a corner of my cloak, I realized we were not alone. A crowd of pilgrims and merchants were sleeping on the ground, little bundles of poor cloth and coarse wool, scattered here and there in the hollows of the terrain or sheltered by the surrounding vegetation. Passover was only about ten days away, and already the people had begun arriving from all over the country. They had camped wherever they could, according to their modest means. Our small group soon reached the little outer walls of the bethsaïd, and I jumped down to the ground. The building of earth and stones was partly surrounded by olive and fig trees, and it was usually crowded with pilgrims, beggars, women about to give birth, and the ill. It would hardly be easy for us to gather there without attracting attention.

Before we had even crossed the threshold of the bethsaïd, we heard shouting and the sound of hurried footsteps, coming from behind the shelter. We headed at once in that direction, with great caution. In the deep shadows of the fig trees we could barely make out six or seven shapes that seemed to be running in all directions, waving their arms about. The altercation was sharp in tone and the atmosphere tense. We were able to recognize some of the voices, so we approached. The tension was so high that we did not even think of the possible danger of our position, and nor did those gathered in the darkness make much of our arrival.

We found six of the Master's close disciples in an indescribable state, violently at odds with the Iscariot. Simon Peter had grabbed him by the collar of his tunic and ruthlessly stood him up against a tree. Levi* alone among the disciples seemed able to maintain his calm, standing to one side and doing his utmost to soothe the others, though without much success.

"Can you believe it? He dared to come back here!" shouted Simon, gripping the Isacriot even tighter, and silence closed over them as if all had been said, as if there were nothing more to be added in the face of the unspeakable crime.

Levi stepped forward and laid a hand on Simon's shoulder. The fisherman was trembling almost uncontrollably, and he loosened his grip. The Iscariot burst into tears, sinking to the foot of the tree.

It seemed to me the maddest, the most horrible night of my existence. Everything we came close to, all the beings we met seemed to exude failure and despair. How could everything be brought to naught so quickly? All the words of love sown over hill and dale, all the eyes full of peace gazing toward the new land—all these efforts were now coming apart.

It was cold and I began to shiver, the exhaustion and the night breeze getting the better of me. I could think of nothing else than to huddle closer to Simon, who drew me to him.

Once again, a voice tore through the silence and the darkness.

"Why? Why? Why?" and as the question was repeated, it faded from hearing, absorbing all our strength.

The Iscariot, at last, lifted his head. Beneath his blazing chestnut hair, his eyes seemed to have sunk deeply into his face, which looked like a tormented landscape, a land devastated by earthquakes.

"That was not what I wanted!" Judas cried, racked with sobbing. "I never wanted that! They betrayed me. They were not supposed to take him. For pity's sake listen to me, believe me, even if it is the last time!"

It is true that in these awful moments, he did inspire pity in us. In all our eyes, anger had given way to discouragement. Many eyes were closed, as if to see more deeply within. Many exhausted bodies

*Matthew.

had found a stone to sit on, and the Iscariot went on talking, opening his heart—a heart that had until now expressed so little.

"The Master had to meet the Romans," he said in a dull voice. "I thought we could no longer go on like that, and that only an official encounter, taking place in secret, could help. Have you seen what has happened in the past few days? People rebelling everywhere, being tortured on all the roadsides, and the Zealots always surrounding us! The Master had to meet the Roman command of the city. It was the only way to save him, and to save ourselves as well. A clear explanation to Pilate would certainly free him from the charge. One of Pilate's envoys approached me yesterday. He insisted that the high authorities at the palace wished to speak with him in all safety. All I did was to tell them where they could find him, away from the crowd. I swear it!"

His sobbing prevented him from going on. We searched each other's eyes in the darkness, perhaps to share our pain, perhaps to share the hundreds of questions we were unable to express.

What were we to believe? I almost tried not to think at all. There was only a drastic sequence of facts. There had been no discussion, they had thrown the Master in chains and taken him away, and our hearts were paralyzed. Our souls wandered in the winter of our despair, seeking desperately the slightest trace of a smile to warm them; but all around were only to be seen hollow faces, closed eyes, tightly clasped hands.

Once more Judas was addressed vehemently. This time it was Philip who burst out.

"I cannot believe you, Iscariot! We have seen you too often with the Zealots lately! You wanted to bring about this altercation. I think you wanted to force our hand, hoping we would react violently and that it would set the whole city against Rome!"

Philip had tried to restrain himself, but had nonetheless been carried away by his indignation. His words troubled me as his reasoning was convincing, and this added to the complexity of the situation. Whether it had been a betrayal or a mistake, little did it matter now as we were faced with a yawning abyss.

Not for a moment did it occur to any of us that the Master might be released, as had happened in Magdala. Too much had changed. Footsteps made us look up: two figures loomed up out of the darkness. It was one of the Brothers from the bethsaïd followed by Joseph, who seemed much calmer than the rest of us.

"Do not quarrel, my Brothers," he said, his voice full of great sorrow. "I was there in the olive grove, and we are all guilty of not having understood earlier. Anyway, the Master did not want a fight, perhaps that is why I saw him go with the Romans unfettered, of his own free will."

Joseph caught his breath, sat down beside John who remained quiet, and continued: "I have just been through the city with Nicodemus and several others. All of our people who could be contacted have been told the news. I spoke with the Master's mother myself, as well as with two of his youngest brothers; the others are not in Jerusalem. I thought it would be hard for her to hear the news, but as soon as I arrived, she seemed to know all that had happened.

"As soon as the sun rises, I will go to speak with Pilate. You know that I have good friends among his entourage, which will ease my way to him. Caiaphas too may see fit to receive me, but this is not so certain. For now, I see nothing better than to wait here."

No one could see Joseph's face for he was hidden by surrounding branches; yet his words came as the comforting balm we were all longing for, and we followed him into the bethsaïd. At this point Nicodemus and four other Brothers arrived out of breath, and at the same moment we saw the Iscariot shuffle off in the opposite direction, on a tiny path that seemed to lead nowhere. Philip wanted to stop him, but Joseph held him back.

"Let him go," he said. "The forces we are working with, are far beyond our understanding today. The Master himself explained that to me this morning. I think he knew!"

It was not easy to find a place to lie down among those who were asleep and the pilgrims who had spent the night praying in the bethsaïd. The air was heavy with the smell of incense and of the food that the Brothers were already busy preparing for the next day. I was no longer sleepy, and it was not long before the first rays of sunlight spread pink hues on the mountain tops. In the hearth of the main room, a wood fire was crackling and some people were preparing a hot herbal drink.

Our heads empty, our nerves frayed, Simon and I left the bethsaïd to take a walk among the brambles and the red and white flowering bushes on the mountainside. We needed to meditate, to recover our strength, as we had been taught by the Master, by old Zerah, and by the elder Brothers who had nourished our childhoods with the dew of their hearts.

From high on the ramparts, at the top of the pinnacle of the temple, the low and strident notes of the horns and trumpets blended together in a renewed call to life.

CHAPTER · XII

THE BROTHERS
FROM HELIOPOLIS

I t was Friday morning, and none of us knew where to go nor what
to do. We thought it unwise to remain in a group, but then, we
could not bring ourselves to separate and disperse throughout the
city. In the course of the morning, the rest of the one hundred and
eight began to arrive at the bethsaïd, and from then on it was clear
that our gathering in force would inevitably lead to a massive arrest.
Therefore we agreed to part, and each of us resume his or her
normal daily activities. It was better to wait for the return of Joseph,
in the hope that his intervention with the Roman authorities would
be successful.

Simon and I remained at the bethsaïd to help with the healing
of those pilgrims who were not well. We noticed the presence of
three copper-skinned men, dressed in white, who seemed to be
waiting discreetly out of the way. Now and then, John, who had
also remainded at the bethsaïd, went to speak to them briefly. They
seemed to me to be the very embodiment of kindness and authority,
and their faces reflected wisdom, inspiring great respect. Something
within me murmured the name of Heliopolis, and at the same
moment, one of them stepped over to me. He was about thirty years

old, hardly more, and I was attracted by his pale blue eyes that brought light to his dark complexion, framed by abundant ebony hair.

"You are right, Myriam," he said to me in Greek as, with a gesture of his arm, he bade me come closer. "My Brothers and I come from the very great temple of Helios in the land of the Red Earth. For many years, a great number of orders have come to you through our intermediary. We have been in Jerusalem for nearly one moon, and we have observed you, for we have been working with Christ ever since his arrival among us. We are here for the completion of his mission.

"Tell the others, Myriam, that they must stop their present behavior. Your personality is naturally suited to the role I am asking you to take on. Each of us must once more find clarity in his mind, for what is happening in these days goes far beyond our own understanding. The Brothers from Heliopolis and the high council now request you to regain your previous openness, unshakable calm, and even joy, for the love that must guide our tongues and our arms cannot blossom in sadness.

"You have in your heart all the necessary tools, do not overlook them because you are lacking in lucidity. Seek within yourselves the key to whatever may happen from now on, it must be there, for it was placed there a long, long time ago.

"You are not alone in your struggle, Myriam; let the others know this. The Brothers from the stars are among us, and the Father expects you to act as their representatives. Be now more than ever the children of Moon-Sun, the children of love."

The Brother with ebony hair put special emphasis on his last words, and his face lit up with a broad smile. I could find no words to reply, and my right hand found its own way to my heart, in sign of agreement and gratitude.

"I have already spoken with John this morning," continued the envoy from Heliopolis. "He too knew, without knowing. You will follow him after the Master leaves. For the time being, make ready to support your Brother, Joseph; his burden is a heavy one."

As he said these words, the sound of hurried footsteps reached our ears, and we both turned our heads. It was Joseph. His long, earth-colored robe stuck to his skin in places, his face glistened with sweat, and his little eyes, wrinkled more than ever, revealed a serenity that was tested to the limit.

Most of those present rose as one. It was decided we should go outside to find a quieter place to talk. There was too much coming and going inside the bethsaïd, and more than anything else we feared some hostile presence. Beyond the walls, it was like a furnace; the sun was already high and forced us to seek shade in the valley below, where the trees grew thicker. We walked slowly toward the rocks of Hinnom, where we were almost certain of meeting no one. There was no clearly defined path, and the rugged stones scratched and bruised our feet.

When we reached a place where the bushes grew abundantly enough to offer us shade, we came to a halt. We were not far from the area reserved for the pariahs, where the city refuse was left, and no one would come to disturb us there.

"Well," began Joseph, rested after our slow pace, "I was able to see Pilate, along with a good number of influential people at his palace. He himself did not seem hostile to the Master's liberation. He told me so openly but seemed uneasy, as two people of his entourage were present. I was able to learn more when he sent them off on some pretext. It is not he who ordered the Master's arrest. He insisted on this, and I believe he spoke in good faith.

"It was Caiaphas then?" asked Philip. "There is no doubt that the Master has caused his authority to waver recently, with everything that has been said and done in the streets of Jerusalem!"

"No," replied Joseph, "the order came from Rome, from the counselors of Tiberius themselves. Pilate was notified after the fact, last night, at about the same time as we all were."

John spoke up: "But yet he must have known. He himself tried to warn us yesterday afternoon."

"He told me he had been approached many times about the arrest," said Joseph, "but that he had always opposed it. He has nothing against the Master, you understand! It is our only chance! I even overheard some words that seemed to half indicate he was favorable to the Master's actions. But we must be wary, this is only my understanding of the situation. Anyway, he immediately sent a messenger to Rome to try to postpone. . . ."

Joseph did not finish his sentence. Did he hope we had already understood? No doubt! But we wanted to hear from his own mouth what had been decided and we pressed him with questions. He remained calm, and replied as naturally as he could:

"Pilate added that Rome had required the Master should be sentenced to death by order of the emperor Tiberius. He said he received the missive last night, after it was all over in Gethsemane. I met with our people in the palace, and they all confirmed this detail, one after the other."

The news fell like an executioner's blade, though we all did our best not to react.

"Caiaphas," suggested Simon, who until then had not said a word all morning.

"It was to Caiaphas that the Master was taken immediately after his arrest. You see, my Brothers, how all was carefully planned. Rome did not want to transgress the law. I found out from a priest of the temple that the great Sanhedrin was already called to meet, and almost everybody was present when the arrest took place!"

"Did you see Caiaphas and Ann?" asked Simon.

"It is impossible to get near them; they don't want to see anyone. All that I learned about the Sanhedrin, as I have said, came from one of the priests who is rather favorable to our cause. It seems there was a close interrogation, and that Caiaphas left the room livid with rage. There is no question that the decision from Rome suits him very well. I think we can expect no help from his quarter; he is consumed with jealousy."

Joseph cut his account short at that point. Did he know much more? Probably. He seemed like a man that keeps dark secrets, one of those rocks whose strength is based on prudence and discretion.

As far as I remember, none of us dared question him further, fearing to open some new wound in our souls. We sat lost in silence for a long time, among the rocks of Hinnom, suspended between our supplications to the Nameless One and our meditations on the possible events to come.

Only the presence at the bethsaïd of the three Brothers from Heliopolis gave me renewed courage. For me this was a sign of destiny that indicated that all was well, and that each of us was acting according to commitments made in other times. But reason always progresses on a tightrope and I had the tormenting feeling that I was caught up in a process I had worked toward as much as any of the others, but whose complexity now made me dizzy.

The memory of all the initiations I had undergone whispered to me confusedly that we could have lived only for these very moments, when it seemed that so many veils would be rent asunder. We had no idea what we were going to witness, but I am certain that in these hours of shared solitude, each of us was conscious of struggling around some gigantic symbol, and that anything, even the inconceivable, could occur within its light.

We felt it was best to stay close to John, Nicodemus, Joseph, and a few others. Most of us were waiting for a signal from the Brothers from Heliopolis who had mysteriously vanished. The others, among them Simon Peter, Philip, and James, had decided to spread out throughout the city in an effort to gather all those of good will. If things had been intended differently, perhaps they might have managed to instigate a popular rising demanding the release of the Master in front of Pilate's palace. When they scattered into the streets thronged with pilgrims and were then swallowed up by the restless crowd, we understood that the one hundred and twenty were about to be divided.

Some were nearly ready to join the Zealots if need be to put pressure on the Roman command, while others, though there was no logic behind such a decision, felt that it was better to wait. Simon and I were among the latter. Our attitude, however, was in no way passive. We chose to enter into long meditations, in order to contact forces we felt to be more and more present all around us. John and Joseph were pillars of strength in this conviction.

Late in the evening, following a frugal meal that we shared in the house of friends, a striking phenomenon occurred. Our meditation technique was based on an old Essene principle that consisted of letting one hand drift about in the dust of the ground in order to draw, within a circle, figures with no apparent meaning, dictated by our inner beings. This served to create an unquestionable state of emptiness in which the meanders of our minds followed symbols that we would have to interpret in silence.

The mental emptiness we sought as a means of revealing another and higher self was suddenly pierced by a high-pitched whistling in the centers of our heads. Immediately, the Master's voice echoed within us with astonishing clarity.

"It is all being fulfilled, my Brothers," he said with the purity of crystal. "You have nothing to fear concerning my Father's plans. Joseph holds the keys, follow him in everything."

That was all. The room was almost totally dark, but I saw all the faces look up and seek each other out at the same time. The message had been heard by all of us in all its detail. Nicodemus and Levi could not keep from exclaiming. What had just occurred was a relief for us all, the reply to our innermost longings.

"This is the sign for me," John said gravely. "This is the very proof that our feet are still on the path. I believe it is now possible for me to reveal certain things to those who were not at the Master's side last night at this hour. It is not by chance that we meet in the darkness tonight.

"As on every Thursday evening, we were gathered to share the meal in our usual meeting place. To tell the truth, no one was very talkative, and the atmosphere moved us to contemplation. According to the custom we observed, we were sitting on the ground in a circle around the meal. Following the common prayer, we began talking briefly of this and that, although I seemed to guess that all of us were forcing ourselves to speak, for what we said had little relevance to what was happening then, and is still happening in the city.

"The Master felt this clearly, and very quickly he interrupted our conversations.

"'Is this all your hearts have to tell me this evening?' he asked. His remark was all it took to bring us back to the reality of the moment, and the anxieties that were buried beneath some sense of propriety burst forth. It was Simon who best expressed our questions.

"'Master,' he said, 'we are worried. We do not know what may happen from one day to the next. Passover is drawing near and the emotion is intense here in Jerusalem and the whole of Judaea. It seems to us that no one in this city is able to maintain his integrity or even his common sense. Hearts are inflamed with problems that are not usually present in celebrations. When I walk through the city streets I see only hatred or excessive enthusiasm in all eyes. I fear both feelings equally, for they are fed by fires that make them uncontrollable. Moreover, the Roman troops have never been present in such great numbers in our streets and on the roads. You are aware that our Zealot brothers are acting in the same way, striking again and again. As for the doctors in the temple, you know as well as we do that we find them to be more publicly concerned with Roman affairs than with the coming Passover. What is happening?'

"'What is happening, my Brothers,' the Master replied his eyes seeming to me unfathomably deep, 'is that the cosmic cycles cannot be ignored any longer. What is happening is that my Father is getting ready to turn a page in the hearts of humans, and this may not be done without pain, for your humanity is imbued with habits it refuses to give up.

"'All these beings you meet daily cannot manage to think for themselves, nor for the universe. They do not listen to their spirits but to their minds, which react according to the moment's interest. They have adopted the ways of thinking and the mentality of their fathers' fathers. Understand me well, they do not yet see the coming of the law of balance and gentleness. This is a simple law, spoiled by long speeches and dogmas. This is the law of those who are no longer satisfied to be, but also want to become. Do not blame, however, those who do not understand, for they are the ones who do not know. They do not need your pity or your feelings of fear, but rather your unconditional love. Their beings are still too young, and only their flesh and their dense souls feel the winds of the great sun.

"'You must realize, my Brothers, that most of the beings of this Earth suffer the law of their blood, that is, the commandments of their race. How many of them, in this land alone, claim to be of the race of David. It is the memory of peoples' children that expresses itself in that way, in the sap of their bodies, rather than the essence of their spirits. Their language reflects their attachment to the All Highest, YodShaba,* the Lord of all races, for their eyes do not see the coming of the Universal Force of the Nameless One. I tell you,

*Jehovah.

my Brothers and my Father are in the heavens, understand this well. From now on, you will no longer drink the blood of the Earth, but that of the Spirit. You will drink the breath of the immaterial celestial grape, and thus your attachment to the cosmic roots will be renewed.

"'From now on, you will no longer live on the flesh of the Earth, but on the eternal body of Nature. You will eat the sublime grain of Form, and thus your link to the fertilized energies will be reasserted. The true Human Being is the child of the Earth and the Heavens.'

"In absolute silence, the Master then took a wheat cake and shared it with us after breathing on it. Then, as we were trying to grasp the meaning of his enigmatic words, he poured a little wine into a stone cup, brought it to his lips, and then passed it among us. We did not know what to think as the Master was so solemn. He had spoken very slowly, and more than once his eyes remained shut for a long while. During this time we felt a sort of numbness spreading into our limbs, as if the food we had taken acted progressively and tangibly upon them.

"The glow of the oil lamps seemed brighter to my eyes, and the cloud of incense that spiraled up in one corner of the room turned a deeper shade of blue. I sensed moving forms and at the same moment I perceived invisible presences hovering all about us, a soft coolness that came and went, and then the prickling of fire rising up our spines. It all happened very quickly, but it was so totally present, my Brothers, that not one of us doubted that something had really occurred.

"'You have absorbed my blood and my flesh,' the Master went on, as our confusion reached its peak. 'You have fed on the double energy that this world receives; my love has placed it in you, for I am the meeting point of these two forces, I am the Cross of ancient times. In me the mysteries of the Taw are comprehended through those of the Mem.*

"'Henceforth, you will do this in memory of me. You will learn to do as I did for all those who want to walk. Your pure love

---

*Two letters of the Hebrew alphabet.

will enable you to communicate some of the flame of all life to the food that you will distribute; but I can assure you, my Brothers, that if your hearts and your spirits are not unified at these moments, your act will be no more than a symbol. It is not this symbol that I ask of you, but the material and spiritual creation of a real force of cohesion on subtle levels. From now on, do this with those who wish to hear you. Free yourselves from this time and have no concern for the coming day.'

"Then the Master was silent for a moment, and the Iscariot chose to speak.

"'Master,' he asked, 'how could we possibly do as you do? I doubt my own strength, as my Brothers probably do. Our wills are weak. How could we speak and act as you do? Could we not clarify our position in the eyes of all? There are ears that are strained to catch something, but all do not hear yet. Could I, as far as I am concerned, talk to those who are deaf . . . or give jewels to those who are blind? We all need a real material support in this land, otherwise I will be the first to fall; my hands will be empty and my voice silent.'

"'Never will the Spirit be nourished in such a way,' replied the Master. 'It is the bridegroom who comes to seek the bride and not otherwise. Stay far from Rome, Judas, far from the pretense of this Earth, for it may happen that before tomorrow you will have encouraged the bride to take the first steps. Go, my Brother, do not weep in your body.'

"Judas' reaction had shaken our newfound tranquility, and the discussion became lively. Some of us seemed, I must admit, very close to the Iscariot's opinion. As for the others, some reacted rather violently.

"Judas fell silent, and withdrew within himself; then after the Master had taken a long look at him, the Iscariot left our group, alleging some vague excuse. No one commented on his departure, and for the first time we began a rite I may not speak of here. You know what has happened since that time; Judas failed to read what was in the Master's eyes."

With the end of John's account, the night enfolded us. We felt no need to separate, and tacitly agreed to spend the night there, busying ourselves with looking for a cloak or some old blanket to roll up in. We felt sleep stealing over us rapidly as the many events that had taken place since the day before acted as an anesthetic. For a time, all seemed to be swept away.

I dreamt we crossed over the oceans with the Master at our sides. The leaping sea reached out for our bodies in vain as our feet glided over the foam and we slid effortlessly over the shattered crests of the waves.

The following days brought their burden of news. Through our many contacts with people from the palace, we learned that Pilate ran the risk of a severe sanction for having sent his messenger to Rome. Indeed, the Master had been arrested by special order of the imperial prefect, who demanded in the same missive that he should be executed rapidly.

Nicodemus learned from Pilate's wife that Rome had ordered the sentence be carried out before Passover so as to lessen the risk of an uprising. He was given to understand that the attempt to sway the emperor's decison was obviously a desperate one, the time left for action being, in any case, insufficient.

For us all, this came as a new thunderbolt. We saw no more hope of a way out, and from that moment, the only strength left to us lay in the words the Master had breathed into our spirits. We went over and over these words, letting them echo in our inner silence like a refrain.

The news of the arrest of the "Great Rabbi" had, by now, reached the whole city, adding to the exasperation of the people of Jerusalem. I even remember having to hide a number of times along with Simon and some of the others, to avoid running up against the Roman militia.

The crowd was nervously impatient and displayed a sometimes unhealthy curiosity. Our faces were known to some and this occasionally put us in a difficult situation, hindering our comings and goings throughout the city. Two days after the Master's arrest there were two altercations between a sizable group of people marching through the city streets chanting his name, demanding him as sovereign, and the Roman army who showed no pity in their brutal repression. This time it was not the Zealots who led the movement.

Levi had spoken with one of their leaders and there could be no more room for doubt as to their position.

"Your Master has nothing to give to the people of this country," said the leader. "We know this clearly now. He is the ally of Roman power, Tiberius' Messiah who has come to break the back of the revolt. He is undermining our command and we can only hope that he will disappear!"

On Monday, the two envoys from Heliopolis mysteriously reappeared among us. They themselves attempted to calm those minds that were once again in turmoil.

"Have no fear," said one of them. "Well before the departure of Pilate's messenger, one of the Brothers had taken care to contact Tiberius. There are no barriers for souls who have learned to speak to each other from continent to continent. Had you forgotten this? A message has already left Rome. All we need is for it to reach the palace on Friday. Even now it is time to distribute very specific tasks among yourselves. Nothing must be left undone, you must understand this.

"You must also know that everything must be done in a certain way, very precisely, for from this moment on, we are participating in the minutely detailed elaboration of an active, living symbol.

"Some of you must observe the crowd and its slightest reactions; others will glean as much information as possible from the Roman command and the priests. Finally, a third group must be formed to remain in constant inner contact with the Master, and they should gather as soon as possible around his mother, who is already working in this way with Myriam of Magdala."

With this, the Brother from Heliopolis changed his tone. I remember his two large eyes half-shut, as if to hold in a deep emotion.

"Now you must know that Master Jesus has just been physically tortured, twice, by men whom Rome sent for that purpose. They hope he will reveal some plot. You will understand that because of the wounds his body has suffered, the Master needs your help. The bonds that unite him with the spirit of Christ are subjected to a strain you cannot imagine.

"The High Council ask you to offer him a little of your vital force. Through your love, through your mastery of the art of breathing, you can project it to him. This is the smallest gift that the Brothers from the stars could expect from you."

During the endless days that followed, Simon and I had the impression that we were hanging from a thread stretched over an abyss. We did not move about much, preferring above all else to join the group that had formed around the Master's mother. We spoke little, but went through inexplicable phases of joy, despondency, or total ataraxia, sometimes even feeling the touch of great slabs of cold stone beneath us, with enormous pillars of stone towering over us. It then seemed that time was melting away, and we were at the very side of the Master in a dark courtyard, partially open to the sky. He had chains on his wrists, and his long white robe, bloodstained in places, stuck to his skin. Small groups of soldiers marched by, and approached him with other men in chains, then walked off again. Then our hearts rose in our throats, and all this vanished; our bodies of light were scattered and we were more miserably than ever reduced to our daily selves.

Friday, early in the morning, Joseph and one of the Master's brothers came hurrying to the little dwelling where we stayed.

"Quick! Come quickly!" they cried. "The Roman council condemned him at dawn, but Pilate refuses to execute the orders. He wants first to speak to the people! Come with us!"

We made a mad dash through Jerusalem. My body was weak and I barely managed to elbow my way through the throng of pilgrims and indifferent merchants. The sunlight dazzled my eyes, and for the first time, I found the odors of Passover quite oppressive. The sweat of the camels, the smells of the spices, and the wafts of fragrant herbs combined in a way that distressed me. I followed the others without really thinking. We finally found ourselves not far from the temple, in a sea of violent, shouting people. There was a little courtyard lined with columns, packed with screaming men and women. In one corner the Roman legion was present in large numbers. In the middle, a few centurions, their hands on their swords, were waiting impassively, while their horses fretted and snorted nervously. High on a terrace several figures appeared, but I could barely catch a glimpse of them. I thought I could make out the Master with another man draped in dark material, who was no doubt Pilate, and about ten others in various styles of dress. Voices rang out, but with all the commotion I could not tell what was said. The one who must have been Pilate tried to make himself heard by raising his arms for silence, but the crowd only sent up an even louder roar. Fists were raised everywhere, and a scuffle broke out. Only then did I realize that all around me people were demanding the death of the Master with an incomprehensible persistence.

"Come Myriam, there is nothing we can do here."

I felt a hand on my shoulder, pulling me backward. I turned to see Joseph, whose face had taken on a livid pallor.

"Come, only the Zealot people are here . . . all they want is blood; they are asking for revenge."

Then, searching in vain for a look of love, I let myself be drawn away from the yelling crowd. I could hear other smaller groups of people calling for the Master's liberation, but their voices had no effect, and fists were raised against them.

Simon and I walked together down the little street flooded with white sunlight that led to the city gates. My limbs were trembling. When the high walls rose before us, with their brilliant color of baked clay and their clusters of heavy white and red flowers, my drained mind was only able to formulate but one thought: How could Jerusalem still dare to be so beautiful?

CHAPTER · XIII

GOLGOTHA

We walked quickly on the path to the bethsaïd. High on top of the ramparts, small flocks of doves could be heard cooing in the sun, and the constrast between their love songs and our wounded souls accentuated our despair. In the shade of the fig trees, even the stones on the path rebelled against our feet, seeming to form a torrent of bitterness. We soon came within sight of the white and ochre walls. Then, for an instant my thoughts stopped, and I had the feeling that the bethsaïd remained the only place in the world where life had meaning, where we were needed, where the justice and love of which we had tried to sing were wanted.

On the wooden threshold, three white figures, straight and solid, seemed to be waiting for us. We recognized two of the enigmatic Brothers from Heliopolis. They saluted us ritually, with smiles on their lips, imperturbable. Something about them told me they already knew. Perhaps they had read it inside us, or perhaps they had leafed through the book in which Nature has always inscribed all that is great in this world. We were silent for what seemed to me like a long time, then one of the Brothers gestured toward the person who accompanied them, and who was unknown to us.

"This is Brother Lamaas, who long ago became one of us, joining the sons of Helios. Today, the crown of man's head will also be the place of his heart. Our Brother has made the long journey from his land to ours to be fully present at the supreme moment."

Lamaas. This name awakened a distant echo in my memory: the road to Bethany, the tales of Manethon—Lamaas, the instructor from the land of Ishwar! The person who was introduced to us had the features of an undeniably noble old man. His skin was very brown, and from his face shone two incredibly deep, clear eyes that penetrated each of us, one after the other, to our innermost being. He smiled a little sadly, then pronounced several words in our language, a language that he spoke awkwardly. I could not fail to notice his robe, worn and yellowed from years of use, the robe of a high priest from the temples of the East who had long ago fled the honors of his position and had guessed the presence of a sun elsewhere than in the sky.

We all went into the bethsaïd, where a few of the Master's disciples were already waiting. Without further delay the envoys from Heliopolis set about giving us precise instructions. The facts were only too clear, and the two Brothers never once questioned the reality of the fact that the Master would indeed be put to death. They spoke of it as something obvious, as an event that had always been foreseen. They mentioned coldly the conditions of the execution and what our roles should be. The way they acted and talked shocked me at first. I thought it indicated a coldheartedness to which I was not accustomed; however, this feeling vanished when my gaze met that of one of them. There I saw, without any possible doubt, all the love, and all the good will, stretched to its limits, of a high initiate who was transcending his own pain in order to finish what he had assigned himself to do.

We were sitting in a circle in the cool half-light of the bethsaïd, as tense as the survivors of a shipwreck waiting to be thrown the rope that would save them. The two Brothers were like rocks, distilling their words, half whispering orders to one or another of us.

Each of us was given a precise role that was a link in a chain that had been skillfully forged. Joseph, who seemed to know which role would be his, sat a way off from the group, his eyes closed.

Some of us were to follow Joseph wherever he might go. Others were given the task of contacting Pilate once more and of watching the palace area, to be on the lookout for a possible missive from Rome. Two final groups were formed: one was to remain at the bethsaïd and to build through prayer a mental force able to help the Master; those of the other group were to disperse among the crowd, ready for anything that might happen, and to benefit, if possible, from any ultimate contact with the Master.

Not one of us questioned them, and when I look back in my soul at all the pain contained in these moments, it becomes clear that we were the hardly conscious actors in a play that was far beyond our understanding. How far we were from our village of tranquility, perched on its hill! And what was Simon looking at, when his eyes searched the darkness around him? The stones of the Krmel? The faces of his masters of long ago who had prepared his mission?

We went out quickly, lumps in our throats, and the merciless glare of the sun fell upon us. Hundreds of men and women, whose presence we had not suspected, soon surrounded us in silence. We stepped forward into the crowd, but at once low-voiced questions shot at us from all directions. We neither could nor wanted to reply. We felt them to be harbingers of death, and that alone was enough to silence us. Like the crows of ignorance and lack of love they escorted us all the way to the ramparts and even beyond. As planned, we separated once within the walls, amid insults from those whom our silence exasperated. The anonymity of the crowd, of the winding streets, and of all the peddlers was a blessing for us. Simon and I dared not speak, for fear of shattering some invisible force that enabled us to move freely about the meanders of the city. The custom was for any condemned person to walk all the way from his cell to the place of execution, usually with his hands chained. According to our information, the route was traditionally the same, with death waiting beyond the walls on a promontory that dominated the valley. Our role was to locate the positions that a number of our people could occupy so as to be seen by the Master as he

306 THE WAY OF THE ESSENES

made his way, and to be able to help him if need be. By occupying key points, the Essenes who were among the one hundred and eight knew also that they could easily master the reactions and the movements of the crowd.

The news of the execution had quickly spread throughout Jerusalem, and we noticed that it caused more indignation than satisfaction. Nonetheless, the preparations for Passover were in full swing, and for some, what was going to happen simply added one more source of interest to the coming festivities.

It became more difficult for Simon and me to progress through the throng of pilgrims. We were suffocating between the thick clouds of incense escaping from every house along the way and the endless flocks of sheep that milled about among the market stalls. From time to time, the strident blare of the trumpets reached our ears, already deafened by the shouting of the camel drivers, the hammering advance of the small groups of soldiers, and the harangues of the temple doctors who had taken up positions in the public squares. Trancelike, we moved on, and soon there was neither pain nor joy in our hearts. The Brothers from Heliopolis had said little in fact, and we did not know exactly what they anticipated as the result of our coordinated action.

As we threaded our way across the city, I thought I had gone beyond the threshold of mental pain. Was it discouragement that had slowly numbed my soul, or was it the effect of a hope which could not be expressed, of some wild dream of light? It almost seemed to me that the Master's execution would force us to grow even more, by fixing his imprint upon us forever. It was a fleeting impression, perhaps a prophetic vision dimly perceived in those hours of chaos, when our past initiations left us with the bitter taste of still being children. How much more would we have to grow before we could finally understand?

We passed several doctors and priests in long, fringed robes and Sadducees in rich cloaks who were followed by a dozen armed men beating drums. Then came a giant of a man with a flat nose and a long black beard. He was exhibiting a sparkling gold censer and chanting incomprehensible litanies while casting scathing looks upon the crowd.

After communicating to the others the information we had gathered, Simon and I decided to post ourselves not far from the porch that led to the road out of the city. The sun was high, and seemed wrapped in a milky mist. We were very aware of this, as the tradition of Essania called such a mist "the milk of Isis" and held that its presence was a sign of a transmutation of a cosmic order. We sat on a round stone post to which camels were usually tied.

Little by little, a crowd gathered along the way, closely watched by armed patrols, and an eerie atmosphere settled over us all. It was as if minds were unable to concentrate on anything, and people's eyes revealed a curiously haggard glint. Jeers gave way to whispers, and whispers to jeers. Finally a quarrel broke out and two centurions, gleaming with gold and purple, intervened violently with the flats of their swords. At this moment I felt my hands trembling, and I was overcome with a desire to rebel. How could we just wait there, under this porch, doing nothing? Could we dare to even look at the Master when he passed, his hands in chains? Were we unable to talk to the crowd, and make them rise up and prevent such an atrocity? Where was it now and what good was it, after all, the soft and persuasive voice perfected by the Brothers of Essania?

Two eyes met mine—a look of tranquility a thousand years old. It was Lamaas, and my anxiety melted away. His peace went straight to my heart, a little jewel of green light. The old man with the dark skin was walking slowly out of the city with an air of absolute serenity that only belongs to the sage.

A clash of arms and a barking of orders made us turn our heads. A group of legionaries, spears at their sides, marched briskly down the street energetically clearing a path. They were preceded by a gray-haired man draped in red, mounted on a white horse. The animal, exasperated by the crowd that increased by the minute, was beginning to get restive and pranced right and left, his rump pushing the people to the side. His rider had the look of a high Roman official. He rode past us quickly, not even so much as looking right or left. As he passed under the porch, we felt the crowd surging. A figure slipped surreptitiously between two soldiers and came our way. It was Massalia. His place should have been at the palace of Pilate.

"The Master is coming," he gasped, his eyes full of tears. "They have tortured him. I saw it when they brought him out! It is horrible! I have just seen Nicodemus: Pilate's wife told him that the envoys sent by Tiberius will not accept an ordinary execution. They speak of nailing him, instead of breaking his limbs . . . we must do something!"

I said nothing. Lamaas's eyes were still in mine, and all desire to revolt had vanished. I saw Simon grasp Massalia by the arm, pulling him firmly to the side. Simon's jaw was set, and he maintained his grip.

"Do not be afraid, Simon," Massalia said. "I know, I know what we must do . . . but it is unbearable!"

He had trouble catching his breath, and we could barely hear what he was saying.

"I know the Master did not bid us farewell and I cannot believe that he will leave this way, but watching his ordeal is just too much! I saw him stumble several times; he barely has the strength to go on. They have tied his arms to a tree trunk that he has to carry on his shoulders!"

"Be silent, Massalia!" The curt order made us look up. Nicodemus was there before us, with Myriam of Magdala and John and a few others. Two legionaries were escorting them.

"Be silent! Pain only engenders pain! Do not forget who the Master is, and remember that Heliopolis is with us!"

A dull clamor rose from the far end of the street. A tall white figure staggered into view, flanked by two armed men and a troop of men wearing short tunics and carrying lances and heavy ropes. We recognized the Master, and it felt as if a dagger had been plunged into our hearts. No words could describe what was happening in my soul. I had thought I could be strong enough, but the earth trembled beneath me.

The Master was slowly coming our way, holding himself as straight as he could, his eyes riveted on the paving stones of the street. His arms had been firmly roped to an enormous, barely trimmed stake that he was carrying across his back. I would have turned my head away, but nothing in me seemed to obey. An indescribable force had taken the reins of my being, and compelled me to look on, to engrave forever in my heart these two deep eyes, this bleeding heart, this eternally white flame that moved toward us.

The Master's white robe had been ripped in countless places, and his body bore traces of many wounds that had dried stuck to the cloth. Upon seeing him appear at the corner of the street, the throng had been struck silent, amazed by the presence of the "Great White Rabbi" whom they had misunderstood and who, so close to his doom, still radiated such nobility. Everyone seemed petrified, trying to catch his gaze, which remained fastened on the ground. When the Master passed before us, he held himself straighter than ever, and seemed to smile at some invisible presence. It was then I saw that his face was bleeding, and that there were thorns tangled in his hair.

The soldiers shoved us back against the stone post with grim determination, and we stood there frozen in dumb astonishment. I heard John bravely stifle a sob, heard him make a vain effort to breathe, to call to himself a bit of the life that was fleeing from us. Then he shuddered violently and broke out of the throng of people, running as fast as he could toward the porch. We watched him as he went away, and suddenly saw the Master from behind, his back streaming with blood. Then my eyes closed; at last they could close. My heart shut its doors inward, full of a pain that an eternity, it seemed, would never be able to relieve.

For two thousand years now, my soul has been keeping the secret of these images, for two thousand years these sentences have been waiting, longing for expression at the tip of a pen, little chains of pointless words that could never really tell. . . .

Simon clasped my hand still tighter, and we were submerged by the wave of people that closed in behind the Master. The crowd's impulse was short-lived, however, as a group of soldiers on horseback followed, shouting raw orders, and once more the street was cleared, this time amid screams. Two half-naked men appeared next, poor figures almost beaten to death and bathed in sweat. Heavy chains hindered their progress. They stumbled, and could hardly hold up the lengths of wood that they, too, had roped to their backs. Thus Rome had not wanted to give the impression of being only interested in the Master, who by this time had disappeared, beyond the porch.

Nicodemus and the rest of us could bear the waiting no longer. There was a scuffle, and we seized this opportunity to dive into the crowd between the soldiers who were trying to hold it back. Nicodemus wanted at all costs to approach as near as possible to the place of execution, where, as he had learned from Pilate, the Master's mother and a few others had already been admitted.

"We must believe! Still believe!" he said aloud; "Those from Helios are expecting a missive from Rome. It could still arrive!"

"Everything will be done," someone replied. "Do not forget that we have friends at the palace."

Strangely, the silence intensified as we passed the ramparts; I met lifeless gazes. We were no more than figurines that destiny had placed where it would. I had the vague impression that we were a multitude of hearts on whose doors life had knocked, and which had remained adamantly locked. Why did humanity have to nourish such a strong death instinct? Was this the great power of Essania, the final scene for which we had forever been prepared? The Brothers from the stars with their clouds of fire and their promises of missions were far away.

Up in the sky the sun was white and here on the paved streets, on the pebbles of the path, on the thin tufts of grass—we were suffocating. Hope was not enough . . . we wanted to understand! Carried along by the wave of people who were overcome by a silent excitement, we stumbled up the little path lined with hawthorn bushes that led to the place of execution. Soon the gallows came into view standing out against the pallor of the sky, the morbid evidence of earlier executions. When we reached the place, a sizable detachment of legionaries was attempting to restrain or disperse the curious onlookers who gathered there, so it was said, as soon as the sentence had been pronounced. Several sword blades and spearheads jutted, flashing, over their heads, and the air was filled with cursing.

The place of execution was quickly cleared, then surrounded by a line of soldiers with impenetrable faces, their weapons in their hands. The Master and the two other condemned men had already been relieved of their burdens, and three bearded men with heads half hidden by wide bands were unclothing them. According to the custom, most of their clothes—or what remained of them—were to be distributed to the pariahs of the valley of Hinnom. The three condemned men were then pushed a few paces farther by one of the centurions, each a good distance from the others, to where the ground was strewn with many ropes, wooden beams and badly trimmed tree trunks. Meanwhile, another group of men using rudimentary picks was finishing digging holes in the rocky soil. Three holes had been dug, and from their gestures, I understood they were now estimating the depth of each.

Once more the vision of what was about to happen struck me, and I felt waves of nausea pass over me. I just wished I could flee.

"Simon," I said, in a constrained way, "let us go; we cannot watch this."

"Do not look, Myriam," he whispered hoarsely, his voice as dull as mine. "But stay, please, your place is here with us . . . his man's heart needs to feel that we are present."

I looked up and saw that Simon had let his head fall, desperately staring at the pebbles on the ground. Suddenly he started.

"He cannot see us here! Remember the Brothers' orders: 'He must know you are present, up to the end.'"

I tried to rouse myself, and followed Simon, who was already making his way through the crowd to a place where it seemed less congested. I hardly had time to catch a glimpse of the Master's tall figure, in pain from the blows he had received, as he was laid on a wooden beam.

I wanted to breathe, to cry out. I cannot remember, but I could barely manage to keep up with Simon, who was now almost brutally clearing a path through the massed bystanders. Three or four times, I met familiar gazes, those of some Brothers, looking like great white birds, their nerves stretched to the limit.

Suddenly a group of soldiers caught my attention: standing behind them were several motionless figures, as rigid as statues. I recognized the Master's mother, one of his brothers, John, Myriam of Magdala, and several others among the one hundred and eight. Then, in the heavy silence I heard a quick, sharp blow and then a hoarse cry, painfully stifled. I stopped in my tracks, unable to follow Simon, who was trying to reach Nicodemus.

I stared at the ground, and the hammer blows fell again and

again in a painful rhythm, punctuated by drawn out gasps. A moaning then rose up, but I realized it was coming from the crowd. I closed my eyes, and felt a hand on my shoulder; I guessed it was Simon's. Keeping my eyes closed, I felt penetrated by the ringing hammer that struck now slower and slower, ending with a deadened thud. Then a flame shot through my mind, something clicked, and I tried to recall the ancient technique of love taught by the masters of Essania.

This was how it had to be. I could perceive this more and more clearly. I had to find the flame of all life, rather than let myself be submerged by the flux of death; I had to form around myself the supreme egg of white light, the egg of cosmic peace. This was the answer, this was what the Master and the Brothers from Heliopolis were expecting of me, of us all. In a last great effort, we had to mentally weave the gigantic cocoon of love, the egregore, dear to the race of Essania, a rampart against all aggression, a torrent of joy and love flooding the heart! Instinctively, my hands had formed the ritual cross over my heart. Deep in my inner silence, I heard cries, hoarse shouts, barked orders, a creaking of straining ropes, then a dull shock, and a long drawn out moan.

My eyelids fluttered, and I barely managed to open my eyes. There, before my eyes and over the still heads of the silent throng, a silhouette stood out against the sky, arms outstretched. It was an enormous Taw, and the Master was hanging on it, his body held close to the cross by heavy lead-colored ropes.

It was done, then; they had gone through with it.

Once more I turned away. Two successive impacts signaled the positioning of the other condemned men. One of them began screaming, splitting the sacred silence that had fallen over the scene. Shouts and curses immediately shot from all directions, and the man was silenced by the insults.

I looked up again. As we had been told, only the Master had had his limbs pierced by thick spikes. Dark stains at the bases of his palms and at the ends of his feet attested to this. Thin trickles of blood were running from the wounds; I could barely see them. His body rested on a massive wooden chock and was held to the cross by tight coils of rope at his arms and around his hips. I held my breath, and peering between the heads of the murmuring people, strained to see the Master's face. I stared at him a long time until my eyes could no longer stand to gaze into his, which looked straight ahead, seeming to see something that escaped us.

Then slowly, the Master lowered his head and searched the sea of faces gathered on the rocky hillside. Several of those in the front rows tried in vain to move closer, but the barrier of spears was impenetrable. A weak voice cried out from the other end of the raised ground, a voice whose source I could not identify, but which must have been that of the Roman dignitary we had seen earlier on. His words came to me in snatches, scattered by the light breeze that had risen. They were repeated from mouth to mouth among the crowd and I understood that he was saying the Nazarene Jesus was executed for plotting against the imperial power of Tiberius, and that the men at his sides were criminals recruited by him long ago, in an effort to destabilize Palestine. Then there was an outburst of voices, and we saw a red figure aggressively making his way through the crowd. Facing him I briefly saw a man I recognized as someone I had sometimes seen escorting Pilate when he went through the city. The news spread that he was arguing with the Roman officer, whom no one knew, about nailing a notice at the foot of the Master's cross, as he was authorized by law.

The man in the red cloak, who was probably an envoy from Rome, must have won his cause, for soon we could hear hammering. I have no idea what happened then, nor how much time passed. It seemed, however, that the mountain as well as all of Jerusalem began to be enveloped in a yellowish white light. Birds flew overhead, sending out long, shrill cries, and the temple trumpets suddenly echoed in the valley.

The Master had still said nothing and was not even uttering the slightest cry of pain. Perhaps this disappointed some who were expecting declarations, for the crowd became less insistent, and clusters of people broke away, heading down the path to the city gates: a disappointed withdrawal by the cold and hard-hearted; an amazing inability to understand what was really happening.

Time passed. Nicodemus and others had joined us. They felt that the Master had not been able to see them where they were, and their eyes were full of tears. There was a movement among the soldiers at the foot of the gallows, and we saw little cups raised on poles to the three condemned men.

As the blood circulation had stopped, their bodies had begun to contort, and it was customary to offer them a painkilling potion. The Master refused it at first, then requested it at last. One of us noticed that his limbs were turning blue in places and that his chest was severely contracted. Nicodemus went off silently, and when he returned, two soldiers were busy wedging supports under the Master's armpits. I found this atrocious. The tearing of the muscles would be prevented, but his asphyxiation and agony would be prolonged.

"Wait until the end!" we had been told at the bethsaïd. These few words haunted me. So that I might pray better, in order to enter into contact with the beings of the invisible by whom we knew we were surrounded at such times, I walked a little from the crowd, which was drifting more and more toward the ramparts.

Suddenly a cry, a low phrase escaped the Master's lips. I felt it like a final breath, like a question and a hope, a call from the light to the light . . . but the words had been unclear. I turned toward my companions.

"He is calling the Brothers from Helios!" said someone.

"Where are they?"

"No! No! Silence! The Master is calling Christ, who is leaving him! Open your souls!"

It was Nicodemus who had spoken and who had at once buried his face in his hands.

Simon pressed my arm, and I gazed up. The Master's face had dropped forward onto his chest, which rose no longer.

Was that all? Was it for this that we had waited like marionnettes with our hands tied? It seemed to me that my little egg of peace was going to burst, to shatter like a crystal submitted to unbearable pressure . . . but nothing. I had the impression that a milky veil was slipping over us all, like some virginal springtime aurora.

Nicodemus jumped up, murmured several incomprehensible words, then cried out, almost roared:

"Quick! Quick! . . . What are they doing?" Then a soldier strode up to the Master, carefully placed the point of a spear level with his diaphragm, and jabbed it in with a quick jerk.

"Let him be," said Nicodemus, who appeared to be much calmer. "The man knows what he is doing. He is one of us and is acting according to the orders of the Brothers from the Red Land. The Master must absolutely continue to breathe."*

Meanwhile, the sky had curiously darkened, and the white light we had observed only minutes before was rapidly fading. We could feel a slight wave of fear passing over the people who had remained. Then I saw that the legionaries were looking up at the sky, relaxing their surveillance.

In no time, a thick blackness seemed to rise from out of the ground itself. It was like a sigh coming from the Earth . . . as if the Earth were trying to reach out, to get closer to the sky. The air became heavy, turning a dark gray.† Around us we glimpsed wheeling forms, white and blue streaks, subtle tongues of gold and silver whirling over the valley. It seemed that all life in the flesh was being extinguished, and instinctively we felt like crying out—not in pain and fear of death—but in hope: a cry of victory! We felt strangely that everything was all right.

Suddenly we heard pounding hoofbeats. Not far from where we were gathered beneath a huge rock, a harried-looking soldier rode up, leaped from his horse and rushed to the Roman officer.

"He is handing him a letter!" cried Simon.

Just at this moment, a strong blast of wind swept across our faces. It was a heavy wind that seemed to bear on its wings all the deep forces of Nature. Then a dazzling streak, the color of the moon, rent the dark cloak in which the heavens had been wrapped. A sharp peal of thunder shook the countryside all around. Instinctively we looked at each other, and in spite of ourselves, we could not help smiling. Our hearts, initiated in the faith of Essania, grasped the message. It was the sign from Christ to the Earth Mother. In a flash, he was relieving her of her pains.

The clouds burst and a heavy rain poured down all at once. There was nowhere to turn for shelter, but this didn't matter. The

---

*Spearing below the last rib must have had the effect of a pneumothorax, delaying the asphyxiation of the body. This did not awaken the suspicions of the Roman officials, for it was sometimes practiced as a way of cruelly prolonging the agony of crucified criminals.
†It was a total eclipse of the sun . . . whose origin could well be a subject for reflection.

huge drops were warm, invigorating, and we welcomed them like a caress.

Lightning flashed and thunder rolled and a good many of those who had wanted to remain until the end fled wildly toward the ramparts. Only about twenty people were left, scattered over the rocky promontory. The soldiers themselves had drawn off to one side to take cover from the violence of the rain. From their group finally emerged the man who, a few moments before, had arrived with what seemed to be a missive.

"Take your Master back, if there is still time," he cried, running toward some silhouettes streaming with water. "The emperor Tiberius has expressly ordered further investigation concerning him."

As he finished his sentence, he went up close to the Master, looked at him briefly, then declared, "I am sorry, it is too late."

He turned to the soldiers and cried to them, "You there! Finish off those two while they are unconscious!"

Two or three of the soldiers hastened toward the gallows, which had been raised apart from the Master's. With long, iron-tipped poles in their hands, they stumbled clumsily in the puddles of water. We averted our eyes, and it was over in a moment.

We heard labored breathing and looked up to see that the small group to whom the Roman messenger had spoken was now quite close to us. There was John, the Master's mother, one of his brothers, and a few others. Their faces were ashen, but I saw their eyes were burning intensely.

"They refuse to lower the crosses!" exclaimed John. "They say they want to wait until the storm is over! This is not possible, Brothers!"

"Everything has been fine up to this point, do not worry. . . ."

The breathless voice, hardly perceptible, was Joseph's.* The persistent darkness and the falling rain made it difficult to see his face clearly, but we noticed immediately that he glowed with some knowledge that we did not share.

"Come, Sister," he said softly, to the Master's mother. "Everything is fine, I assure you."

*Joseph of Arimathea.

The rest of us waited in silence, and Joseph issued a series of orders, the first of which was to hasten the release of the Master's body, at any cost.

"It must be done immediately," he said tersely, "even if you must bribe the soldiers, against our rules!"

Then John, who had stepped away from the group for a moment, rushed back. He was mute for a long moment, his eyes misty, then a short, half-whispered phrase came from his lips.

"The Master—blood is still flowing from his wounds. He is alive!"

CHAPTER · XIV

THE MYSTERY

The storm continued to rage over Jerusalem. It seemed it would never stop. It set both Earth and sky ablaze, like a reaction on the part of the cosmos against the atrocities that had been committed. The sky had been pitch-dark for a long time now; since the moment when the Master had lost consciousness, daylight had not dared reappear, and time had passed in a confusion of bodies and souls. We sat, huddled one against another, sheltering in a tiny cave on the side of the mountain. The night was cold and we were shivering, but in our hearts a short phrase kept coming back again and again, then bursting like a sunrise: "He is alive!"

There were seven of us waiting there, trying to fight off sleep. Joseph's orders had been explicit: we were to stay awake all night long if necessary, so as to watch any comings and goings on the mountain path that led to the tombs. Once more, we had to be ready for anything, for we might be asked to intervene. Nothing seemed certain, but little did it matter; we felt streams of love, overflowing with indomitable energy.

While some had carried the apparently lifeless body of the Master, Joseph and Nicodemus had sent us some way from there, to the part of the valley traditionally reserved for sepulchers.

"Act quickly," Joseph had said to us. "You will easily find an open tomb that has been recently dug according to my instructions. As a precaution, I told Pilate that it was reserved for one of my relatives who is presently dying. You will see it, it's deep. We will lay the Master there. Go and make sure that all is in order. I had balms and sheets of linen put there."

Without delay we had run through the darkness and the beating rain, and had found the site. A Brother clothed in white was already waiting there. He had planted a torch in a crevice in the rock and was standing there waiting, not in the least worried.

"Set your minds at peace," he said, when we arrived, "all is in order, and has been for three days. With the help of the Father, all will come to pass as foreseen."

We could not find words, and indeed there was nothing to be said, so strange it seemed that a secret plan had been carefully prepared by the Brothers from Heliopolis and by Joseph himself.

The sepulcher was vast, with a number of recesses as well as a sort of back chamber large enough for a number of bodies. I noticed immediately that uncommon care had been taken in the fashioning of the walls. The angles seemed perfect, and the proportions harmonious. A natural fissure ran deeply into the vault of the ceiling, forming a sort of cone. A tomb of pink stone waited open before us, and four earthen vials, a linen robe, sheets, and woolen blankets had been discreetly placed on the ground.

We waited there a long while, lost in thought, the many things we had seen that day rising up before our eyes. At last there was the sound of footsteps, of stones clattering on the path, and in the flashes of lightning we saw a dozen men coming, carrying a body wrapped in a thick white cloth. It was the Master's. When they laid his body on the ground of the tomb, he seemed to be sleeping. Only the dried and blackened blood on his temples, his pinched lips, and the dark blue circles around his eyes attested to the suffering he had endured. I recognized John and two Brothers renowned throughout Palestine for their medical knowledge. They immediately uncorked one of the vials that we had seen on the ground, and a strong, undefinable odor pervaded the sepulcher. Simon and I followed the others who had already gone out, to let them work on their own in accordance with their art.

Joseph was standing at the entrance to the burial cave, and it was then that he had asked us to wait not far away.

"Station yourselves in the hole of the rock that rises over the path," he said. "In a while you will probably see a legionary coming this way. I have asked Pilate to send a guard or two, for the people may go to excesses we cannot imagine."

We had indeed seen two soldiers pass by, armed with spears, protecting themselves awkwardly from the rain with a heavy shield and cursing as they ran as fast as they could. We had not revealed our presence and had let the time pass by, now and then looking up at the sky.

Suddenly an enormous ball of fire appeared over a clump of trees, immediately stretching out to form an ellipse that lay horizontally in the air. At first immaculately white, it then surrounded itself with a green, vibrating glow. The sphere remained immobile for a long moment, both peaceful and palpitating, radiating an undefinable aura of peace. The vision stirred something deep within me, something that could not have faded. . . .

"The Brothers from the stars!" murmured Simon. "It has been so long."

The immense glow then began sparkling even more and slid slowly and soundlessly towards the sepulchers. We did not move as we watched it disappear behind the rock wall of the mountain.

The cave where we were waiting suddenly resounded with cries of joy, followed by a respectful silence. There had been something solemn in this vision of emerald and fire, something that made us reluctant to make any comments.

I had the impression of knowing without completely understanding, a knowledge that went beyond the intellect, one of those impulses of the heart that allow the transcendental soul to whisper within, lovingly comprehending the multitude of causes and effects. It was a fleeting sensation, like all those that leave their imprints in the soul. Then, blown on the wind, I heard a wonderful melody. I let myself drift on it, until four or five silhouettes loomed up out of the darkness of the night, climbing up toward us over a little rockslide. We recognized Joseph and a few others, including the two Brothers who were healers.

"Now we must pray," they said, sitting beside us. "Everything has been done as it should. The Master has been anointed with unguents, and we were able to push the stone in front of the opening. The guards are posted; now we must mentally offer our vital body to Master Jesus."

I raised my eyes and sought Joseph's face. For the first time in a long, long while, the Master's name had been explicitly pronounced by one of us. To the heart of an Essene, it was the undeniable proof that something had just changed.

The rest of the night was spent in silence. The heavens had stopped their rumbling but the rain kept beating down. Shortly before dawn, Joseph and the two Brothers broke the silence.

"Come," they said, rising together, "now it is time to rejoin the Master. He must have had time to revitalize his body."

It was the call we had all been secretly waiting for. During the night, no one had dared question Joseph, but something we could not define had let hope grow within us. In no time we were on the path to the sepulchers. In the first gray glow of dawn, we could hardly recognize the Master's tomb. There seemed to have been a landslide, and the rock had been split asunder in several places, as if by lightning.

There was no sign of the guards sent by Pilate. We concluded that the storm must have sent them running for cover. They were probably sheltered in some cavern or thicket somewhere. Following Joseph's orders, Simon and four other Brothers set their backs against the rough-hewn boulder. The ground and the rock were running with water and the men slipped and struggled in the mud, but finally the rock gave way, and a gaping black hole was revealed. Joseph went in alone, and we heard him murmur something we could not understand. The two Brothers who had assisted the Master then entered the tomb. There was a long moment of silence, interrupted at times by metallic sounds. Finally a tiny glimmer appeared in the darkness, growing quickly into life, and I saw a torch being passed from hand to hand.

Then we heard Joseph cry out, his voice echoing off the rocky walls, insistent and elated.

"Massalia," he shouted, "run and get a horse! A Brother should be already waiting with one not far from here, in the first house on the road to the valley."

Massalia leaped up and was off. Not daring to enter the tomb, we all thought it a good idea to post ourselves a short distance away, to keep watch over the surroundings. We had to find the guards too, for we did not want the authorities to accuse us of having secretly carried off the Master's body. He had been declared dead by the centurion, and we saw no reason to run the risk of being suspected of some sort of plot. But it was still dark, and we did not wander far away. Calling out seemed useless; the falling rain and the wind swallowed up our calls no matter how we cried out.

When we returned to the tomb, an unforgettable scene awaited us, a vision that thrilled us to the depths of our being. The Master was standing before the sepulcher, lightly supported by two of the Brothers. He stepped forward a bit, turned his head our way, and a small smile stole over his face. We approached, dumb, to look closer into his eyes, those eyes that had so often spoken to our hearts of all the love in the world, and that still reflected the unbearable pain of the day before. Again he smiled at us. We could barely see him in the dancing light of the torch that Joseph was holding.

We did not know what to do, what to say. We felt like throwing ourselves at his feet, but he had always refused such gestures, and besides, it would have been ridiculous compared to what we were feeling. The wind carried a distant sound of hooves on stone, then we heard pebbles clattering on the path and the gradually awakening dawn revealed the silhouettes of the two Brothers from Heliopolis, then of Massalia, leading a horse. There was an exchange of looks, with eyes full of fever and peace, brief messages laden with meaning.

We did our best to help the Master mount the horse, and a heavy blanket was thrown over his shoulders. This happened quickly, in an economy of gestures. Then we saw him slowly ride off, slightly bent over the horse, the two Brothers from Heliopolis walking on either side.

I do not know how long we stood there in the timid dawning of a new day, in the blustering wind and rain. What was going to happen now? Words and images were whirling through my mind, and there was nothing I could do to discipline them. I was happy, quite simply and selfishly happy. I had no idea where our mission lay now, nor what was becoming of the Master's own mission. Everything took on a new face, perhaps an infinitely greater one. One thing alone mattered: he had been able to regenerate himself, he was alive. . . .

Finally we struggled up a sharp rise toward the city gates. A pale sun had barely come out, revealing an astonishing spectacle. The storm that lasted all night had been so fierce that trees lay uprooted and broken across the paths. Some sepulchers seemed to have been so shaken that their stones, perhaps struck by lightning, had been loosened and had slid in the muddy ground.

This worried us somewhat. We foresaw therein signs that would nourish the verve of fanatics ready to make fire of any wood, in order to embellish upon the tales they would tell about the Master.

The reality of it all was so wonderful that in our eyes it needed no spectacular framework such as the unleashed fury of Nature.

The rain had ceased, and we felt no need to sleep, nor even to seek shelter. It seemed so much simpler, so much more appropriate, to stand there looking out over the valley that stretched broadly at our feet. We gazed far into the distance to the desert mountains of Judaea. They rose against the skyline sometimes white, sometimes crowned with gold in their incredible bareness.

A heavy beating of drums reached our ears. The temple and the city were awakening, and with them the final preparations for Passover. Nicodemus, who had left us while we were still on the path to the city, returned after a short while. Following the orders of the Brothers from Heliopolis, he had gone to give Pilate the news of the Master's state of health.

"I could not tell if he believed me," he said while scrambling

324 THE WAY OF THE ESSENES

up the last rocks that separated us. "It seems to me he thinks rather that we have stolen the body; but do not worry, we have nothing to fear, at least for the next two days. He does not want any trouble in Jerusalem until Passover has come and gone."

We strolled along the mountainside, meditating on what we were to do now. Between the rocks, we could see the gardens of Gethsemane, the huge arcades of the road and the peddlers' multi-colored figures. The sun began warming everything progressively, and long serpents of mist uncoiled, stretching upward over the landscape towards the Cedron.

It was agreed that our group would split in two. The Master's close disciples who were still with us would try to rejoin him farther north, on the road to Galilee, where we learned he was to be cared for in secret. Thus John, Jude, Andrew, and Levi left us, after having discreetly met their companions and the Master's mother. As for us, we spent the whole day wandering in the mountain near the city. We had so much to share with one another that we felt the need to be together in the solitude of the rocky landscape.

The singing and calling out that rose from the ramparts left us indifferent. Our hearts and our eyes yearned in another direction, toward a narrow green path where three men in white and a horse were progressing. One of the Brothers from Heliopolis had stayed among us, and his smooth, timeless face, the dark complexion of his skin, and the flame burning in his eyes would remain forever engraved within me. Indeed, on this morning of the high Shabbat, he gathered us around him with a sober gesture of his hand and told us the following story:

"Brothers, my words are aimed at the depths of your souls, to awaken what is still asleep in you hearts.

"You must know that Christ is no longer among us. He departed from this Earth yesterday when the Master endured his ultimate suffering. He has regained the ocean of light that is his own, after having cleansed this world of humanity's failures.

"Understand this clearly, my Brothers, you who are aware of the deeper nature of human beings and of our mother, the Earth.

"Christ has taken into himself, and transmuted, the monsters of past humanities. It was a necessary step, for they were poisoning the heart of this universe and of its creatures; they were slowing down the forward march which had become too heavily burdened.

"The mystery was fulfilled last night. Christ wished that the vital body of the Earth might be totally purified. Thus the human etheric soul has been cleansed of the poison that it has distilled ever since the times of the people of Atl, and even before. The density of our world, as well as its very vibrations, have now been changed.

"This was accomplished, my Brothers, through the strength he gained from possessing the twelve bodies of the true Man, but also through love. Within him, the Master held the force of all lightning, combined with that of all gifts.

"All was prepared in secret by the greater Brotherhood; however none of us, I assure you, could have controlled the exact unfolding of the Mystery, up until the last instant. The forces that surrounded us were not of this world, and we could only act as children, posting ourselves here and there. We knew that Master Jesus had offered his flesh as a vehicle for the Logos, and we knew that he must not perish, that he could not perish.

"The lives of great beings, my Brothers, are written in the stars; we try to read them letter by letter, but our vision is still short-sighted. Think of the past masters—Yoshiri, Cernunnos, and others—whose lives you have been taught. Nothing is new. All has already been said, but this all transcends itself perpetually through the force of love, the love that opens like a flower with a ruby-red heart. I may tell you no more, for your path is your own and you must live it alone. The one who unveils must never insist, for while revealing he casts another veil. You already have enough tools to pave your own road.

"My heart alone may now guess what may happen tomorrow—for we have not planned it, and it will come about because the cosmic plan wished for by all the spirits intends it to be so.

"What is it to be reborn to life? Who has really come back to life? That is the question I am asking you."

Exhausted by the questioning and the impulses of our hearts, we returned to the bethsaïd at nightfall. On the following morning, Passover day, as we were rolling up our sleeping mats, we heard people crying out near the bethsaïd. Then Massalia rushed into the shelter where we had slept, looking both happy and worried.

"They are the men and women from the city," he half stuttered. "They managed to get by the guards, and discovered the Master's empty tomb—and you can guess what they have concluded!"

"Let them be, Massalia," I was moved to reply, and some inner voice incited me to add, "Let them be; the spirits of all human beings wish it thus. It is the people themselves who are rising from the dead! At last they raise Christ from the dead within themselves!"

CHAPTER · XV

REUNION

The days passed, and the news spread like lightning through the harsh land of Judea. We felt the need to get out of the city, to walk in the sandy soil of the mountains, and we soon realized that there was not one humble dwelling, not a single palm grove, where one version or another of the facts was not related.

So once more we put our white robes aside and tried to gather those of the one hundred and twenty who were still in Jerusalem. It was during this gathering in a cellar of the city that we learned about the account given by the two guards we had vainly sought near the Master's sepulcher. The story they told was vague, and we readily understood that two not entirely similar versions of the events had been presented by the men. They probably had needed to account for their absence from their posts near the tomb. We supposed they had invented a story based on the occurrence of the great flash of light, seen by all and following which the stone blocking the sepulcher had rolled away. Thus they confirmed in the eyes of the people the powers and the divinity of the "Great Rabbi."

We were at a loss to know what to do. Orders from the higher levels of the Brotherhood still had not arrived. Several of us had been accosted in the streets of the city and had been begged with enthusiasm, admiration, mistrust, or aggressiveness, to give an explanation of the facts.

In reply, some of us had mentioned the great capacities of regeneration that the Master had developed during his life. But the truth did not satisfy everyone and in less than a week three different points of view spread throughout Jerusalem: that of the resurrection, that of a work of magic—which gave the priests an occasion to condemn us with all their fury—and finally, that of some political intrigue. The Roman command gave no sign of life. Pilate became unapproachable, even to Joseph. We concluded from all this that it would be best to leave the region in small groups, heading for the shores of the Sea of Galilee. Although uncertain as to when, we knew that the Master would await us there and that there would certainly be work for us to do. We had had no precise information about this, but something within us refused to admit that it could all stop here. A mysterious mechanism had been set in motion, and we had to follow its course.

The Master's mother had already left Jerusalem a few days earlier, and we felt the time had come to do the same. By now our faces were known to the whole city, and we served as a point of reference to a group of fanatics devoted to the Master whose reported resurrection had aroused in them a rash sort of zeal, moving them to flout the authorities. Some of them would point at us and run proudly up to us, priding themselves on being among those who each day paraded to the tomb with their arms full of palm leaves and flower petals. We remained silent with what was perhaps an excessive determination, but there were many who wanted to see rather than know.

So we left Jerusalem, for what was to be the last time. From the parched heights we looked down on the white ramparts, and our gaze was drawn to a long, motley file of men and women. Far below on the flank of the mountain, among the uprooted trees and the fallen rocks, a gaping hole was attracting a curious and contemplative crowd.

We walked briskly, certain that he was awaiting us at the end of our path. It was a path that led toward springtime, toward the cool shade of pomegranate and almond trees. Gradually the dusty road turned into a greener footpath that passed through olive groves, and once more we found shelter beneath the roofs of isolated dwellings. The smell of the donkeys in the stables and of new, dripping cheeses, and the crackling of a fire at night reminded us of the time when the Master had traveled with us before, on this very ground. Time seemed to have galloped like some stallion wild with newfound freedom. Had centuries passed during this time? We watched for a glimpse of any human figure at a turn in the path, or sitting on a stump, or leaning up against an olive tree the way He had loved to do. For the first time, the journey seemed a long one. Would we not see the Master before we reached the shores of the lake and the city of Tiberias? Doubt began to creep into several of us.

Or what if the Master's regeneration had only been temporary? What if his body lay somewhere between life and death in some secret home of Essania? At last we rejoined his mother in a sheepfold belonging to the Brotherhood, several kilometers this side of Tiberias. She was waiting in the shade of an arbor, together with John, Simon Peter, Martha, and several others. The sheepfold was discreetly hidden, nestled in a valley, and as we came down the steep hillside, she (whom out of respect we dared not call Myriam,[*]) rose and lifted both hands to her heart. We had recognized her at once, in her gray robe and her two superposed veils, one the color of dawn, the other the color of the night. In our language, they attested to her devotion to the ancient temple of Helios.

"It is true," she said, advancing toward us with Martha, "the Master is indeed alive. The image of his soul[†] appeared here yesterday confirming this. I was longing for you to learn of it."

The news came as a relief, and we embraced her, our hands on our hearts. I could not resist staring at her, at her large clear eyes and her smile that was fresher than any we might have managed. I had

[*]Mary's original name.
[†]His astral body.

always found it strange that she should call her own son the Master. There were ties other than blood that had become apparent to her long ago. They were not those linking a disciple to a Master, but those between two allied souls who, to the very end, respect the roles distributed in other times. This now seemed clearer to me than ever.

We gathered quickly into a circle, and Joseph suggested we sit and break bread together. We all took our cups out of our bags, and the shepherd, a member of the Brotherhood, served us an amber-colored liquid, probably made from honey. It was our first meal since the day before, and we could not have wished for anything more wonderful. We spoke little, and it was as if we were surprised to find ourselves once more together, alive, sitting in the warm sunlight. We felt cleansed, relieved of an immense burden, as after some impossible victory.

Pleasantries were exchanged, but I felt them to be somewhat artificial, for we suspected there remained so many things to say and to do. I saw the world as an ocean, waiting for us to dive into its flow so it might carry us from one land to another, from one heart to another; everything was opening, being transmuted through our presence.

Was it a dream? Was it a subtle perception of the trust the Master had placed in us? Toward the middle of the afternoon, a voice came calling at the doors of our souls, a soft voice that nevertheless hushed the birds singing in the valley. At first it came in a vague ripple, like the unexpected melody of a mountain stream.

We all looked at each other, interrupting our conversations, and plunged into the silence that Nature was offering us.

"Brothers," I then heard clearly, as if the voice came both from within and from without—as if I were one with the sheepfold and the mountain, and the word emerging from that whole.

Instinctively, however, I turned my head toward the little stone-walled building. There was a sort of white whirlwind, amazingly sparkling, standing out against the darkness in the embrasure of the doorway . . . then something began moving.

At that moment a veil separating two contiguous worlds—perhaps two states of consciousness—was ripped asunder. A silhouette, at first as if hastily sketched, took form in the dim light of the sheepfold, then came toward us.

We could have thought it had just shaped himself, taking its form from the very particles of Nature. It was the Master. We heard his voice again, soft yet firm, as he stepped forward into the sunlight.

"Brothers, Brothers," he said, "I thank you for your presence. The Nameless One's plan is now and forever inscribed within you. Do not be concerned about my appearance; my body is resting some distance from here. It is a worn out garment for the moment, but I expect to wear it for many more years."

The Master broke into a broad smile, to which we replied at first in an amused murmur, then in an explosion of joy. We jumped to our feet under the arbor, ready to run toward Him. Yet some force held us back and we could only stand there, our hearts beating wildly, gazing at the glistening curls of his hair, the flowing folds of his robe, and the iridescent glow limning his body.

"The One who loves can shape the light, my Brothers," he said, "like the best clay there is. Thus you must understand that death, distance, time, are nothing, nothing but impossibilities, conjured up by those whose hearts are blind. Thus, let each instant of your lives be pure energy, and your presence will become mine; you will manifest it beyond space, beyond the ages and the worlds.

"No, my Brothers, I am not mouthing the terms of a blind, sanctimonious belief. I have not prepared you to receive the credo of a new faith based on a system that may be analyzed and taken to pieces. I am revealing to you the perception of the unique Essence, for everything exists beyond the duality of consciousness and words.

"Thus, when you speak in my name, I ask you not to establish a new religion. Your world has already known so many of them. They are all shadowed by their dogmas, as are cities by their walls. They forget that the Earth rumbles and that winds blow. Live and help others to live; feel and help others to feel; think and teach others to think. Do not impose what you know to be true, but help others to love the search for truth. People have always recited the thoughts of others. Let them, at last, recite their own thoughts that come from the deepest parts of their beings where they will see the light; where the Father—the Force—dwells; where they themselves dwell and always have. Thought is the essence of light, so let them learn to think.

"Soon, you will speak about this to the people of the Earth. Try to live forever in each of the words you will pronounce. Set no bounds through your words; be without limit in heart and in mind and in your words, lest your language become a barrier.

"You will reach out to others, although you may not travel the road for them. Be the stone from which springs the genuine spark. Understand my words, my Brothers. Never implant my Father's truth into human hearts. Let it take root of itself lest you become craftsmen of power and illusion.

"Do not speak to them of me, but of my heart which slumbers within them. Teach them, at last, to want to love. That is all the Father asks of you.

"Soon you will see me one last time, I promise you. Not because I will leave this Earth—I will remain attached to it until its whole awakening—but in order to offer you some last counsel."

The Master smiled again, and the glow that haloed his body suddenly seemed to disintegrate, to disperse into the atmosphere. Then we could see him no more. Once more Nature resumed her rights, with her birds singing, the rustle of the wind in the trees, the heat rising from the Earth.

One of us stepped forward to the spot where the Master had been standing a moment before. The blades of grass were still bent.

No one felt like speaking. It was one of those moments of plenitude when just to be alive is to know that anything is possible and that there is a golden gate standing wide open before each of us. Not the gate of some Eden, but that of our own force, of the energy of peace and knowledge that we refuse to see within us straightaway.

"No doubt it is too near for you to see it," the Master used to say. "Do not expect from me a liberating formula, some technique for salvation that will help you to flee the evils of this world! You are not asked to accept, you are not asked to run away, but to go beyond. Right now stop turning in circles like a wheel around its own axis!"

The following day we continued on our way until we reached

the shores of the lake. The news about the Master had preceded us. The throng of fishermen and merchants asked us to speak, to tell them what we had seen. We were caught up in a sort of dream, or rather a total awakening that we had not experienced before, and we all caught ourselves instinctively imitating the Master's attitudes. It was as if each of us had received him within us. Joseph and Nicodemus started off toward the heights of Gennesaret, and hundreds of men and women followed them. Simon borrowed a fisherman's boat and began speaking soberly in the little port of Capernaum. Others went through the streets addressing the crowd from the terraces of houses. Within several days, the whole land of Galilee was ablaze with love.

We spoke of resurrection—not of the resurrection of the Master, but of the only one that ever was: the resurrection of humanity itself, of the human spirit that regenerates, rediscovers its source, and regains its true nobility.

We did not speak in words, but with the breath that one person unconditionally transmits to another.

It was only after a month, in a little house on the road to Magdala, that at last we saw the Master again in his body of flesh. His wounds seemed to have completely healed and the suffering that had pervaded his eyes had vanished. He was no longer Christ, but neither was he only Master Jesus. He was like a rock, a mountain of energy, but also a source of gentleness.

Our meeting was brief; he left that night on his way to the Krmel, accompanied by most of his closest disciples. We knew this encounter would be the last; he had told us so himself.

"I leave for the Krmel," he had said simply, "I have yet other work to do. My words will sometimes reach you in the dark of your night, over the seas and the mountains wherever you may be. However my Brothers, never forget that you do not work for me, as I am only a little part of yourself; you work for That. . . ."

And with a vast wave of his hand, he traced a circle in the air around him, and it seemed that it was the whole universe he designated. Then time flew on wings.

Soon there was not a mountainside in all of Galilee and Samaria that we did not know. Stones were occasionally flung at us in way of greeting, but our hearts only remembered the flowers. I realized that the one hundred and twenty had rapidly grown to three hundred and sixty, and that the circle had been completed. Our paths often crossed and it was not unusual to find ourselves gathered with three or four others around a shepherd's fire, or at a craftsman's table at the back of his shop. When these images pass before my eyes today, I see them like so many pearls we strung together clumsily, but with complete joy.

The seasons and perhaps the years passed; the faces of our companions from Golgotha whom we met now and then on our path displayed a few more wrinkles than before. The sun, the road, the cold, the stones, the flowers, the road again—this was our daily bread, and we would not have longed for any other.

From time to time a little persistent gleam in the sky strengthened our hearts by showing us the way. It was a greeting from the Brothers of Moon-Sun, the Brothers of the little eight-sided star of our childhoods. They sent us their eternal sign, subtle but so clear and strong. It was the song of those who were never alone.

An evening in the month of Elul* found us once more reunited with Joseph and quite a large number of Brothers. It was in a village located not far from the Krmel, some distance inland.

I can still see some men with their donkeys returning from the hillsides, their heavy baskets laden with freshly picked olives. We had set up camp a little way apart from the flat-roofed houses and no one paid much attention to us.

We numbered twenty-two, and in turn we each ritually threw handfuls of incense into the flames of the fire around which we sat. It was our way of purifying the ether of those places where we came together. Everything had to be as pure as crystal, our beings as well as the soul of the air we breathed.

Twenty-two! This number echoed within me; it was the number of initiations to the Brotherhood of Essania. Each of its components corresponded to a test that challenged the psyche as well as the physical body. These twenty-two initiations originated from the land of Atl, where they were practiced in the temples of

*Toward the end of summer.

the One. For us it was not like that; most of them did not take place in the secret of a building and no notion of rank was attached to them. Long before, the eldest members of the Brotherhood had let it be known that according to the will of the great beings presiding over the destiny of our world, these tests should henceforth be stripped of any useless glamor and be mingled with everyday life. Their number had never been arbitrary; they corresponded to humanity's sacred architecture, to the mysteries of the three and the seven that one must solve for oneself.

So each time twenty-two Brothers found themselves gathered through no will of their own, their hearts felt all the more ready to open. This was regarded as a sign and everyone was willing to listen.

Joseph was the eldest of us all, and we knew him to be very close to the Master. It was he who spoke.

"My Brothers," he said simply, "we must now leave this land. The old land of Canaan has now sufficiently nourished the soles of our feet. Yesterday, for the last time, I was able to meet Master Jesus. He told me that he would go on leading his existence within the walls of the Krmel and could consent to see only two or three of his close disciples, at specific times. I am pained by this news as much as you are, but we must respect his decision. The Master himself acts according to the counsel of the Brothers from the stars. In spite of all the obstacles, his destiny is written in the cosmos. The imprint he will leave complies of itself with the patterns demanded by this humanity. You see what I mean by this. Thus it is useless to oppose the principle of the total resurrection of his body, which contains the seed of the ideal nourished by the people of this Earth. Moreover it corresponds to a possibility he did not have to resort to, given the actual circumstances of his crucifixion.

"But as I have said, we must leave now. We are asked to cross the open sea and to land on a shore known to our fathers long ago as the land of Kal,* which means the land of stone. You may meditate on this name. For us it will be a bridge. It is a land of independent tribes, experienced in the art of abstraction. It is said that the people there are rough, but that a certain form of poetry

*Gaul.

flows through their veins. According to the information given by the Master, this land, owing to the interplay of the forces in its ground, carries within its heart the sign of the star of equilibrium, of balance. It then calls out for the initiatory seven, whose image has been entrusted to me.

"We will leave as soon as tomorrow, if the Eternal allows it, and we will bring to the land of Kal all that we have within ourselves. We will confer upon this land the book of our existences and the buds gathered in the presence of the Master.

"We will not arrive as conquerors of souls, as you know. We will simply follow the spirit that Christ has long ago instilled there, not as reformers, but as eternal allies. It could not be otherwise."

That night seemed long. Sleep would have nothing to do with us. When morning first crept over the mountains and the forests of oak trees, a group of twenty-two shapes were already under way, progressing briskly along the hillside.

It was cool, and we had our cloaks wrapped around us, with only small bags over our shoulders. Thus it was that, for the last time, we walked past the Krmel, towering above us in all its majesty, all its beautiful austerity. No one breathed a word. Through its walls, in the silence of the dawn, we were all searching for a face.

· BOOK THREE ·

BOOK THREE

CHAPTER 1

THE TWENTY-TWO

A fresh breeze gently brushed our faces and the two skiffs were cleaving the waves with perfect harmony.

"Look!"

A hand pointed from the stern towards the horizon.

"Look one last time!"

The bluish mass of the coastal mountains could still be seen in places between the crests of the waves. Little by little, it seemed to sink into the sea and then there was nothing left but the monotonous dance of the iridescent foam to capture our gazes.

Myriam was leaning on her elbows in the bow of the boat, absorbed in the contemplation of the mist. As for myself, Simon, I would gladly have given all the energy of my heart away. I was torn between despair and enthusiasm, between bitterness and gratitude. Was it all over? Was it just the beginning? I knew the answer, but probably like many of the others on this timid morning, I had trouble expressing it clearly. We knew so little about this land where we were to go. The Brotherhood had given us several items of value so that we might provide for the primary necessities of life, but after that? . . . We would have to make a completely new start.

When we had arrived at the still sleepy harbor below the Krmel, we found two frail boats already waiting for us. It had not been possible to find a single boat large enough to hold us all. Anyway, according to Joseph, some had thought it wiser to split us into two groups for the crossing. Several of us who had been fishermen were perfectly skilled at handling both sails and oars. They took command of our two groups of eleven, and we accomplished the maneuvering as best we could. Among us were seven women, including Myriam of Magdala. We certainly did not look like conquerors! Burdened with all the anxieties and all the hopes on Earth, we set out like the nomads we had always been in some ways, our hair in the wind and our rough cloth bags at our sides. One of us had expressed the desire to write so that nothing would be forgotten; to preserve what we all felt, however, would be impossible to recount.

Joseph had opposed this, not as a master, but as a conscious being who held unsuspected keys. He had suddenly risen, and clinging onto the mast to maintain his balance, had tried to explain his view.

"My Brothers," he said in his strong voice, "there can be no master among us. We can hardly claim to be apprentices. If I ask you not to write, however, it is because this is not your task. Our energies are our most precious possessions, but they do not belong to us. We are entrusted with them for a specific purpose and we must not scatter them. Moreover, you must now know that Master Jesus is apprehensive about certain things that will be written. You are all aware that he has spoken to me at length about a number of things recently; I assure you, this is not your task for the moment."

Joseph had gathered us around him, as the sail was flapping noisily in the wind and making conversation difficult. Only one Brother remained in the stern, one hand on the scull, watching the sky to measure the course of the sun. I had no idea how long we would have to travel like this, our only support being a voice that had not stopped echoing within us. But little did it matter. Our skiff offered no shelter other than the sail that we could stretch over the hull if necessary. It had to be a strong fire that burned within our hearts for us to set out in this way, leaving everything behind, with no clear idea of where we were going!

We wanted to reach the land of Kal, located far away, somewhere to the north. That was all that most of us knew, and no doubt it was not necessary to wish for more. What comes from the depths of the human soul may only be accomplished in a single impulse, and when I look back on these hours, I wonder . . . . How many today would do what they did then, would dare live from day to day, according to what they believe, to what they know? Are we perhaps today at once too rooted to the Earth and too far from the pulsations of its flesh?

In spite of the wind, Joseph wanted to talk. He hid his long hair in a veil, whose edge he tucked under several times, then he finally sat down.

"There are so many things I have to tell you, so many things, that I am not sure I can. First look at this!"

Without another word, Joseph thrust his hand in the big woolen sack he carried over his shoulder. He took out a number of little items, one of which was wrapped in a cloth of the purest white linen. With great care he unfolded it, revealing another cloth of a lighter texture, dark blue in color. The second wrapping was taken off with just as much care as the first, and in his open palms he revealed a small cup carved out of stone. It was identical to one of those we occasionally used with the Master during the traditional meals we shared together. There was nothing extraordinary about it, nothing more, apparently, than the nobility of the material from which it was made, or the simplicity of its form. It was no more than a hemisphere, like a fruit cut in half and hollowed out.

Joseph lowered his voice and said: "Look carefully. The Brothers from Helios put this cup in my keeping. The Master used it daily for a long time, and I was given the mission of collecting a few drops of his blood that was still flowing from his wounds when he was freed from the cross.

"I can guess your thoughts, my Brothers . . . no, this is not a mindless attachment to matter, neither is it some morbid symbol, even less a hint of idolatry! According to what I was taught, and am sharing with you now, the Master's blood, invested by Christ, was endowed with a great number of properties. I collected this blood from five places on his body, five key points where five little wheels of fire still whirled in the ether. Five subtle energies were flowing from the different types of wounds sustained by the Master. These forces, I was told by the Brothers, play a role that is both concrete and abstract, a precise function in relation to our physical organisms and our spiritual essence. I cannot say much more; you will clearly understand that the solution to such a mystery may in no way be communicated. This is not for concealment's sake, but because words can only betray what is not accessible to simple human understanding. The enigma of this cup and its contents is none other than that of the evolution of any life form."

With great care Joseph folded the two little cloths over their precious contents. He seemed to be looking for words, then went on:

"This cup, my Brothers, will be for us a source of strength as well as a symbol. Its subtle radiation distills an unsuspected energy in all the places where it is kept. You know that our eyes see so little. Be aware, however, so that everything is perfectly clear, that its possession gives us no privilege, nor does it convey a mastery of any of the powers of domination coveted by all the magicians on Earth. When I have buried it where it is destined to go, any physical quest for it will be futile. Remember this! A force of this sort may only be found by someone who deserves it, and thus we realize that its material possession is useless to us, for we have already absorbed its contents of light. Therefore, those who will seek, but to no avail, will first have to learn to find themselves. There is no philosophy in this; the symbol goes back to the object, for this symbol is precisely a living being, a loving form on the planes of light.

"You must know, my Brothers, that every man, and every creature, animate or not, has his own cup that is waiting somewhere, outside time, in a place of peace that only his pure consciousness— though perhaps still germinating—will enable him to attain. It is a matter of harmony between each being and his own self."

"But Joseph," a voice asked, "if the spiritual force represented by the Master's cup is essentially the image of the one that we must awaken within us, why preserve the physical object in this way? Since the Master does not want us to establish a religion, in the full sense of the term, why protect a cup that is likely to become an object of worship?"

Joseph buried his face in his two hands, then after a long while in silence, he looked up again, and his smiling eyes fathomed the depths of each of us.

"The important thing," he said in reply, "is that the Master's cup be in prolonged contact with certain parts of the Earth. Its mission is to fertilize these places spiritually, for it radiates an extremely purifying aura. I do not think the effects are something spectacular, but on the contrary, they are of a slowly maturing nature. The cup acts upon the earth where it is placed in the same way that it acts upon a person, clearing a secret and open ground that may receive the flow of all the energies of the Spirit.

"But I do know that we cannot prevent idolatry; but then, tell me what we can do in this world that might not be distorted? There will always be people who will deify what should not be deified; there will always be ears that will hear only what they want to be told. This is why the truth is so often hidden. The guides of our humanity have seen it soiled so frequently that they are now preserving it, and distilling it, drop by drop.

"We project our impulses and our needs even into the realm of the Spirit—our memories and hopes as well, fortunately. So do not worry about that. All the living organs of this Earth—by this I mean its great centers—possess their own cups; whether they are simple native stones or some works of art, the same energy is given off, quenching the same thirst and inspiring the same, the only reality to strive for: the harmonizing of humanity within the cosmos."

Joseph spoke to us in this way for a long time. He appeared to enjoy challenging our thoughts and feelings with a sequence of statements at times perfectly clear, and at other times enigmatic.

"Symbols and images are not only simple, arbitrary games for the mind," he said, paraphrasing the Master with an amused look. "They are the marking stones loaded with the multitudes of contributions that delineate the path we follow."

He also told us that it was imperative for the precious cup to be set upon a hexagonal foot, a detail that contradictorily tended to identify it as an object of worship. At last we understood there was not one single solution to the enigmas he presented us, but ten, a hundred, a thousand, as many as there were beings in this world.

"You want recipes, my friends? The key that suits one person is just a joke for another, it is just an illusion! We must now learn to open our eyes and look, rather than calculate."

Several days passed, punctated by Joseph's words, by our questions, by the breath of the wind, the rolling of our skiffs on the waves and the burning of a yet pale sun. Several times we sighted land, arid rocky coastlines or pleasant green shores; we hailed the boats of fishermen or merchants, but the reply was always the same, coming to us in a very succint Greek: "Much farther still!"

Nevertheless, the sadness and the anxiety of the departure had been driven from our hearts by the enthusiasm of discoveries to come. We would certainly have to give, to explain, as we had learned to do, but might we not also receive, and undoubtedly come to understand much more? For how long can one who never brings a jug to the fountain continue to offer water to others?

We sailed our two crafts side by side as much as we could, now and then thwarted by crosscurrents, or joyfully accompanied by dolphins. When the weather was at its calmest, we called back and forth to each other for no reason at all, simply to express our joy at being there, on the way to "somewhere," which for us meant "everywhere." We numbered twice eleven: twenty-two! And certainly we were a little mad, but stricken with that madness to which, unfortunately, people so rarely surrender! We were twenty-two who reasoned differently, not outside the norms, but without norms, without that little something that always wants to define everything and make it old by giving it a designation. The true fire, that of love, has no name, because it does not obey humanity's laws!

Twenty-two was for us a sacred madness, a way of closing the loop with our own selves, a form of stability. For the Brotherhood of Essania, in this number twenty-two was the solution to the proverbial attempt to square the circle.

As we awoke one morning, drenched with the spray from the night before, a long white ribbon glistened on the horizon. We all stood at once, in silence, our eyes riveted on the coastline. Soon we could make out a cliff the color of amber. Thick vegetation grew on its top and in the many crevices of the rock, in places seeming to reach down to the water. Farther inland, high ochre-hued peaks gave the landscape an aspect of peaceful, protective majesty.

Up close, the coastline appeared to be too rocky, and landing there might have been risky, so we sailed westward along the coast that seemed to fit the description we had been given. We could not contain our joy. Little by little the shoreline softened, and we noticed tiny boats with patched sails, hardly hoisted. The land of Kal seemed to be still asleep. In the distance, smoke from several fires rose straight into the azure, the first sign of settlement. After a moment of hesitation, we brought our boats about, and sailed shoreward. There, however, the land seemed to encroach upon the sea. The waters were divided into several tongues, bordered by rushes and tall grasses. We quickly realized we would soon be able to go no closer, and that we ran the risk of being stranded in the shallow waters. One of us bravely leapt into the water, with a coil of rope in hand, and sank up to his neck before his feet reached the bottom.

It was then we heard a call—a long, modulated cry. We held our breaths in silence, searching the tall grass. There was the sound of water lapping and the rustle of leaves as two huge birds took to their wings. Then, a frail boat slid out of the rushes, with two men aboard. They were wearing short white tunics and stood thrusting long poles into the water.

Suddenly they stopped still and stared, studying us. No one spoke, and I had the clear impression they were testing us. Finally, one of them, with a timid smile, raised a hand to his heart.

A hand raised to the heart! This was the only language we could have hoped to hear.

CHAPTER · II

TOWARD THE GOLD
OF TIME, MYRIAM . . .

The days following our arrival in the land of Kal were peaceful ones. Though we were treated as guests, it was with great reserve, and we observed each other intently. We had been immediately led to a sort of village, three-quarters of which was built on the water where the marshes met firm land. Everything was made of wood and woven rushes, and the dwellings that stood high over the water were connected by movable footbridges. The whole village was hidden in an inextricable tangle of reeds, rushes, and trees clinging to thin strips of land. Scores of boats were always waiting here and there, moored to enormous piles that were washed by the eternal lapping of little waves.

A few huts were farther off, where the firmer land could bear the weight of stones. Most were surrounded by little palisades, which seemed to be more a matter of esthetics than of defense. The lacustrine village, almost lifeless on the day we arrived, proved to be very populated. A big fire was continually burning on firm land, watched at all times by an old man in a gray tunic who was wearing

346

a great many strings of beads around his neck. This seemed to be his role, while most of the men in the village spent their time fishing with nets. The women showed great skill at weaving the rushes and were busy repairing the precarious roofs of the dwellings.

We did not know why they welcomed us so, but they offered us a large cabin built on piles and caught in a web of ropes and ladders. The walls were hung with old fishing nets into which were cleverly woven thin branches, partly covered with dried mud. The floor was strewn with straw, thick mats, and skins. It was our new home, and we felt at ease there.

Did they know who we were, and what we had just done? Perhaps not, but Providence was a force in which we put faith. Their hospitality was for us one of those manifestations from the ray of energy that had always cleared our path.

Three of the men in the village were distinguishable from the others by the long white robes that they wore, somewhat like ours. For a long time they kept looking at us from afar, with occasional smiles.

The language spoken in the land of Kal was totally different from our own, and for many days we communicated through rudimentary gestures. We decided to get to know this village, something of its language, and to wait for a sign before undertaking anything at all. We made a point of becoming involved in their daily activities, while carefully preserving our own identity. Also, as Joseph suggested, we made no effort to hide our rites. Daily prayers and ablutions quickly attracted the sympathy of a great number of men and women.

I cannot say how many weeks or months passed in this way. Time's memory keeps the secret of those days we spent meditating, observing, and helping as much as we could this people with whom we had decided to mingle. We felt as if we were drinking at a newfound spring, though we still could not understand the reasons behind such a tolerant, if distant, behavior.

After a time there was more mutual understanding in the looks we exchanged, and then we managed a few clumsily articulated phrases in their language. While we were still in the elementary stages of learning their tongue, something strange happened. The more we learned to use this new vocabulary, the more we had the impression that it was as one with ours. This feeling was not rooted in logic, and no doubt it would have been futile to compare systematically the words of the two languages. The parallel was based on a subtle pattern of sonorities, without any attempt to divide the sentences into individual words. Some expressions, cut in half and joined with others, some sentences heard differently according to a rhythm which was perhaps that of the heart, took on precise meanings that went much further than the surface of things. A form of enchantment was achieved in terms of pure sound, or of phonetic relationships between the words. This realization puzzled us a lot, and Joseph, who remained the soul of our group, helped us to understand better the notion of "original language," a smattering of which had been revealed to us at the Krmel, through ancient vocalization exercises. Better than ever, we understood there is a way of working with sound that enables one to absorb its substance directly.

It is a matter of relationships between sounds, rather than words, and this detail contains one of the keys to the understanding of all earthly languages. The laws of Nature, and of what is summarily termed evolution, are given to the use of anagrams at all levels of life. It is a game, for when the heart and the mind are joined together, they do not take the paths of sadness. According to the Master's expression, as it was reported by Joseph, "one who finds neither joy nor amusement in study is not yet on the path of learning, but is still working to clear the path."

At last the day came when the men clothed in white took a step in our direction. It was at nightfall, and we were assembled, sitting on the little platform attached to the front of our cabin. They came in single file over the footbridge that led to our dwelling, with long white veils over their faces that they removed as they arrived, revealing their first real smiles directed at us. We all rose at once, both hands over our hearts in sign of welcome and respect.

"Brothers in Esus," said one of them in a loud voice, "this will be your name among us."

"Esus"! This sound found a strange echo in our hearts. It brought us back to the Master, several years before. It brought me back, also, to the cold walls of the Krmel, where we had studied the religions of peoples none of us had ever imagined we might meet one day.

Essania, Isis, Esus, now Master Jesus, and how many more to come? One would have to be deaf not to notice a sign in these sounds. The word coincidence was without meaning for us, and when the man in the white robe pronounced the name of Esus, we could not help but greet him with open arms. It was a bit as if he had pronounced the very name of the Master, and to our hearts, his simple words had the force of an acknowledged Brotherhood between them and us.

"We are the priests of our people," continued the eldest of the three. "The light has spoken to us, and now we can see in you the guardians of Ashas. We have long been waiting for the coming of strangers to our shores. The stars guide our steps, our knowledge, and our acts, and have always done so. Set your minds at rest, Brothers, for their envoys have prepared your path. They spoke to our fathers of the flame you have brought to this land, thus renewing an ancient alliance. Your ancestors and ours are descended from the same branch of the great tree; we know this. So speak and we will listen, we could do no better. Perhaps we have lived only for the moments that will follow. We are familiar with the reading of souls, and we understand now that we are welcoming those who have lived. So speak now, and your burden will be lighter."

"Our burden is not a burden at all," Joseph replied warmly, "or if it is, Brothers in Iesus, nothing in the world could take it away from us. It is the weight of years lived near the sun. It has penetrated our veins, and our hearts are full with it. It is the weight of the sacred art of medicine, for we are the healers of the true being.

"We will speak of the Master who has sent us, for he is yours as well. So, from now on, we will no longer say 'our Master,' for he belongs to all. He is the Master without servants, for his only image is that of the flame that springs from the summit of all human foreheads. Brothers, we have not come to tell you the story of a god, nor of a man who wanted to be a god; we have come to remind you of the story of true humankind, as it acknowledges itself and undertakes to regain its wholeness.

"Today the great stag that leads your people crosses his antlers and joins them to form a ladder.

"You know what may lie hidden beneath the surface of words. With your aid we will attempt to heal those who have forgotten, but you may be sure that we have not come to erase anything. It is a long road that has led us across the millennia to these shores, and we only add one more milestone along it, for it does not belong to us. Truth is not a matter of a people, or of a robe, this you know. Truth is the ideal of those who move forward without turning back, helped by their groping in the dark. We will bring you all the light of a heart and a sword united, because with them we unveil humanity, and thus offer you a small part of the truth that is so sought after. Now that you know us better, listen to the story of the One who awakened, the story of the Master who received Christ."

Then Joseph went to fetch animal skins and mats, and we all sat facing the three priests. One after another, they slowly lowered their veils over their faces, and a peaceful silence descended upon our assembly, a dense silence, inhabited by all the thousands of beings in Nature.

And thus for the first time in the land of Kal, was told the story of Master Jesus, who had opened the door for other people to follow. When Joseph had finished speaking, it was late at night. The three priests had listened intently, and had not interrupted him. For a long time we remained under the charm of this narration and of the memories it evoked. On the shore, we saw the silhouettes of men and women piling branches and grass on several fires, and it seemed to me that they were sharing in the journey of our inner beings.

After a long while, the gentle lapping of the water brought us back to the present moment, and the priest who spoke in the name of the others, once more addressed us.

"What you have just said, Brother, has no need of commentary. I am not one to analyze stories as scribes and masters in the art of speaking do, without knowing that they waste the most precious marrow. Their mental attitude distils a water of death. Your account is true because it speaks to my heart, because it stirs within me memories contained in no book. It draws deeply from the very roots of the Great Ash Tree! I do not want to kill it, for it brings life to the stories of my own people. You must know, too, that at the same time I see proof in your story of our ancient brotherhood. The most hidden accounts entrusted to me long ago contain the same signs as yours. I am well aware that the spirit of your Master appears at the crossroads of our ascent. The many crosses that serve as symbols for the people of your race, remind me of a story that does not belong to those of us here, but to mankind as a whole. Some say it is a legend that poets have embellished in their way. They do not know; they set their minds at rest for fear of the dizziness that comes from contemplating something so much bigger than they are. Here then is the story I may tell you tonight, though perhaps you know it already.

"Tens and tens of thousands of our years ago, probably even longer than that, the skies were not formed as they are today. The great energy of Esus that eternally renews everything had placed the stars in patterns different from those we know now. Our world was not so far from the others as it is today. In that way the bright light you name Moon-Sun shone more brightly on this Earth than it does in our days. As for human beings, they did not live on this Earth; the worlds they peopled were many in our universe. Their faces were not the same as ours today, and had already undergone many metamorphoses in the great life cycles decided by Esus. Their power was such that they could visit the stars in the heavens, and find there the manifestations of the Great Existence. Little by little, they learned to choose their paths, and it happened that the paths differed according to which star they lived on. Our ancient teachings tell us that one of those stars let itself be led into the cycle of destruction. The people who had lived there up until that time were drunk with power, and thought themselves beyond the whole in its capacity of generation. When they understood that for this reason, their world was going to disintegrate, they became afraid and began searching for a virgin world in the skies. When they found one, they went there on board great machines that looked like multicolored chariots. This world, as you know, Brothers, is the one we walk upon today. Hardly had they arrived, when they saw the heavens ablaze with a gigantic cross, which was the farewell of the old star they had killed. Many were those who had not managed to flee in time.

"The celestial fire burned for moons and moons, consuming worlds in all directions, thoughout the universe. Moon-Sun and others suffered. Thus the race of destroyers settled on what has become our world, bringing with them their pride and their hunger for power. The children of some stars had to seek refuge among them as they fled in terror from their wounded planets. Others swore they would not abandon the Earth to a people of such destructive ways. Thus it was, Brothers, that the races of our world were born. The memories of the evil that consumed them still infest the air we breathe. This is why the envoys from the stars illuminate our skies at times of great anxiety. They want to drive out forever the image of destruction that is ingrained in all forms of life on this Earth. Your Master is ours for all eternity. He is the force of humanity within humankind, the resurrection of forgotten love, the transcending of the knowledge of death."

With these words, the priest removed his veil, and approaching Joseph, embraced him at length. Meanwhile, Myriam of Magdala, who had been so close to the Master and who for so long had remained silent, entered our dwelling and returned at once with a little violet vial in her hand.

"Take this," she said to the priest, still standing. "Tonight we exchange and unite our energies. This oil was blessed, charged with the life force by Christ himself. It has been in my keeping until today. I know the moment has come to give it to someone who will know how to use it."

Without waiting for a reply, Myriam of Magdala returned to her place. I saw her long gray cloak become lost among the others as she rejoined our group.

Then one of the priests who had remained seated, lifted a big horn that hung at his side. He brought it to his lips, puffed out his cheeks, and a deafening low note filled the air. It was an endless, nostalgic, heartrending call, able to awaken the memory of the great love we all longed for.

On the shore, around the fires, songs arose in answer to this cry of the soul. I had the feeling that some extraordinary pact had thus been sealed. The monotonous chants continued until dawn; they kept us awake in a sweet torpor until we became aware of the birth of a new day.

From then on, our position in the land of Kal was assured. We concluded that we would soon have to divide our action. We would travel throughout the land in groups of two or three, not with the intention of preaching, which seemed contrary to logic, but in order to share our knowledge and to give, here and there, all the pearls of love we could possibly generate. Why compel a being to believe, when his deeper being does not open? Can something that forces a lock be called a key? We knew there was a different word for each sort of heart, as there is a gardener for each variety of plants.

It was decided that Myriam and I would leave together, on our own, and head west to make contact with those from Palestine who were said to have settled in this land long before. We did not know how far we would have to walk, nor where we would find these people. It was the same for each one of the twenty-two. We were each given a specific destination and we would radiate outward from the hub of a wheel. In this way we hoped to weave a web, in order to spread the teachings of Christ. Our common goal was to awaken and then to train beings whom we could trust in the small areas for which we were responsible. These people, in turn, would extend our action, by doing the same wherever they went. We no longer wondered how we might speak to the crowds. We were aware that it was enough to be present and to tell with simple words what we knew, without trying to convince. What is obvious needs no proof, and cannot be communicated. It may only be offered, and it will be received when a being is at the crossroads of his life. It is intended only for those who have understood they long for it.

We would act as we had always done, our only luggage being the strength that He had given us, and that remained to be chan-neled. We would heal, we would speak, but we would also be silent and listen, and let those who would, come to us.

When we took leave of the village built upon the water, and of its three priests, a ceremony was organized during which each one of us was presented with a little sealed wooden pot, containing a coarse powder that was dark gray in color. It was, we were told, made from the ashes of stag antlers that were ground in a certain way, at a specific time of the year, and was used to prevent and treat heart diseases.

Our departure was staggered over a period of several days. When at last it was our turn to leave, we set out, with our bags over our shoulders, and did not look back. The first days of our journey were arduous. The population of the land of Kal, though peaceful, seemed to be ensconced in a sluggish comfort. The crowds came to us, however, drawn by some force we could not quite understand, but we felt that they did not quite grasp our message. For the people of this land, Christ was a combination of both Esus and Cernunnos. They could not always understand what had moved us to cross the sea, and they were astonished by our ways of healing. Following the teachings of the Master, Myriam and I attempted to reharmonize their bodies in relation to their basic musical tone. This was obtained through the use of sounds, of etheric energy channeled at specific points, and also through very localized manipulations.

Our progress toward the west was painfully slow. We lived on the road for many months with no real difficulty, but in constant dread of the Roman army. The region through which we traveled was overrun with soldiers and even Roman merchants, who seemed to have settled there for good. We feared bearing the burden that, to the end, had plagued the Master: the accusation of intrigue against the empire. Perhaps the officers we saw sheathed in steel and wrapped in purple had had news of the suspicions hanging over the "Great Rabbi" and his followers clothed in white. In any case, we had no problems, and the cohorts passed at our very elbows without even paying us any attention.

It was a harsh, uncertain life, but also a time of absolute peace. We might no doubt have gone on like that for a long time, nursing the sick, and speaking to those who would listen to the words flowing from our hearts—if fate had not decided otherwise.

Indeed, one day when the wind was wild, the world took on a new face for me. We had found a broken-down hut, on top of a little round mountain, inhabited by a number of insects and encroaching brambles. The road from the last village had been long, winding through the fragrant countryside, and as the sun was setting, Myriam was overcome with violent shivering.

I wrapped her in my cloak as best I could, and she lay down on a makeshift bed of dried grass. The wind increased, making it impossible to light a fire. There was nothing to do but face the facts: the night would be long, cold, and difficult. Darkness fell, bringing with it all the cries of the world of Nature and the sighs of the elements. Overhead the hut creaked as the wind blew through it without pity. We found ourselves without even the most elementary comfort, and Myriam was rapidly consumed by a high fever. With astonishing rapidity, trembling shook her whole body. I can still see her eyes, filled with a strange gleam in the light of the moon, searching me with their questioning rays. I placed my hands on Myriam's burning face, and began a long prayer, as I focused all my strength into my palms. Then I tried to localize the root of her suffering by vibrating in rhythm with her body, which I attempted to soothe through my breathing. However, the long darkness had only begun. The fever at one point seemed to fall, then it rose even higher. Perhaps that night I was lacking in the energy, the trust, that had so often made us come out victorious even before we had begun our battle? Perhaps one path had to end there?

Myriam's limbs quivered even more intensely, and I realized she was losing consciousness. Between the contractions, a few odd, incomprehensible words escaped her lips. For the first time, I felt myself totally at a loss. How many times had we relieved the worst fevers, delivering beings from the grasp of epidemics? Could the art of Essania be of no help to the one who had practiced it so long? I would have burned herbs, but I had none! For a good part of the night my palms worked on the fire wheels of her body, stimulating the ones whose energy was weak, and draining those that were in excess. When dawn came with its first feeble rays, all my energy had fled from me, and my body felt like a cold stone. Myriam's face was livid, streaming with perspiration. Outside the wind had calmed down a little, and I got up hoping to be able to kindle a fire. Myriam's shuddering had subsided, coming now in distant spasms, and her slow breathing gave the illusion that she was in a deep sleep.

But as I moved toward the door, I heard a rustling come from the bed of leaves. I turned around at once, and saw Myriam stretched out on one side, her skin gray and taut. Then . . . I understood . . . I understood that Myriam had gone to seek the gold of time.

I fell to my knees, drained of any remaining strength, bewildered. I cannot speak of that moment of torturing heartbreak. It is enough to have relived it, and to still feel its full weight. It is always one's own suffering that makes one weep and rage against injustice, without trying to understand.

Myriam's vigil lasted three days and three nights in the silence of the bare little mountaintop, and I buried her near the hut in the rocky soil among the brambles and the lavender.

CHAPTER III

THE GARDENS
OF IESSE

T he weeks that followed Myriam's departure found me in a deep depression, and I just wished to be left alone. I struggled with myself—with that part of myself that made me selfishly want to call out to her, though I knew she was then perfectly happy where she was. I felt as lonely as I had been in the dark labyrinth beneath the Krmel, in quest of a source of air and light. Myriam's death was a trap for me, and I knew it. It was like a thick veil with which some insidious force attempted to stifle that which had been awakened.

I spent several weeks meditating near the little hut. I might have called Myriam, or projected myself to where she was, but I knew this was not the thing to do. Each one of us has a role to play, and if it is not a pleasant one, we must not accuse fate. We are our own fate.

In my still-confused mind, I could not order my thoughts. I remember asking for a sign with all my might; I called out to the Master, to all the energies I felt present, but which remained cruelly silent.

One morning at last, in reply, I heard a cry ring out on the mountainside. It seemed to be carried to me on the wings of the air. Someone was calling me! I caught sight of some figures standing at the top of a gray rock. There were several men there, waving to me as they approached. For the first time in a long while, I thought I could hear my name, echoing among the hills. I walked toward them. Four men, wearing wide trousers and long tunics belted at the waist, emerged from behind a hillock.

"Are you Simon, Brother of Iesus?" one of them asked.

Brother of Iesus? I almost said no, so strangely did this name resound within me. Never had I been called thus, and never, probably, had I less deserved to be so.

A Brother in Iesus could never slumber like this, beside a grave and a hut. Something was wrong, and the title conferred upon me threw me into deep confusion for a short but terrifying moment. It was at once a balm to my pain and a salutary slap in the face.

"Is it you, Simon?" one of the men asked again, one whose face seemed familiar. "We have been looking for you for days and we were beginning to despair of ever finding you. You must come! There are many who are ill among us. Our priests have said you should come with your companion."

There was something imperative in the request, something direct, and the man's voice was both rough and musical. Our gazes met briefly, and I saw in his eyes the response to my call. It was an order, the signal that it was time to leave. I said nothing, only smiled; without delay I gathered in my bag what few possessions remained to me and acquiesced with a nod of my head.

That day marked a new beginning, a new sun. I had stopped going toward others, and they had come to me. This thought went round and round in my mind and was soon enlightened by one of Christ's reflections: "The others? How can you speak of the others? You should speak of yourself, in other places, with other faces! Do you not see how you are linked ? The light of your heart complements that of another. Be the other, and you will be everywhere at once, in all minds; you will be what I am, which is yourself!"

That day I felt a living flame spring from my chest. It was like a cool, green, soothing ray. In it, I felt the strength of Myriam being added to my own and reflected in even the slightest of my acts.

Once more I was called to wander the land, from village to village, and I combined my knowledge with that of the local priests. Occasionally, I was told of "another Brother" who had been seen several miles from where I happened to be at the time. I did not, however, feel the need to go toward him; for me, it was enough to know that he, too, worked for the awakening of the great cosmic consciouness that is still asleep on this Earth.

During that period I tried a number of times to make contact with the followers of Moses, who had settled long before in the region. My attempts were fruitless. I felt the hearts and lives of these people to be singularly closed. Their Moses was not the one I knew, and it seemed that in them vibrated only the letter of the law. Even more than those of the high temple of Jerusalem, they feared the Father.

It was with fear, then, that they sealed their doors to the words of the Master, he who had taught us to banish fear from our hearts. Today I understand that their reaction, their history, was not exclusively that of one people or of one particular caste, but was that of all those who refuse to look at anything other than what they have always been shown. The spirit of immobility bears the face of the spirit of sleep; whereas the spirit of movement is often confronted with discomfort, and occasionally even with scandal, but a choice must be made. "The Force of the Two belongs to the one who marks time, who hammers the ground with his double step," the Master used to say. "The force of the Three is propelled, through all the risks, in quest of omnipresence and identifies itself with the energy of the One."

Joseph had entrusted me with a manuscript belonging to the Brotherhood. I was supposed to deliver it to these people. Yet, it was not to be so. My efforts, as well as those of all who had set foot upon this ground, were then concentrated on selecting and training the men and women whose foreheads already bore the mark of the flame of Christ. I did not have to seek them out, nor to walk among the crowds searching their eyes; they came to me, to us, and there was no need to exchange profound and serious words. The vocabulary of love is always simple. It frightens away those who are not simple and who do not dare to display a form of joy. The Brothers of Essania were never sad in their manner of expressing themselves, for the true spirit in expansion is not the realm of the recluse.

Many of the men who presented themselves to me (and also, I learned, to my Brothers) came from families of warriors. They possessed vast domains and had servants at their bidding. They lived in relative harmony with Rome and had become accustomed to seeing its armies marching through and controlling the region. At first, their personalities and their social positions bewildered me. They came to me clad in leather and skins studded with metal, with rich daggers hanging from their belts. Some of them offered me the hospitality of their stately homes made of wood and strongly fortified. They listened to my words of liberty and peace, and I rapidly won their hearts without always understanding what I had done. Some force must have placed them there, at a precise moment—and made them hear me!

Against my hopes, they neither abandoned their arms nor their positions of power over their domains, which I judged to be abusive. I understood, however, that there were reasons for this, their reasons.

None of us could make them full Brothers. We had been born of the line of Essania, and for us it was a matter of ancestral wisdom. This line was bound to die out one day, in order to arise in another one whose face we could not then even guess at.

Was it possible that these coarse warriors, even if versed in the concepts of peace and love, would be our successors in the land of Kal? Night after night this question burned in my heart. Did I have the right to give all to these men? Were Joseph and the others going to do the same wherever they were? My soul said "yes," but my mind refused to hear.

One evening, in the rich home of carved wood belonging to one of the warriors who had welcomed me, I decided to resort to an ancient method used by our people when confronted by a dilemma. The room that had been placed at my disposal was vast. The walls and ceiling were made from a multitude of trunks of little fir trees, some of which were cleverly worked, representing faces that evoked the forces of Nature. I had been given a massive chair, to which I was hardly accustomed, and a low bed with several cushions. According to my wish, the many skins that had covered the walls and floors when I had first arrived had been removed, as their etheric vibrations hinder the purity of spiritual work, except in certain specific cases.

Fortunately, my host possessed resins that could serve as incense. I burned pinches of them in the four corners of the room, and I placed a layer of the sandy soil of the region in a metal tray on the floor. By the light of a torch, I traced an equal-branched cross and an even spiral circling outward toward the periphery of the tray. Having done this, I lost myself in the humming of the consonant *M,* the sound proper to the Brotherhood, then I went to sleep, my mind empty.

The night passed, and when I awoke, the answer I had looked for awaited me. The spiral had vanished, carefully erased by a sort of breath that had spared the cross. According to the code defined by the Brotherhood within the walls of the Krmel, this meant yes. Yes, I should trust the rough chiefs of this harsh land. Yes, I could bequeath to them the contents of my heart. The answer was clear, all the clearer as the operation had nothing to do with magic. Those of Essania were not at all keen on handling forces external to themselves and to the Great Universal Agent. It was myself, my body of light, that had been projected toward the soil in the tray. There are no questions to which we do not unconsciously know the answers, and we would be far less blind if we understood that each night we drink from a pure spring. We must reunite with who we are, our first strength, if we wish to know to be able to act.

It was so simple: It is our lack of faith that ruins everything!

So it was that I shared the entire teaching of Christ, the life of the Master, the methods of Essania, and the existence of the Brothers from the stars with a few proud lords of Kal. And so did others.

At Joseph's request, a symbolic pact was sealed: the chiefs initiated into our teaching vowed to wear their hair long, in memory of another, and much more ancient pact.*

Everything went quickly then. Before the eyes of my soul still

---

*The descendants of these chiefs were those known as the Merovingian kings.

pass the images of these rough men haloed in silver fire, speaking to their little bands of warriors or their servants of a great Master of justice who had lived across the seas. They told them the life of the one in whom Christ had dwelt, thus proving that all were able to receive him in turn. The priests who recognized the turning of the cycles soon associated themselves with this movement, and I saw assemblies gather in village squares, even in the marketplaces. They spoke of doing away with chains, of independence, and of the union of beings.

But in the eyes of Rome, beings are but bodies, wills to be broken! These public meetings gave rise to fear on their part and countless scenes of upset market stalls and dispersed crowds took place before my eyes. The Roman legion, spears at their sides, imposed their own law and watched in distrust.

And finally the day dawned when I was to turn one of the main pages of my own book. It had been arranged that I would speak to a crowd in the market-place of a tiny coastal village. Those present knew me well, having seen me many times in the company of their lords. The images of these moments still fill me with emotion and with a strange feeling. Space had been cleared for me on a wooden table, and men and women of all sorts were beginning to gather noisily beneath a pale sun.

Before I had been able to say anything at all, a troop of armed men suddenly appeared at the corner of a street. They were Roman legionaries. They charged forward, their spears ready at their right side, raising a thick cloud of dust. Their quick and silent approach over the sandy ground triggered a mad panic. In no time, those present were brutally dispersed. Baskets were overturned, jugs broken, stands with their racks of fish trampled or abandoned. I cannot say why I stayed there, why I did not react: Was it the memory of the Master in Magdala? There was no fear in me, no apprehension—just trust, or prescience! Twenty spears were thrust at my chest and held there for a long time, awaiting an order. Finally a centurion appeared, and in a calm voice, uttered several brief sentences. My wrists were quickly bound, and I was led out of the village. I did not know where they were taking me. No one had questioned me or even spoken to me. I walked in silence, closely tied to the harness of one of the horses. We probably walked several miles through the flat marshy countryside. In the distance, a thin line of little blue mountains emerged from the haze. I gazed at them, thinking of a tiny hut perhaps still swept by the wind.

Suddenly my escort decided to come to a halt. On our left was a clump of stunted trees with gnarled trunks. Two legionaries pushed me roughly toward them, and I was overcome by a deep, irrational feeling of coldness. I had no time to wonder at this, but turned abruptly toward the soldiers. At the same moment I glimpsed an arm in movement, something being hurled at me and then a rending flash. I felt a dull sound, a shock in the hollow of my chest. Then, nothing. Nothing more for the space of an instant; a fleeting sensation of dizziness, then an image formed with unusual clarity. I recognized myself at last, lying beneath a tree, a short, heavy spear planted in my chest. There was no terror, no pain, and everything vanished. Slowly, the image of my lifeless body was blown away by a white breeze, disintegrated in a soft breath. I abandoned myself to a sort of torpor, bathed in the coolness of myriad spinning tongues of fire.

Again my body appeared before me, as between parted curtains. The soldiers had moved it and were rapidly covering it with branches and stones. It was a short flash, and then I felt myself drawn into the heart of a force, toward an energy that I was incapable of localizing. How could I describe what happened afterwards? How could the words not sound ridiculous compared with what I experienced?

I saw a white world, whiter than all the snows of our dream; I saw its whiteness come to life, then breathe out all the shades of the rainbow. I saw mountains and forests, trees and multicolored chalices, seas and shores of diamonds. I saw Peace, the Peace that is unknown to humans.

It was thus that the gardens of Iesse opened their doors to me. I awoke, and the images of my life on Earth returned to me with all the force of the love I had sought. There were the houses of my village, the shores of Capernaum, the Master's eyes, Myriam's smile, my errors, my joys.

I contemplated the drop of water that we had tried to add to the great ocean for which all hearts long. As I was pondering, beneath my feet I felt grass wet with dew, the land of souls! A crystalline voice invaded me, happier than any I had ever heard.

I cannot say where it came from, nor what it patiently distilled in me. Yet I know that it was no one's voice. The force that prevailed in it belonged to the Long-Desired One. It was the force that does not write the word *end* anywhere. It had a name, just one, like a thousand suns: Love.

Master Jesus went on teaching in secret at the Krmel into his old age.

When the time came, he left his body of his own free will. His resplendent form of light, whose density was such that it seemed to be his physical body, was seen rising slowly over the Krmel.

His body of flesh, kept in a perfect state of incorruptibility, remained in the monastery for many centuries, before it was taken away with the help of the Brothers from the stars, farther to the East.

Thus did the memory of time express itself to us.

BOOKS OF RELATED INTEREST

The Mystery of the Copper Scroll of Qumran
The Essene Record of the Treasure of Akhenaten
by Robert Feather

The Secret Initiation of Jesus at Qumran
The Essene Mysteries of John the Baptist
by Robert Feather

The Brother of Jesus and the Lost Teachings of Christianity
by Jeffrey J. Bütz

The Gospel of Mary Magdalene
by Jean-Yves Leloup
Foreword by Jacob Needleman

The Gospel of Thomas
The Gnostic Wisdom of Jesus
by Jean-Yves Leloup
Foreword by Jacob Needleman

The Discovery of the Nag Hammadi Texts
A Firsthand Account of the Expedition That Shook
the Foundations of Christianity
by Jean Doresse

Jesus the Wicked Priest
How Christianity Was Born of an Essene Schism
by Marvin Vining

Jesus in the House of the Pharaohs
The Essene Revelations on the Historical Jesus
by Ahmed Osman

Inner Traditions • Bear & Company
P.O. Box 388
Rochester, VT 05767
1-800-246-8648
www.InnerTraditions.com

Or contact your local bookseller